Daughters of Sarah

Daughters of Sarah

Anthology of Jewish Women Writing in French

Edited by

Eva Martin Sartori
and
Madeleine Cottenet-Hage

HOLMES & MEIER

In association with *ejps*
European Jewish Publication Society

Published in the United States of America 2006
by Holmes & Meier Publishers, Inc.
PO Box 943 • Teaneck, NJ 07666
www.holmesandmeier.com

In association with The European Jewish Publication Society
PO Box 19948
London N3 3ZJ
www.ejps.org.uk

The European Jewish Publication Society gives grants to support the publication of books relevant to Jewish literature, history, religion, philosophy, politics and culture.

Copyright © 2006

All rights reserved. No part of this book may be reproduced or transmitted in any form or by any electronic or mechanical means now known or to be invented, including photocopying, recording and information retrieval systems, without permission in writing from the publisher, except by a reviewer who may quote brief passages in a review.

This book has been printed on acid-free paper.

Designed by Brigid McCarthy
Composited by JoAnne Todtfeld

Library of Congress Cataloging-in-Publication Data

Daughters of Sarah : anthology of Jewish women writing in French / edited by Madeleine Cottenet-Hage.
  p. cm.
  Includes bibliographical references.
  ISBN 0-8419-1436-2 (hardcover)—ISBN 0-8419-1445-1 (pbk.)
 1. French literature—Translations into English. 2. French literature—Jewish authors. 3. French literature—Women authors. 4. French literature—20th century. 5. French literature—19th century. 6. Jewish women—Literary collections. I. Sartori, Eva Martin. II. Cottenet-Hage, Madeleine.
  PQ1113.D38 2006
  840.8'09287089924—dc22
                                                      2006001292

Manufactured in the United States of America

For our mothers,
Cyla Stolowicka and Germaine Spiegelstein

Contents

ACKNOWLEDGMENTS ix
INTRODUCTION xi
BIBLIOGRAPHY xxxi

Eugénie Foa 1
The Jewess 4

Pauline Franck 9
A Woman's Life 11

Julienne Bloch 15
Letter to Monsieur Eugène de Mirecourt 17

Elissa Rhaïs 21
Children of Palestine 25

Irène Némirovsky 39
Fraternité 42

Sarah Lévy 51
Beloved 53

Clara Malraux 61
And Yet, I Was Free 64

Jacqueline Mesnil-Amar 75
Those Who Sleep Through the Night 77

Simone Weil 87
What Is a Jew 90
Israel 92

Anna Langfus 95
The Lost Shore 99

Viviane Forrester   111
Tonight, After the War   115

Liliane Atlan   123
Mister Fugue   127

Sarah Kofman   139
Rue Ordener, rue Labat   143

Hélène Cixous   147
Dawn of Phallocentrism   151
Bare Feet   155

Elisabeth Gille   161
Shadows of a Childhood   164

Régine Robin   173
Yiddishkeit   176

Michèle Sarde   187
The Disaster   190

Annie Cohen   205
La Rivière des Gobelins   208

Paula Jacques   223
Light of My Eye   226

Brigitte Peskine   241
The Sweet Waters of Europe   244

Chochana Boukhobza   251
A Summer in Jerusalem   253

BIBLIOGRAPHY OF ADDITIONAL JEWISH WOMEN WRITERS IN FRANCE   263
CONTRIBUTORS   269

ACKNOWLEDGMENTS

It is a pleasure to acknowledge all the people who have had a part in the creation of this volume. We are most grateful to the scholars who have selected, translated, and/or introduced the texts that form the body of this anthology. Special thanks are due to Ralph and Suzanne Tarica who not only translated many texts, but also reviewed translations by others, to Elissa Gelfand who helped us refine our introduction, and to Miriam Holmes whose attention to language improved our translations. Zahava and Israel Cohen solved computer problems we encountered along the way. Jean-Claude Kuperminc and Eva Harbon of the Alliance Israélite Universelle in Paris made the library's collection available to us and suggested texts for this volume. Eva Sartori benefited from a year's residence at the Five College Women's Studies Research Center on the campus of Mount Holyoke College. Financial assistance from The European Jewish Publication Society and the University of Nebraska-Lincoln Judaic Studies Department helped make possible the publication of this book

Finally, we would like to thank Ken Schoen of Schoen Books in South Deerfield, Massachusetts, for providing Sarah Lévy's *O Mon Goye* which gave the impetus to this project, and Jenny Sartori for making a gift of it to her mother.

Introduction

For the last thirty years, literary scholars have shown an increased interest in texts by authors from outside mainstream culture and established centers of power. In French studies, they have broadened our literary horizon by bringing attention to the works of writers originating from the French-speaking Caribbean, from North and sub-Saharan African countries, from French Canada, and to the works written by minorities recently settled in France, in particular the "Beur"community.* To this chorus of voices, we would like to add those of Franco-Jewish women writers, a group with its own charged history which has not yet received much attention.

Scholars of the literature of Jews in France only occasionally mention women writers, even though Jewish women in France have been writing and publishing since the middle of the nineteenth century, often with great success.[1] Although many of these women are known to the French-speaking public, most are unknown to Anglophones. We hope readers will find the translated works in this volume both interesting and meaningful, and will be motivated to further explore the lives and works of the represented Jewish women writers. We also hope that this anthology will serve as a tool in considering the ways in which ethnicity and gender intersect. As Jews, these writers have been marked by their forebears' experiences in a host culture that was often ambivalent in its attitude toward the Jewish minority. As women, they struggled to find a place in a society, reluctant to grant them equal rights and equal opportunities. Because the experiences of Jewish women in France differed from those of Jewish women in other countries, we think it important to situate these writers within the social, cultural, and historical context that shaped their writing.

Defining a Franco-Jewish Writer

The existence of a Jewish literature in diaspora is the subject of an ongoing debate.[2] The answers are complex and inconclusive in the context of the United States. How much more so in regard to France! Cultures and countries categorize knowledge differently. In the area of literature, the French have had a marked preference for larger categories: periods, movements, genres. Furthermore, the French preferred the concept of the larger nation over ethnic minorities and communities. The notion of a Francophone, that is, a French language, Jewish literature is therefore not one they have accepted as a meaningful

---

*Beurs are second-generation immigrants from North Africa.

Introduction

one. Ethnic—if we accept Jewishness as an ethnic category—and/or geographical origins are not considered useful distinctions. One may argue that the concept of a Beur literature, for example, has been gaining ground with greater acceptance of "emerging literatures." But the existence of Jewish writers in France is hardly a recent phenomenon; thus the label "emerging" literature is inapplicable.

We can, however, begin to define the "Jewish writer," even if the existence of Jewish literature as a traditional category might be contested. A writer who happens to be Jewish is not *de facto* a Jewish writer. Accepting the definition proposed by Vladimir Rabi, we define a Jewish writer as one who is writing from within and about a Jewish community, and in the words of Ben Siegel, about characters "motivated to action by their sense of Jewishness."[3] We recognize that not all of these writers examine the Jewish experience exclusively, but they are nevertheless imprinted by it. **Viviane Forrester, Clara Malraux, Hélène Cixous,** and **Michèle Sarde** are cases in point. Jewishness is not the sole focus of their writings even though, we would argue, it is implicit in their work. So, while being Jewish does not make one a Jewish writer, a writer who is writing about Jewish communities, creating Jewish characters, examining the future of Jewish exiles—their relationship to Israel, to their host countries—does give credence to the label of Jewish writer. These are the Jewish writers we have chosen for our anthology, selecting texts in which they have expressed what Jewishness means to them.

Some critics will claim that a cultural Jew, even when not exploring Jewish themes, partakes in "Jewish" qualities, modes of thinking, of being, of acting that translate into her work, justifying the Jewish writer label. An example is **Simone Weil,** about whom critics have written that her lifelong commitment to left-wing causes and social justice—as well as her ceaseless probing of history, philosophy, and theology—bore the stamp of her Jewishness in spite of her, to some unforgivable, denunciation of Old Testament Israel. Another example is Nathalie Sarraute, whose sole reference to her Jewishness is in her autobiography, *Enfance [Childhood]*. It is said that an obsession with words is "the hallmark of the Jewish heritage to the world."[4] Sarraute's works are about words, about unmasking the layers of meaning beneath banal utterances. Then too, sarcasm, derision, self-flagellation—commonly used by her characters—have been said to be characteristic of Jewish writing. Not to mention the supposed existential condition of Jewish moral anguish and guilt. No doubt many will argue that this invoking of essentialist characters is unfounded, but it merits that we give them some thought.

Bold type indicates writers featured in this volume.

Introduction

Strangers in the Land:
Jews In France Before the Revolution

Azoi vi got in Frankraych—As [happy as] God in France—is a Yiddish saying often used by Jews in Eastern Europe to express their special cultural and political affinity with France. For them, France was a land of great beauty and high culture, but it had a special hold on their imagination because it had been the first nation to grant Jews full citizenship rights. However, there were also many troubling periods during their long history in France when Jews were marginalized and even excluded as the ultimate epitome of the "other."

Jews have lived in France at least since the fourth century. Their material conditions, indeed their survival, depended on the benevolence and economic needs of the various lords and kings under whose jurisdiction they lived, as well as on the disposition of the Catholic Church. However, they lived as free people, were integrated into society, and practiced a variety of professions. But from the end of the twelfth century their conditions worsened, as new accusations of blood libel and of desecration of the host were made. Jews were vilified for their practice of moneylending, one of the few occupations permitted to them. During periods of economic depression and plague they became the scapegoats for all the country's ills. In 1394, Charles VI formally expelled the Jews from his kingdom for practicing usury and seized their lands and possessions.

In spite of the edict of expulsion, Jews began returning to France during the fifteenth century when, for economic reasons, Louis XI allowed a few "Portuguese" merchants (Jews who had converted to Christianity, but who had continued to practice their religion in secret) to settle in the Bordeaux region. During the sixteenth and seventeenth centuries Louis XIII and Louis XIV authorized Jews to settle in Lorraine and Alsace to help maintain and supply the French garrisons.

No Longer a Stranger in the Land?
French Jewry After the Revolution of 1789

Emancipation—the attainment of full citizenship rights—came in two stages for French Jews. In 1790, the Jews of Bordeaux, wealthier and more acculturated, and those of the Papal States became citizens on a par with their Christian neighbors. The Jews of the northeast and those scattered over the rest of France became citizens in 1791. Citizenship meant that Jews could participate fully in French culture, then considered to be the most enlightened and the most brilliant in Europe. The fight for emancipation was led by the Count of Clermont-Tonnerre, who declared, "We must deny everything to the Jews as a nation, in the sense of a constituted body, and grant them everything as individuals," and by Abbé Henri Grégoire, who argued that Jews were not inherently inferior but that their behavior and appearance resulted from the way they had been treated. Full citizenship would make it possible for the Jews to be "regenerated." Both the Count of Clermont-Tonnerre and Abbé Grégoire argued for the integration of Jews into the community, demanding that they shed their particularism in favor of a republican universalism. Many, if not most, Jewish leaders agreed with this approach. "Let there be neither Jews nor Christians, except at the hour of prayer for those who pray! That is what France proclaimed on 26 August 1789, in the Declaration of the Rights of Man. From that day on France recognized only citizens," declared the assimilated Ernest Crémieu-Foa.[5]

As Michael Marrus has observed, "emancipation was thus from the start linked with assimilation."[6] Putting into practice the revolutionary notion that Jews should integrate into the general population, Napoleon obtained the consent of the leaders of the Franco-Jewish community to a series of "reforms" that encouraged the assimilation of the Jews. Judaism was to be viewed as a private matter, not a way of life. Jews were to blend into French life by adopting French manners, the French language, French clothes; they were even asked to shed names that did not sound French. Marriages had to be contracted in French civil court before being celebrated in the synagogue. Whereas previously Jews had handled their own disputes, the Civil Code now replaced religious law. The leadership of French Jewry eagerly accepted the bargain offered by the state and stressed the harmony that existed between Republican and Jewish values. Berr Isaac Berr declared in 1791, "As long as we do not change our customs, our habits, in fact our entire education, we cannot hope to deserve the esteem of our fellow citizens or participate in ways that will show the patriotism in our hearts."[7]

During the nineteenth century, the Jewish population as a whole generally blended into the majority culture, and made great economic progress. After restrictions on their mobility were lifted during the Revolution, they increasingly migrated to urban centers, especially to Paris, and entered the ranks of the bourgeoisie. A few made large fortunes. Many Jews distinguished themselves in music, law, philosophy, banking, publishing, and in the theater.

Assimilation did not mean that Jews severed their ties to their community. Cases of conversion and intermarriage were rare, since professional advancement did not depend on conversion. Many highly assimilated and wealthy Jews felt solidarity with their less fortunate brethren and contributed funds to the building of synagogues, schools, hospitals, and charitable institutions. Two anti-Semitic incidents abroad motivated community leaders to establish the

Introduction

Alliance Israélite Universelle in 1860.[8] Its purpose was to defend Jewish interests throughout the world and to "rehabilitate" local Jewish populations around the Mediterranean by providing a secular French education, supplemented by Jewish subjects. Two important and enduring Jewish French-language periodicals were created: the *Archives Israélites* in 1840 and the more conservative *Univers Israélite* in 1844.

Emancipation had given Jewish men equal civic and legal rights as well as economic opportunities. But what did it mean to women who even after emancipation could neither vote nor have the educational and professional opportunities that were available to Jewish men? As the Jewish community integrated into French society, many Jewish leaders adopted rhetoric regarding male and female roles that had much in common with bourgeois Western European notions. Most notably, in contrast to traditional Jewish gender norms, which considered official religion largely a male affair, women were assigned the task of preserving the Jewish traditions and rituals that many men now neglected in favor of participation in the broader French public sphere. Women were supposed to maintain the family's connection with the synagogue and ensure a proper Jewish education for their offspring. At the same time they were to supervise the acculturation of their children into the surrounding society. Theoretically, and again in contrast to traditional Jewish communities, where most women worked and contributed financially to the family, women were to live their lives largely in the private sphere, leaving the public realm to their husbands and fathers.[9]

In practice, women's tasks in the post-emancipation world were far more complicated than these neatly delineated roles would suggest. Based on the new beliefs about mothers' responsibility for training children for participation in the Jewish and French communities, important improvements were made in both the religious and secular education of girls, and most Jewish girls now received at least a primary education, whether in a Jewish or a non-Jewish school. Yet despite the new rhetoric, girls' religious instruction continued to lag significantly behind that of boys, and little evidence exists of women preserving religious traditions as their husbands discarded them. The lines between the public and the private spheres, moreover, were often blurred. Not only did many women of the lower and lower-middle classes have to work, especially before marriage, but Jewish women—like their gentile sisters—built upon their traditional roles as mothers and caretakers to move into such activities as teaching and philanthropy.[10] Occasionally they would write for publication. In this anthology, the highly assimilated **Pauline Franck** exemplifies the life of a Jewish woman of the bourgeoisie concerned with the welfare of children and family, with the transmission of high culture, and with the imperatives of a

Introduction

moral life, while her husband Adolphe enjoyed a successful career as a philosopher and a leader of French Jewry.

It is not surprising that there are only a few works written by Jewish women of the nineteenth century. The sparse number reflects women's exclusion from the Jewish scholarly tradition, inadequate education, lack of civil and political rights, and the minimal opportunities to publish available to women in general.[11]

Within the Jewish tradition women were generally excluded from serious religious education, and French culture did not offer them much in the way of secular education. Even after the Camille Sée Law of 1880 made free public education available to girls, it included only the homemaking arts and a modicum of religious learning. Few women possessed a sufficiently broad education that would have encouraged authorship. Furthermore, under the Napoleonic Code, women were considered minors for their entire lives. They lived under the control of their fathers and husbands, confined to the roles of wives and mothers.

Thus, only three nineteenth-century Jewish women writers appear in this anthology. **Eugénie Foa, Pauline Franck,** and **Julienne Bloch** can be viewed as anomalies because they benefited from unusual upbringings. Foa came from a wealthy, assimilated Bordeaux family; her education was encouraged by an uncle who had recognized her talents. While little is known of Pauline Franck's life, as a young woman she earned her living as a private tutor and was intellectually ambitious. Julienne Bloch had the good fortune to be the daughter of the publisher of a leading Jewish journal.

Jewish women then generally wrote in non-traditional genres. **Foa** and **Bloch** were journalists who promoted a political agenda and published in uncommon venues; **Foa** wrote for a feminist journal and **Bloch** for a Jewish one. **Franck** wrote occasional pieces for the magazine *L'Univers Israélite* but mainly confined her writing to private letters that were not published until after her death.[12] As members of the first emancipated Jewish generation, these women embraced French culture, which offered exposure to modernity. Although they were sometimes angered by incidents of anti-Semitism, they did not question the fundamental compatibility of Jewish beliefs and traditions with the broader French culture.

Not until the 1880s did right wing and clerical circles and anti-capitalist and socialist groups adopt a new pseudo-scientific concept that declared Jews an inferior race. The most virulent anti-Semite of the period was Edouard Drumont, author of the vicious diatribe *La France Juive* (1886). The depth and breadth of anti-Semitic feeling was to find its greatest expression in the Dreyfus Affair. In 1894, army captain Alfred Dreyfus was found guilty of treason by a

Introduction

secret military tribunal on the basis of forged documents. Dreyfus was exiled for life to Devil's Island, off the coast of South America. After much pressure from left-wing intellectuals and the 1898 publication of Emile Zola's famous article "J'accuse," a second trial was held in 1899. In spite of evidence of forgery and of a cover-up by the military, the court still found Dreyfus guilty, although with extenuating circumstances. Shortly afterward, he was freed by presidential pardon, but he was not vindicated by a civilian court until 1906.

The Affair divided the public into Dreyfusards and anti-Dreyfusards and was the occasion for expressions of a virulent anti-Semitism not heard in France since the Middle Ages. Under the banner of pro-military sentiment, anti-Semitic newspapers such as *La Libre Parole* and *La Croix* felt free to publish bitter attacks against Jews. The army "is France itself," wrote the prominent critic Ferdinand Brunetière in *La Revue des Deux Mondes*.[13] The Jewish press was largely silent, fearful that support of Dreyfus would put into question Jews' loyalty to the army and their patriotism. Some Jewish militants defended Dreyfus in print, among them Bernard Lazard and André Spire. The only Jewish woman who referred to the Affair in print was Louise Weiss when she noted in her memoirs that her grandfather was distressed that Dreyfus continued to be denied a second trial. She writes tersely, referring to her grandfather, "He was an Israelite."[14]

A Stranger in a Strange Land: French Jewry Between 1900 and 1945

Largely assimilated and with scant interest in religion, French-born Jews felt that the successful outcome of the Dreyfus Affair had confirmed their faith in the inherent justice of the Republic and in the bond that united French Jewry to the state. But after World War I, they were no longer the only face of French Jewry. The composition of the Jewish community was dramatically altered during this period by the arrival of new working-class immigrants from Eastern and Central Europe and North Africa. By 1930, there were some 200,000 Jews in France. These immigrants generally did not speak French (they favored Yiddish) and were readily identifiable as Jews in appearance and behavior—factors that strained relations between the two groups of Jews. Nevertheless, the immigrants possessed a vibrant and multifaceted culture and developed organizations and cultural activities to meet their needs. They were also politically active in a variety of political movements, principally Communism, Bundism, and Zionism, all movements to which French-born Jews were generally hostile.

Soon, however, a new interest in Zionism, a recurrence of pogroms resulting

Introduction

from the arrival of great numbers of Jews from Eastern Europe, and the stirrings of Nazism spurred a number of intellectuals of Jewish birth to return to the exploration of Jewish themes in literature, art, and music. Vladimir Rabi lists several dozen Franco-Jewish writers active in the interwar period, among them Armand Lunel, Jean-Richard Bloch, Edmond Fleg, and André Spire.[15] Aroused by the anti-Semitism of the Dreyfus Affair, public intellectuals, such as Fleg, Spire, Darius Milhaud, and Gustave Kahn, portrayed the positive aspects of Judaism in their publications and in meetings of the Jewish group "Les Amis du Judaïsme." They presented the possibility of an "alternative, non-religious form of Jewish identity."[16] The journal *Revue Juive* (1925), whose contributors included Freud, Einstein, Proust, Fleg, and Léon Blum, was an ambitious although brief enterprise edited by Albert Cohen. In 1926, the publishing house Rieder inaugurated a series entitled *Judaïsme*, which produced works by Franco-Jewish writers as well as translations from other languages.

In the interwar period, political activism by women in general achieved significant social and political gains. A secondary school program offered the same education for women and men. Consequently, women entered the professions in increasing numbers. In 1938, the legal status of married women improved. No longer considered minors, they could now open a bank account, freely dispose of their earnings, and enter the universities. Some Jewish women joined in these struggles. Among them were Louise Weiss, a pacifist and an early Europeanist; Claude Cahun, a photographer later associated with the Surrealists, who joined a revolutionary organization of artists; the lawyers Yvonne Netter and Marcelle Kraemer-Bach; and Cécile Brunschwicg, active in the International Council of Women.

These social and political gains, however, are not reflected in the numbers of Jewish women who published literary texts. Myriam Harry and **Elissa Rhaïs** took advantage of the Orientalist vogue by focusing on North Africa and the Near East. Lily Jean-Javal wrote travel books and books for children. **Irène Némirovsky's** novels and plays were extremely popular, while **Sarah Lévy's** two novels addressed the controversial topic of intermarriage. Berthe Bénichou-Aboulker's play *La Kahéna* (1933) was the first work published by a Jewish woman in Algeria. The play celebrates the defeat of the Arab invaders in the seventh century by a Berber Jewish queen. The heroine La Kahéna embodies the ancient presence of the Jews in North Africa and their courage and determination in fighting oppression.

Why have we not been able to identify more Jewish women writers in this period? Several reasons could be advanced. While women in general wrote in increasing numbers, and despite the towering presence of the writer Colette, they did not have as many opportunities to publish as did men. The fact that

Introduction

women tended not to join literary circles may explain their lack of visibility. In addition, as some feminist critics have pointed out, women have often been omitted from anthologies and disregarded by critics and compilers. Furthermore, according to Jennifer Milligan, because influential critics, among them Henri Peyre, **Hélène Cixous,** and Susan Rubin Suleiman, held that in general French women of the period "did not produce literature of sufficient caliber to merit detailed study,"[17] their works were seldom collected and are now largely absent from libraries.

Against this background, the paucity of Jewish women writers becomes more understandable. As Jews, these women faced the additional hurdle of coming to terms with their ambiguous status within French culture. Those writings by Jewish women writers that remain reflect the same secular concerns as do those of Jewish men. Like their male colleagues—for example, Fleg, Spire, Armand Lunel, and Albert Cohen—women addressed questions of Jewish legitimacy, identity, and tradition, but in more personal terms. **Elissa Rhaïs** and Berthe Bénichou-Aboulker expressed the yearning for a homeland; **Irène Némirovsky,** the psychological discomfort of the assimilated French Jew condemned to be the perpetual outsider; **Sarah Lévy,** the powerful desire to be accepted into the French bourgeoisie. As the Great Depression of the 1930s gave added momentum to anti-Semitic groups, these issues became more pressing for French Jews.

By 1939, some 300,000 to 330,000 Jews lived in France, of whom only about 90,000 were French-born. After the German invasion in May–June 1940, France was divided into the German-occupied zone north of the Loire and a "free France" south of the river, ruled by Marshal Philippe Pétain in Vichy. The first discriminatory decrees against the Jews were issued by the German occupiers. A law of July 1940 created a commission to review naturalizations that preceded August 10, 1927. A September 27, 1940 Nazi ordinance defined a Jew as anyone practicing the Jewish religion or having three or more Jewish grandparents. Those who fit the definition were required to register with the local police. In the years that followed, the Vichy government and the Germans tried to outdo one another in devising new discriminatory legislation. On October 3, 1940, on its own initiative, Vichy issued its first "Statute on Jews", which broadened the definition of a Jew to include those who had two Jewish grandparents and a Jewish spouse. A second and a third statute increased discriminatory practices, limited Jews' access to industry, commerce, and the liberal professions, and forbade them to take part in any artistic activity. In May 1942, Jews in the occupied zone were required to wear the yellow star.

Roundups of Jews for incarceration and deportation began in 1941. After

Introduction

Hitler decreed the "final solution" in 1942, France was ordered to send 100,000 Jews to forced labor camps. The most severe of these roundups, known as the "Vel d'Hiv roundup," occurred on July 16–17, 1942. From this roundup, 13,152 men, women, and children were interned in camps that became "reservoirs" for deportation. More roundups took place in Bordeaux and other southern cities. After the abolition of the southern zone in November 1942, Jews were systematically hunted throughout the entire country. The last train headed for extermination camps left on August 17, 1944. More than 77,000 Jews, over 24 percent of those living in France at the end of 1940, perished during the war; most of them were foreign born. Only about 2,800 returned from deportation.

Deprived of civil rights, unable to earn a living, and hunted by both the Gestapo and the French police, some Jews managed to survive by hiding, often with the assistance of non-Jews. Others joined the Resistance and other networks, or emigrated when they had the means. Various Jewish as well as some Christian organizations helped with food, money, forged papers, and hiding places.

Reintegration

Writing by Jews in France halted during the Holocaust and its immediate aftermath. During World War II, the urgent question had become how to survive, how not to be engulfed by fascism and anti-Semitic paranoia. After the war, the 200,000 Jews remaining in France, most of them of Ashkenazi (Eastern European) origin, had to locate whomever was left of their families, find lodging and work, and the returnees had to be reintegrated into the community of the living. Thereafter, they felt compelled to be "witnesses." Those who had undergone terrifying experiences as adults or as children began describing them in works of fiction, plays, poetry, and memoirs, even as they questioned the possibility of writing after Auschwitz. For women, the Holocaust was often the defining experience that moved them to write as Jews, sweeping away the illusion that they were citizens *à part entière*, full citizens as the emancipation laws had promised.

Jacqueline Mesnil-Amar's work in this volume is a stirring example of writing as a response to the shock of the Holocaust. Her tribute to the victims and condemnation of those who "were asleep" during the war reestablishes the borders of her own Jewishness, which had become blurred with assimilationist practices. She rediscovers her Jewish identity and her connections to the larger community of Jews, French and non-French; France is depicted as a

Introduction

nation that failed its Jewish population. In their autobiographies covering the same period, **Viviane Forrester** and **Clara Malraux** express the same painful recognition that being Jewish took precedence over and put into question their families' identity as French citizens. Assimilated Jews found themselves on the same side as those "foreign" Eastern European Jews whom they had looked upon with indifference or disdain, those Jews "with accents."

In their testimonies of life in the concentration camps, women writers often position themselves in the context of a culture of Death. In the three novels based on her own horrific experiences in Poland and in the camps, **Anna Langfus** transforms this difficult material into art. Trying to both represent and forget, to unburden herself of the haunting images from her past, she shapes them into a wrenching testimony of tragedy and grief.

Beginning in the 1960s until the end of the twentieth century, a younger generation tried to come to grips with events that had shattered their community and their lives as children. These child survivors describe in memoirs, testimonials, novels, and plays how they avoided deportation. **Elisabeth Gille** was hidden in a Catholic school, **Sarah Kofman** was cared for by a gentile "mother," and **Michèle Sarde's** heroine was adopted by a Catholic family, her Jewish origins kept secret from her. Second-generation writers such as Myriam Anissimov and **Régine Robin** were haunted by their parents' tragic experiences, even as they attempted to make their own way in the world.

Women obtained the vote in 1945, but it was not until the turmoil of 1968 and the emergence of the Women's Liberation Movement that women's grievances were addressed. Women entered the workforce in greater numbers, secured reproductive rights, and won the right to be free of sexual harassment. Feminist theorists—the most notable being **Hélène Cixous,** Catherine Clément, Luce Irigaray, and Julia Kristeva—rejected the binary oppositions and hierarchies that patriarchy uses to subordinate women. They addressed issues of sexual difference as manifested in language, notions of identity, and representation, especially as they concerned women. **Cixous,** an Algerian Jew of Sephardic and Ashkenazi origin, who coined the evocative portmanteau word *juifemme,* urged women to "write themselves," encouraging word play and rejecting traditional narrative structures in favor of a less constrictive, more fluid writing that challenged the stable meaning of words.

The *librairie des femmes,* of which **Cixous** was a founder, was instrumental in publishing a number of experimental works, among them the poetic texts of **Annie Cohen.** Another writer, **Régine Robin,** took experimental writing in another direction by mixing prose and poetry, French and Yiddish, the language of the social sciences and that of fiction and autobiography. Although

Introduction

these Jewish writers subscribed to the message of the feminist theorists, none other than **Cixous** established an explicit connection between ethnicity and literary theory.

At the same time as the status of women in French society was changing, an influx of Jewish immigrants from the newly independent North African countries contributed to the altered character of French Jewry, creating a more self-confident, self-conscious and religious community. Between 1956 and 1967, some 235,000 North African Jews settled in France. The Sephardic women who came of age after World War II did not experience the radical trauma of the Holocaust or the devaluation of Jewish culture by the Western European countries. Most of them were already urbanized. Many were literate in French and familiar with French culture because they had been educated at the schools of the Alliance Israélite Universelle in their native countries. For these communities, Judaism remained a way of life as well as a religion. Although the North African Jews had certain advantages over the Jews who had emigrated earlier from Eastern Europe, the transition to a different culture and a different climate still proved difficult.

The arrival of these Sephardic and Judeo-Arab Jews following decolonization created a new audience for Franco-Jewish literature and a complementary new group of writers. In their novels, **Brigitte Peskine** and **Paula Jacques** re-create these communities in the process of transition from their countries of origin to metropolitan France (as had Albert Cohen and Albert Memmi in their work). They and others like Paule Darmon and Marlène Amar write lovingly, if not uncritically, of the milieu from which they came. At the same time, they describe the pain of dislocation and integration into a new culture. In her poems about a Parisian district with a large immigrant population from many parts of the world, **Annie Cohen** extends our understanding of exile by reminding us that many other groups share its pain.

Current Status

With about 600,000 Jews, France has the second largest Jewish population in Europe after the former Soviet Union. New schools, community centers, and synagogues have been built, and discussion groups on Jewish themes have been created. An active Jewish press publishes works of fiction and nonfiction on Jewish themes, and there has been a revival of interest in Yiddish language and its literature. Festivals of Jewish music and films abound. As the historian Pierre Birnbaum has observed,[18] in the twenty-first century French Jews are about to become, by their own desire, a minority among minorities within

Introduction

France—a minority with its own history and its own distinctive practices, unwilling to have its identity defined by the majority culture. However, by and large, French Jews no longer voice unqualified support for the universalist assimilationist principles of the Revolution: They often view with suspicion the politicians' occasional attempts to speak of a Franco-Jewish "community."

A singular event, the publication in 2001 of a novel entitled *La Juive* by a major French publisher, suggests that the integration of the Jewish minority into the broader community remains problematic. A semiautobiographical novel by the gentile writer Colette Mainguy tells the story of a young girl who entertains very poor relationships with her Catholic bourgeois family. The novel is particularly startling in its description of the young girl's pathological fantasies of being subjected to violence in a Nazi camp. To account for her feelings of being a pariah, she imagines that she, the only one of her kin, has inherited traits from a distant Jewish ancestor. In this novel, Jewishness has been turned into an imposture. The Holocaust, a historical tragedy, is appropriated as a metonymy for life in a dysfunctional family. Yet, as disturbing as these misappropriations are, the book is also a telling document, illustrating how powerfully the French imagination has linked the concepts of Difference, Otherness, and Suffering to the image of Jewishness. Furthermore, since Jewishness is embodied in a female protagonist, the story may be interpreted as reviving the stubborn stereotype of the "Jewess" as the tantalizing, impure, feminine "Other" often portrayed in male-authored texts.

It is difficult to assess the current state of integration of Jews into the broader French culture. For many French Jews, the attacks on Jewish institutions such as synagogues, cemeteries, and schools, as well as the popularity of right-wing parties, are not an expression of anti-Zionism or a condemnation of Israel's policies toward the Palestinians, as some contend. Rather they are an indication that the old-fashioned European anti-Semitism they thought had disappeared after the Holocaust still persists. This sense of vulnerability, however, is no longer buried in discussions among Jews. The Jews of France give voice through demonstrations and through dialogue with a government that is taking their concerns seriously. The public posture of the "Jewish community," an unwelcome phrase not too long ago, is in itself a sign that the old idea of a national ideology in the service of universalist values is no longer operative. As the historian Pierre Nora has argued, the "holy legend" of a unified historical past has been replaced by multiple histories, including those of previously silenced groups—workers, women, Bretons, Corsicans, royalists, and Jews. Perhaps it is this new sense of legitimacy and enpowerment that is encouraging French Jews to express their difference in literature as well in historical narratives.

Introduction

Is There a Tradition of Women's Franco-Jewish Literature?

Given that Franco-Jewish women lived in a culture that differed from that of Christian women as well as from the culture of Jewish men, can we assume they produced a literature that shared certain preoccupations, certain ways of looking at the world? The call for a literature by Jewish women in France was heard as far back as the middle nineteenth century.

In June 1854, **Julienne Bloch,** a schoolteacher, administrator, and journalist, called on Jewish women to make their voices heard. Why, she asked, were the Jewish women of France, unlike their British sisters, so silent, even on issues that concerned them? Why were they afraid of being ridiculed as bluestockings?

Bloch hoped her column in the *Archives Israélites* would inspire other French Jewish women to take their rightful place as writers at their brothers' side. As was her wont, she buttressed her belief in women's abilities with biblical texts, quoting Abraham who, on entering Egypt, asked his wife Sarai to pretend she was his sister so that the Egyptians would treat him well (Genesis 12:13). Women writers, Bloch implied, could even make it easier for male writers to enter gentile circles.

Bloch went further in her legitimization of women within Jewish tradition, again supporting her argument with biblical text. Numbers:27 records the demand of Zelophehad's daughters before Moses that they should inherit the land their father would have given them as dowry if he had not died before reaching the promised land. "Give us an inheritance like those of our father's brothers," they demanded. Moses consulted the Lord who agreed with the daughters. In her eyes, women's rights to the Jewish tradition were divinely sanctioned.

Did **Julienne Bloch** get her wish? Can we speak of a French Jewish literature by women? Without a doubt, French Jewish women writers share with their male colleagues certain preoccupations inherent in their common diasporic condition. Both exhibit allegiance to several cultures, a concern with generational roots, an attachment to an ancestral land, and an awareness of the tensions arising from assimilation. French Jewish writers of both sexes explore the status of a religious minority in a Catholic country and the reverberations of specific historical events such as the emancipation decrees, the Dreyfus Affair, and the Holocaust. They also share values such as the importance of the family, an emphasis on book learning, and a concern with justice.

We suggest, however, that women's perspective on these cultural experiences and values may be different from that of men. It is interesting to note that, unlike male Jewish writers, few Jewish women writers belonged to a

Introduction

literary or philosophical movement. During the interwar years, while Spire and Fleg were reclaiming the historical roots and the moral mission of their Jewish heritage, **Sarah Lévy** and **Irène Némirovsky** focused on questions of sexuality, marriage, family dynamics, and their place in the community. Their writings are firmly anchored in the everyday world, concerned more with expressing the psychological and physical struggles of their daily existence than with theory or ideology.

Because according to Jewish law, the mother's religion is determinative, a Jewish woman's relationship to her own identity is of a different nature than that of a Jewish man—perhaps more intimate, more visceral. Issues of exogamy or endogamy, survival, persecution, exile and loss, and freedom from tradition may become more threatening, more definitive, more dramatic. In many ways, personal selves are more tightly bound to the existence and the history, past and future, of the group. Remembering, caring, celebrating, grieving, and rebelling are personal acts performed by these Jewish women *within* the community.

The centrality of the family as a theme in Jewish literature has frequently been noted. "What does one do standing by a grave when one does not know how to pray? One remembers."[19] What does one remember? In **Brigitte Peskine's** novel about Turkish Jews, for example, the author "remembers" the Jewish family members and the local community, their rituals, their foods, their daily life punctuated by colorful Judeo-Spanish or Yiddish phrases, warm protective places, vividly recreated. But one also remembers the suffering of victims, the destruction of families and neighborhoods, the pain of children orphaned by the Holocaust **(Elisabeth Gille, Sarah Kofman)**, the discovery of anti-Semitism **(Clara Malraux)**. Trying to understand and resurrect a time before everything went wrong haunts **Viviane Forrester's** autobiography and Jacqueline **Mesnil-Amar's** essay. Issues of identity tend to be foregrounded more often in texts by Ashkenazi than in those by Sephardic women writers who had stronger ties to the Jewish community.

We have already discussed the special relationship that the Jewish culture has with languages, linked both to a long Talmudic tradition of engaging with and debating sacred texts and to a diasporic history that led to polyglossia among Jewish communities. Jewish language—Yiddish, Judeo-Spanish—ensured the survival of a sense of communal belonging, at the same time that other national languages were required for daily existence in host countries. Such polyglossia has often resulted either in playful, or serious dismantling and recombining of language to extract new meanings, or in peppering French texts with foreign words, expressions and inflections, resurrected in the act of remembrance. The novels of **Paula Jacques** and **Brigitte Peskine** make wonderful use of these linguistic mixtures. On the other hand, **Hélène Cixous's** particularly felicitous dismantling and recombining of language to extract new meanings situates her at the crossroads between Derridian linguistic practices and traditional Jewish creativity..

The condition of women in the Jewish tradition is one of the themes that runs through several of the included works. Sephardic Jewish writers are more likely to denounce the tyranny of the Jewish family, the submission of mothers, the restrictions imposed upon daughters, and their professional and educational options. **Peskine** follows her main character through decades of fighting against family decisions and historical obstacles, whereas **Chochana Boukhobza** chooses a narrower temporal span, a summer in Jerusalem, to examine her protagonist's confrontational reunion with her family of Tunisian Jewish settlers in Israel. More than a century earlier, **Eugénie Foa**, in *La Juive*, a text that has lost none of its freshness, pleaded for the freedom of a young woman to choose a husband. But will such freedom imply the possibility—and the risk—of exogamous marriages? This theme, also raised in **Sarah Lévy's** *O Mon Goye,* is one that several writers in this volume have addressed.

The preservation of the Jewish faith had been much in the forefront of nineteenth-century Jewish thinkers, a concern we find echoed in the writings of **Julienne Bloch.** Twentieth-century writers of the interwar period, however, express little interest in theological questions, with the single and very controversial exception of **Simone Weil,** who applied her formidable bookish culture in religions to examine the Old Testament. For many, after the war, the full knowledge of the tragedy of the Holocaust shattered the possibility of a transcendental being. **Liliane Atlan** is one of the few writers to envisage a return to religion. **Elisabeth Gille,** on the other hand, rejects vehemently the existence of a God who could have allowed the Holocaust.

The discovery or recovery of one's Jewishness, previously erased by assimilation or persecution, is one of the recurrent themes in recent Jewish narratives by women. These texts often ask how one preserves one's identity while becoming part of a nation in which the concept of minority has no legal recognition. And what are the costs of integration into a larger, Christian community? These are questions that nineteenth-century writers had raised after emancipation and that later writers continued to explore.

The feeling of solidarity within the Jewish community is often portrayed as illusory. **Némirovsky's** short story *Fraternité* powerfully illustrates how class divisions can shatter the notion of the "oneness" of the Tribe. While some authors write about nostalgia for a lost shore and a lost community, others remind us that self-hate can also be part of a Jewish heritage. Self-hate is most

Introduction

evident in the work of **Simone Weil**—as many of her critics claim—who repudiated her origins. It is also frighteningly displayed in **Lévy's** treatment of a Jewish middle-class beauty and her rejection of all Jewish traits.

So what do these texts tell us? On the whole, they convey simultaneously the desire to belong, the fear of exclusion—from one's community, one's country—and the fear of entrapment by the Tribe. These tensions tear at the fabric of the self.

Principles of Selection and Organization

This volume offers texts by nineteenth- and twentieth-century women authors in a variety of genres. All are focused on the theme of Jewish identity. While the majority consists of fictional prose, we have also included poetry **(Cohen)**, a play **(Atlan)**, essays **(Mesnil-Amar and Weil)**, letters **(Bloch, Franck, Weil)**, autobiographies **(Malraux, Forrester, Kofman)**, and a hybrid text **(Robin)**. Included in our selection are authors whose names are well known, as well as others whose names are less familiar. In selecting, we gave preference to texts with literary merit, but we also included selections whose interest is primarily cultural and/or historical, or ones that raise provocative questions about a woman writer's problematic Jewishness. Readers will undoubtedly discover that some names are absent. The risks inherent in any form of selection are always present and always great. We accept them and have provided at the end of this volume the names of authors not represented in this anthology. We hope that other scholars will be inspired to do further research.

Each text is preceded by a short biographical introduction and a discussion of the author's work. Represented are the works of French-born and French-educated Jewish women writers, Jewish women writers born elsewhere who came to France as children or adults from non-French-speaking lands and adopted French as their language, as well as the works of Jewish women writers from other French-speaking countries. This anthology celebrates a rediscovered consciousness of Franco-Jewish identity and community. Irrespective of the dates and origins, familiar echoes circulate among these texts.

We hope that this anthology will stimulate discussions on the differences between the texts of Jewish men and Jewish women, and a comparison between the texts of Jewish and non-Jewish women. We also hope that it will lead readers to further explore the existence of a female Jewish literary tradition in France and that it will facilitate comparisons between this body of women's texts and those of other cultures and lands.

Introduction

Notes

1. See Alan Astro, *Discourses of Jewish Identity in Twentieth-Century France. Yale French Studies,* no. 85 (New Haven, CT: Yale University Press, 1994); Pierre Horn, *Modern Jewish Writers of France* (Lewiston, NY: Edwin Mellen, 1997); Vladimir Rabi, *Anatomie du Judaïsme Français* (Paris: Les Editions de Minuit, 1962).
2. The question was posed by Rabi in "Littérature juive et écrivains juifs," *Les Nouveaux Cahiers,* no. 24 (Spring 1971): pp. 24–31. Similarly, Ben Siegel examines the issue in "Erasing and Embracing the Past: America and Its Jewish Writers—Men and Women," in *Daughters of Valor,* Jay L. Halio and Ben Siegel, eds. (Newark: University of Delaware Press, 1997).
3. Siegel, *Daughters of Valor,* p. 20.
4. Siegel, *Daughters of Valor,* p. 25.
5. Quoted by Michael Marrus in *The Politics of Assimilation* (Oxford: Oxford University Press, 1971), p. 87.
6. Ibid. For a somewhat different view of the project of assimilation, see Phyllis Cohen Albert, "Israelite and Jew: How Did Nineteenth-Century French Jews Understand Assimilation?" in *Assimilation and Community: The Jews in Nineteenth-Century Europe,* Jonathan Frankel and Steven J. Zipperstein, eds. (Cambridge: Cambridge University Press, 1992), pp. 88–109.
7. Quoted by Jean-Marc Chouraqui in "L'Amour de la patrie," *Juifs de France.* Les Collections de l'histoire, no.10 (Paris: La Documentation Française, January 2001), p. 50 (Our translation.).
8. In 1840 the death of a Capuchin monk and his servant in Damascus was attributed to Jews. In 1858 a Jewish child was forcibly converted to Catholicism in Italy. See Paula Hyman, *The Jews of Modern France* (Berkeley: University of California Press, 1988), pp. 78–79.
9. Paula Hyman, *Gender and Assimilation in Modern Jewish History* (Seattle: University of Washington Press, 1995), p. 67.
10. For a thorough discussion of Jewish women's education in nineteenth-century France, see Jennifer Sartori, "Our Religious Future: Girls' Education and Jewish Identity in Nineteenth-Century France" (Ph.D. diss., Emory University, 2004).
11. See Michèle Bitton, *Poétesses et lettrées juives. Une Mémoire éclipsée* (Paris: Publisud, 1999). There is no record of female French Jewish writers prior to the late eighteenth century. Even in the early nineteenth century, France could not boast of Jewish women writers of a stature comparable to those in England, such as Grace Aguilar. Edmond Fleg makes a similar point in his *Anthologie juive des origines à nos jours* (Paris: Flammarion, 1951).
12. Interestingly, Marion A. Kaplan was able to locate many more memoirs by Jewish women writing in German than we have by Jewish women writing in French prior to World War II. See her "Gender and Jewish History in Imperial Germany," in *Assimilation and Community: The Jews in Nineteenth-Century*

Europe, Jonathan Frankel and Steven J. Zipperstein, eds. (Cambridge: Cambridge University Press, 1992), pp. 199–224.
13. Quoted by Michel Winnock in "L'Antisémitisme est-il au coeur de l'Affaire Dreyfus?" in *Juifs de France,* p. 72.
14. Louise Weiss, *Souvenirs d'une enfance républicaine* (Paris: Denoël, 1937), p. 19.
15. Rabi, *Anatomie du Judaïsme,* pp. 102–106.
16. Paula Hyman, *From Dreyfus to Vichy* (New York: Columbia University Press, 1979), p. 45.
17. Jennifer Milligan, *The Forgotten Generation* (Oxford: Berg, 1996), p. 2.
18. Pierre Birnbaum, *Jewish Destinies: Citizenship, State, and Community in Modern France,* Arthur Goldhammer, trans. (New York: Hill and Wang, 2000), pp. 275–276.
19. Sylvie Courtine-Denamy, *La Maison de Jacob* (Paris: Editions Phébus, 2001), p. 184. The author, whose ancestors were expelled from Spain, searches for her roots during a long history of displacement and name changes.

BIBLIOGRAPHY

Agosín, Marjorie. *The House of Memory: Stories by Jewish Women Writers of Latin America.* NY: The Feminist Press, 1999.
———. ed. *Passion, Memory, Identity.* Albuquerque: University of New Mexico Press, 1999.
Astro, Alan. *Discourses of Jewish Identity in Twentieth-Century France.* Yale French Studies Number 85. New Haven, CT: Yale University Press, 1994.
Bard, Christine. *Les Filles de Marianne: Histoire des Féminismes, 1914-1940.* Paris: Fayard, 1995.
Baskin, Judith R., ed. *Women of the Word: Jewish Women and Jewish Writing.* Detroit, MI: Wayne State University Press, 1994.
Braude, Claudia Bathsheba, ed. *Contemporary Jewish Writing in South Africa: An Anthology.* Lincoln: University of Nebraska Press, 2001.
Becker, Jacques and Annette Wieviorka, eds. *Les Juifs de France de la Révolution française à nos jours.* Paris: Liana Levi, 1998.
Benbassa, Esther. *The Jews of France.* Princeton, NJ: Princeton University Press, 1999.
Birnbaum, Pierre. *Jewish Destinies: Citizenship, State and Community in Modern France.* Trans. Arthur Goldhammer. New York: Hill and Wang, 2000.
Bitton, Michèle. *Poétesses et lettrées juives: Une mémoire éclipsée.* Paris: Publisud, 1999.
———. *Présences Féminines Juives en France, XIXe-XXe Siècles.* 2M Editions, 2002.
———. and Lionel Panafit. *Etre Juif en France Aujourd'hui.* Paris: Hachette, 1997.
Dugas, Guy. *La Littérature Judéo-maghrébine d'expression française: Entre Djéha et Cagayous.* Paris: Editions l'Harmattan, 1990.
Finkielkraut, Alain. *The Imaginary Jew.* Trans. Kevin O'Neill and David Suchoff. Lincoln: University of Nebraska Press, 1994.
Friedlander, Judith. *Vilna on the Seine: Jewish Intellectuals in France since 1968.* New Haven, CT: Yale University Press, 1990.
Gdalia, Janine and Annie Goldmann. *Le Judaïsme au Féminin.* Paris: Balland, 1986.
Halio, Jay L. and Ben Siegel, eds. *Daughters of Valor: Contemporary Jewish American Women Writers.* Newark: University of Delaware Press, 1997.
Horn, Pierre. *Modern Jewish Writers of France.* Lewiston, NY: Edwin Mellen Press, 1997.
Hyman, Paula. *From Dreyfus to Vichy: The Remaking of French Jewry, 1906-1939.* New York: Columbia University Press, 1979.
———. *Gender and Assimilation in Modern Jewish History: The Roles and Representations of Women.* Seattle: University of Washington Press, 1995.
———. *The Jews of Modern France.* Berkeley: University of California Press, 1998.
Jackson, Julian. *France. The Dark Years 1940-1944.* Oxford: Oxford University Press, 2001.
Lazarus, Joyce Bloch. *Strangers and Sojourners: Jewish Identity in Contemporary French Fiction.* New York: Peter Lang, 1999.

Bibliography

Lebovics, Herman. *True France: The War over Cultural Identity 1900-1945*. Ithaca, NY: Cornell University Press, 1992.

Lehrmann, Chanan. *The Jewish Element in French Literature*. Trans. George Klin. Rutherford, NJ: Fairleigh Dickinson University Press, 1971.

Lévy, Clara. *Ecritures de l'identité: Les écrivains juifs après la Shoah*. Paris: PUF, 1998.

Lichtenstein, Diane. *Writing their Nations: The Tradition of Nineteenth-Century American Jewish Women Writers*. Bloomington: Indiana University Press: 1992.

Lionnet, Françoise. *Postcolonial Representations: Women, Literature, Identity*. Ithaca, NY: Cornell University Press, 1995.

Marks, Elaine. *Marrano as Metaphor: The Jewish Presence in French Writing*. New York: Columbia University Press, 1996.

Marrus, Michael and Robert O. Paxton. *Vichy France and the Jews*. New York: Schocken Books, 1981.

Memmi, Albert. *The Liberation of the Jew*. Trans. Judy Hyun. New York: The Orion Press, 1966.

———. *The Colonizer and the Colonized*. Trans. Howard Greenfeld. Boston: Beacon Press, 1991.

Mendelson, David and Michael Elial, eds. *Ecrits français d'Israël de 1800 à nos jours*. Paris: Minard, 1989.

Monego, Joan. *Maghrebian Literature in French*. Boston: Twayne, 1984.

Schnapper, Dominique. *Jewish Identities in France: An Analysis of Contemporary Jewry*. Trans. Arthur Goldhammer. Chicago: University of Chicago Press, 1983.

Wardi, Charlotte. *Le Juif dans le roman français 1933-1948*. Paris: A.-G. Nizet, 1973.

Woodhull, Winifred. *Transfiguration of the Maghreb: Feminism, Decolonization, and Literatures*. Minneapolis: University of Minnesota Press, 1993.

Yudkin, Leon I. *A Home Within: Varieties of Jewish Expression in Modern Fiction*. Northwood, Middlesex, UK: Symposium Press, 1996.

Zuccotti, Susan. *The Holocaust, the French, and the Jews*. New York: Basic Books, 1993.

Eugénie Foa
(1796–1853)

Eugénie Foa was born Esther Rebecca Rodrigues-Henriques in Bordeaux. As far as is known, she was the first professional Jewish woman writer in France.

Foa belonged to a prominent, wealthy family whose ancestors had settled in the Bordeaux region after the expulsion of the Jews from the Iberian Peninsula in 1492. Her mother Esther was the daughter of the shipowner David Gradis, who had barely missed being elected to the Chamber of Deputies. Her father Isaac Rodrigues-Henriques belonged to a family of bankers and had been a member of the Grand Sanhedrin, the group of rabbis and notables convened by Napoleon in 1808 to decide on the institutional form the Jewish religion would take in France. Her brother Hippolyte became well known as a playwright, and her sister Hannah Léonie was a sculptor and the wife of the celebrated composer Jacques Fromenthal Halévy.

In 1814, Eugénie married Joseph Foa, a businessman from Marseilles. The marriage was not a happy one and she turned her attention to literature. Under the name of Eugénie Foa or the pseudonym Maria Fitz-Clarence or Edmond de Fontanes, she wrote for a number of journals, among them *La Chronique de Paris* and *La Voix des femmes,* and helped to create new magazines for children such as *Le Journal des demoiselles, La Gazette de la jeunesse,* and *Le Journal des enfants.* Contemporary critics praised her vivid imagination and her ability to communicate feelings. Her first published novels, among them *Kiddoushim ou l'anneau nuptial des Hébreux* (1830) [Kiddoushim or the Wedding Ring of the Hebrews] and *La Juive* (1835) [The Jewess] focused on Jewish themes. Then she concentrated on children's literature, an unappreciated genre that she promoted tirelessly. Though her tales are meant for a general audience and portray well-known French historical figures, she also introduced Jewish themes and explained Jewish customs in the columns and short stories she published in *Le Journal des demoiselles.* Her works continued to be published after her death and some of her children's books were translated into English in the early part of the twentieth century. Later she was forgotten, known only to scholars specializing in the field of children's literature.

In *La Juive,* Eugénie Foa portrayed a young Syrian woman caught between the expectations of her parents and her own attachment to Judaism and her desire for emancipation and acculturation to French life and culture. The novel reflects Foa's attachment to French culture, even as she celebrates Jewish customs and values. She reveals both the opportunities offered to Jewish women by emancipation and the losses it exacted from them.

Eugénie Foa

Set in Paris during the Regency period that followed the death of Louis XIV, a century earlier than the novel's publication, *La Juive* consists of a series of scenes or tableaux as intense and tumultuous as they are unlikely. It tells the unhappy love story of Midiane, the daughter of the very traditional banker, Schaoul, and his wife, Donanime, originally from Syria. Midiane falls in love with the Christian André de Prezel, a romantic and melancholy artist. Because her father forbids her union with a Christian and insists that she marry a Jew of his choice, the two young people run away and live together without benefit of marriage; secular marriages being unavailable at the time. They have a child, but, deprived of her mother's affection and her father's blessing, Midiane dies. Her death is soon followed by the death of her parents and of André. The orphaned child is brought up by André's friend Daniel—a Jew—the very man Schaoul had insisted Midiane marry.

The novel is notable for its dramatic presentation of cultural variations and conflicts. By alternating scenes depicting a close-knit Jewish family with scenes portraying the dysfunctional family of the Regent, Foa reverses the usual stereotype of Jews as depraved and Christians as civilized. While order, harmony, and probity reign in Schaoul's bank and in his home, the Regent's milieu, influenced by the notoriously corrupt minister, the abbé Dubois, is characterized by disorder, corruption, lechery, and a passion for easy money. Jewish family rituals, such as Sabbath meals shared by the extended family and the celebration of the Passover, underscore the coherence of Jewish life. Jewish values that emphasize charity and communal responsibility contrast with the profligate and wanton life of the court.

Foa also depicts the shackles that Jewish customs place on women, for the religion demands obedience to the commands of the father and of a God impervious to human needs. Modernity offers women the possibilities of education and travel, not available in the traditional Jewish household. To emphasize the backwardness of the traditional Jewish way of life, Foa creates a setting in which the women are sequestered and wear oriental dress.

In the following selection, which shows her heroine Midiane praying with her mother, Foa portrays customs and aspirations that had never before been described in French literature by Jews themselves.

— **Michèle Bitton**

Selected Works

Kiddoushim ou l'anneau nuptial des Hébreux. 4 vols. Paris, 1830.
Philippe. Paris: A. Levasseur, 1831.
La Juive, histoire du temps de la Régence. 2 vols. Paris: A. Bertrand, 1835.
Le Petit Robinson ou le triomphe de l'industrie. Paris: Ebrard, 1840.
Alexandrine. 2 vols. Paris: Passard, 1845.
Contes historiques pour la jeunesse. Paris: Desforges, 1843.
Le Livre de la jeunesse. 5 vols. Chez l'auteur, 1843–1848.
Les Enfants illustres. Paris: A. Bedelt, 1853.

Translations Into English

The Boy Life of Napoleon, Afterwards Emperor of the French. Boston: Lothrop, 1895.
Mystery of Castle Pierrefitte. New York: Longmans, Green, 1927.
Biographical Sketches. New York: P. O'Shea, 1877.
The Little Robinson of Paris, or Industry's Triumph: A Tale for Youth. New York: Philip J. Cozans, 1843.

Secondary Works

Rosa Buzy-Filgarz. *Eugénie Foa.* Mémoire de Diplôme d'Etudes Avancées. University of Paris X, 1998.
Elisabeth-Christine Muelsch. "Eugénie Foa," in Eva Martin Sartori, ed., *The Feminist Encyclopedia of French Literature,* Westport, CT: Greenwood Press, 1999.
R. Fountès. "Eugénie Foa," in M. Prévost and Roman d'Amat, eds., *Dictionnaire de biographie française.* Paris: Letouzey and Ané, 1979 (14:151).
Camille Lebrun. "Foa, Eugénie," in Fetis Hoefer, ed., *Nouvelle biographie générale.* Paris: Didot, 1958 (18:19).

The Jewess

Two women were standing in an apartment very similar to the one to which André had been taken and from which he had been removed in such a strange manner. They were facing east, each with hands clasped together, their lips moving, their bearing reverent. Everything in their attitude indicated that they were praying to God.

Their veils had been thrown back, revealing their strange costume. You know what the younger of the two was wearing. The other one's clothes were similar, except that a cashmere turban decorated with fine pearls covered her hair. A few strands of hair were visible over her temples, attesting to the passage of time. A thick muslin shawl hid her neck and the top of her shoulders, the pure and perfect form of the younger woman's shoulders remaining exposed.

They had both been praying for a long time, but it was easy to see that the older woman was entirely absorbed by a saintly fervor, while the younger woman seemed withdrawn, sad, and bored. Soon her lips stopped moving, she lowered her hands, still clasped, after bending her head. She remained that way, pensive, her beautiful eyes raised to the sky, until her companion, her eyes closed as if adoring an invisible being, turned around after bowing three times and called, "Midiane!"

The young woman gave a start when she heard her name. Her face colored. Then, tearing herself from where she stood, she ran toward the woman who was calling her, took her hand, placed it on her head, and said in a choked voice, "Bless your daughter, mother."

"May every blessing fall on you, my child," answered the mother, kissing the charming forehead that had remained bowed as if weighed down by a deep and secret thought. "May the God of Israel bless you as I do, my daughter, my Midiane. But tell me, my child, what is this change that has suddenly come over you? What are you feeling? I have been watching you for several days. Your youthful gaiety seems to have disappeared. You seem lethargic in everything you do, when you read, even when you pray, and yet it is such a sacred thing to pray to God. Midiane, do you have some secret sorrow that your mother does not know about? Speak, daughter of my heart."

"It is nothing, mother, but I am sad, and I don't know why."

"A joyous heart makes one beautiful, but a sad heart depresses the spirit. How long have you been sad, my child?"

"My good mother, don't be angry. Ever since I have come to know myself,

From: *La Juive, histoire du temps de la Régence* (Paris: A. Bertrand, 1835), pp. 76–84.

ever since I have had feelings, ever since I have come to understand my existence, it has always seemed to me that something was lacking. This sort of captivity in which we eastern women live and in which we are brought up, seems to me narrow, harsh. I don't understand it."

"My daughter, where do these thoughts come from? What saintly works have given rise in your young head to thoughts whose danger is hidden by your inexperience?"

"Mother, don't be angry with me, for I will not have the strength to tell you anything . . . a kiss . . . another kiss. . . . Oh! Let me open my heart to you. If you only knew how much I need to pour out my heart to you! . . . Dear mother, I love you so much! . . . Listen to me: You remember my childhood, how lively I was, how scatterbrained and playful. Aleppo, or to be more exact, that terrace, that garden where I played as a child with other children my age, seemed to me to contain all the happiness that a human being could wish for. For me that terrace was the whole universe . . . until the day when I was ten years old and you received a letter from my father. You told me about this letter. Oh, mother! That letter suddenly opened my eyes and my head. It contained a faithful description of his travels. What vast and beautiful things were revealed to me, the names of which I didn't even know! What wonderful discoveries! Nature is so vast! My God, I knew nothing of all this! And I, a woman, though more than a slave, I was never to see them, never. It was horrible to think that! . . . Never! Never to be free of this barbaric yoke which holds us women back! I will never be able to admire, free and proud, all the marvels that my feverish imagination probably paints as more beautiful than they are but which, because it is impossible for me ever to enjoy them, seem to me more than desirable, more than essential to my being. They seem to represent existence itself! Oh! Mother, my dear mother! How pitiful is the plight of women! Forgive me for these mutterings. They oppress me and I needed to speak of them to you, my darling mother. If you knew how much I suffer. If you knew how all of my father's letters, so avidly read and devoured by me, increased my excitement, to the point that I felt I was going to waste away every day. . . . Luckily we left Aleppo. You remember my joy. I imagined that by changing cities we would also change our way of life, would change this existence that weighed down so heavily on me. What a fool I was! I had only changed prisons. . . . Mother, please answer me, tell me why there have to be barriers and walls that keep me away from the entire world? But not all women are slaves, nor are they shut in as we are, mother. I know it."

The Syrian woman was rendered speechless by her daughter's words. She felt as though she needed to ask Midiane to start all over, so strange and incomprehensible was what the young woman was saying. Brought up on these ideas which so revolted Midiane's high-minded and independent soul, this woman had never thought that a more expansive and freer life existed elsewhere. Almost afraid of the feelings that were growing in her child and what these simple and naïve questions expressed, the old woman did not know how to answer.

Midiane continued, "Mother, I can't live like this, I feel that I'm dying every day."

"But what have you seen, my child, that makes you speak this way?" cried the mother, lifting her hands and her eyes to the sky.

"Seen . . . nothing . . ." answered Midiane, sadly, "but I have read . . . things that stirred my heart, that made me think."

"What, dear God, what could have so troubled your mind? What books have you found? . . . The only book I have here is the sacred Bible."

"But if I tell you everything, you will perhaps be angry."

"Alas, he who spares the rod hates his son, but he who loves his son punishes him quickly! Dear Lord, I would like to act that way; but where can I find the courage when my child looks at me and when her hand, so soft and so pretty, closes my lips? My darling daughter, tell me quickly what you have seen and then forget it even more quickly, I beg you, for your mother's sake."

Midiane shook her head and answered, "The secret passage my father uses when he comes to see us . . . well, one night while you were sleeping, I took it."

"God of Israel!"

"Don't be frightened, mother, I met no one. I came to a pretty room where the doors were all closed, except the one through which I had come. And there, in that room, I found books, many, many books. I took one."

"What was it called?"

"The Princess of Clèves."

"I don't recognize that name. Let me see it."

Midiane took a little book out of her pocket that she handed to her mother. Hardly had her mother seen it, when she cried out, "Abomination of abominations! This book isn't even written in Hebrew. It isn't a book of prayers or psalms."

"No mother, it's a French novel."

"A novel! Unhappy child, no wonder you seem to waste away, if you read books of the devil's invention. . . . Daughter, forget this princess, forget her, I beg you. . . . Oh! My God, my God!"

"Mother, I am no longer a child. I am fifteen years old and I have my own thoughts. No, our fate is not to live shut in, hidden away. Mother, I want to see the world."

"God of Israel, my daughter is going mad. Poor child! The madwoman talks too much. What she says is only foolishness, she knows nothing. The good child makes her father happy, but the mad child is the enemy of her mother. The demon has taken hold of her; he wants to seduce her, to lead her to ruin. Second Eve, listen to the voice of God. Crush the serpent that is breathing his poison into you. My child, child of my womb, come to your senses. . . . Ah! I was too proud of my daughter, the God of Israel has punished me."

"Mother, I am not mad. And you complain wrongly, without answering any of my thoughts. Dear mother, don't you feel anything inside that tells you that elsewhere one is free, one can come and go, the sun seems bigger, the earth larger, the horizon further away? When you were my age, did you never ask your mother for more air, more freedom of movement than you allow me? Oh! I am suffocating!"

"My daughter, since I was born, I have followed my mother's teachings without deviating. They have always served me well. Do the same, that is all I can answer you."

Midiane became quiet and sighed. In her naïveté, the young woman felt that her mother didn't understand her, couldn't understand her. Then, pursuing her thoughts in spite of herself, she said, "What could have happened to that stranger?"

"Who?"

"The young man whose carriage was knocked over?"

"Why do you care what happened to that Christian? Like all of them, he did not thank us for our help and thinks we are well paid by having obliged him."

"Why judge him that way, mother? There was so much goodness in his face, such a beautiful expression in his eyes!"

"You must have looked at him carefully, Midiane! . . . Believe me, if I judge strangers this way, it is because they deserve it. They heap contempt on us; their society is forbidden to us! I pay them back with the contempt and the scorn they pile on us. I hate them to death, these people, this race of Amalek."

An irritated look crossed Midiane's eyes, she was going to answer; but probably a thought stopped her, for she simply said, "Does father dine with us today?"

"Yes, you have reminded me. I am so preoccupied by your sadness that I forget everything when I look at you. Come, Midiane, cheer up. Prepare the dessert; put fresh flowers everywhere. I'll go down to the kitchen to help Kitime prepare the meal."

Schaoul's wife left and Midiane made herself do what she had been expected to do. Nevertheless, her movements had about them an extraordinary nonchalance and an air of abandon and boredom. When she had finished, she stopped, pensive, in the middle of the room where her thoughts had immobilized her.

"Where is your mother?"

At the sound of this voice, Midiane emerged from her reverie. A tall, thin man was standing before her.

"I'll tell her that you are looking for her, father", she answered timidly.

"Tell her that I've brought two guests for dinner, two rabbis from Jerusalem. Tell her to serve the very best of everything. This is my daughter, sirs. Midiane, come let them bless you."

Midiane noticed then that her father was not alone and that two strangers were following him. Each of the two old men with long beards wore a white turban, a brown cloak, a cashmere sash, wide pants and steel-tipped shoes. But everything was so worn out, so dusty, that from their clothes alone you could tell that they had come a long way on foot.

With an air of respect and submission, Midiane came toward the rabbis and welcomed them. The old men, smiling at this pretty head bent before them, held their hands briefly above her head and, murmuring a few words, called forth all of heaven's blessings upon her. The young woman thanked them with a grateful look, then left to find her mother and help her with the housework.

— **Translated by Eva Martin Sartori,
Ralph Tarica, and Suzanne Tarica**

Pauline Franck
(1809?–1865?)

We know very few facts about Pauline Franck: not her maiden name, the place and date of her birth, or exactly when she died. We only know that out of financial necessity she worked as a governess to a Jewish family in her native province of Lorraine until her marriage. Separated from her future husband, Adolphe Franck, who was busy building his career as a teacher of philosophy in various French towns, Pauline Franck began a correspondence that ended only with her death. Her letters were collected by her friend, Louis de Ratisbonne, and published after her death.

Franck's life is an example of a rich emotional and intellectual existence, happily carried out within the circle of the family. After she married Adolphe, who was to become a prominent philosopher with a chair at the Collège de France and a leader in the Jewish community, she devoted herself to the tasks of being a wife and mother. Her purpose was to teach her children and to provide for her family a haven from the cares of the world. Although she demanded equality with Adolphe, that equality was based on a clear division of labor. Her letters offer no details about her material situation and tell us little about external events. Instead they give us insight into the internal life of an acculturated Jewish woman at the middle of the nineteenth century.

What role did Judaism play in Pauline Franck's life? Pauline Franck rejected atheism, which she believed would inevitably lead to the moral disintegration of society. By nature, she was intensely religious and, like Foa, saw the divine manifested in nature rather than in religious practice. While she occasionally referred to the Jewish holy days her mother observed, these events do not evoke in her an emotional response.

Spiritually, Franck was drawn to Christianity, especially to the figure of Christ, and she admired the abnegation of the monastic way of life. But she maintained that she could never convert to Christianity because its miracles strained credulity. She described herself as *"croyante de coeur et incrédule d'esprit"* [a believer in her heart and an unbeliever in her mind]. Adolphe, however, was active in the affairs of the *consistoire* and she supported his activities on behalf of the Jewish community but she resisted socializing with Jews just because they were Jews. References to anti-Semitic incidents, although rare, aroused her anger, especially when they were directed at Adolphe. When an article used disparaging words about Jews, she remarked, "We feel that we are merely tolerated, but in reality we are hated." This remark is the only one in the published letters that hints at a chasm between the majority culture and the Jewish community.

Her letters are varied in tone, at times lively, at times playful, always inquisitive. But what distinguishes them most is an intense moral life pursued with rectitude and passion.

— **Eva Martin Sartori**

Selected Work

Une Vie de femme. Lettres intimes de Pauline Franck. Tours: Imprimerie Paul Bousrez, 1897.

A Woman's Life

May 1833

If one needs only to love in order to believe, surely I am well on my way. My dear, I told you, my soul needs faith. And doubt, which others bear lightly, withers me and robs my life of magic. And yet how often it has assailed me! How often, when reflecting on the misery of an existence with no purpose, with no future other than death that swallows everything—body and soul, hope and love—I have become discouraged and asked myself: Is it worth it? Belief, on the other hand, by turning me away from earthly existence toward the heavens, seems to carry me above the world's misfortunes. It fills my soul with strength and joy, and accomplishing even the most painful duty gives me a feeling of happiness when I am no longer the slave of a blind and despotic will but the object of a benevolent divine Providence. Am I not rather to be pitied than blamed when I still doubt, or at least when I remember, some of those old doubts which I have put aside without seeking to clarify them, reasoning that you and perhaps others have thought about them for me.

June 1834

It terrifies me to see all this paper blackened with my ramblings. But look! On the subject of my compulsion to tear up all my fancy reasoning, I must confess quite frankly, even though it will earn me a lecture to which I will happily listen but which will not cure me. It is hard enough for me to entertain my correspondents with what happens to me, first because there is nothing about my life that is really all that interesting, and then because outside events leave little impression on me and because I value only the life of the soul. That is why my letters are more like a bundle of thoughts, of daydreams set down without order than full of the details one expects in an epistolary exchange. Well, with you, my dear, you whose image and words are constantly with me, you who share my feelings, why do I sometimes become silent and constrained? Why does my pen stop when my soul is still unsatisfied? Let me confess: it is because your immense superiority intimidates me profoundly and that often, when I have come up with a pretty bundle of doubts—thoughts I wish to clarify, ideas that are new to me that I would like to tell you about—I turn away having done none of this because it seems to me that, with the best intent in the world, the look you would give resembles one that a jeweler would bestow on a

From: *Une Vie de femme. Lettres intimes de Pauline Franck.* Tours: Imprimerie Paul Bousrez, 1897.

vulgar stone. Don't be angry with me because my vanity makes me keep things from you. Admit that I am right. Isn't it true that you are smiling?

December 1834

I think I told you once on an unforgettable day, in the presence of monuments we owe to the Christian fervor of the Middle Ages, what I thought of Jesus and Mary. I admire and wish to practice the morality of the Gospels. I even confess that all those symbols of the Christian religion speak to my heart and to my imagination, and that the practice of Catholicism more than any other seems to me in harmony with my beliefs. But I cannot go any further and accept that the laws of nature can be contravened, that the man-God was not born and died like another. It seems to me that his divinity is like that of all beings who rise above the shackles of matter and become ennobled when they shed their earthly passions. What is human in him disappears and only God remains. I am willing to be a Christian but for the belief in miracles, the Virgin, and the Resurrection, my reason doesn't allow my imagination to believe in them. These miracles are admirable myths and that is all. I hope that as a Jew and as a philosopher you will not think me too impious. I ask of you only a declaration of principles on which I can base my beliefs. When one is too lazy to educate oneself, it is so convenient to find ready-made opinions.

July 8, 1836

I admit that I love the shrewd and nimble mind of these mighty destroyers, the courage of their genius. And most of all, yes, I love the one who was probably the most fanatic atheist, Diderot, the eloquent and fiery Diderot, who brought to the great issues of his century all the ardor of his soul and the power of his genius. Diderot, who, in other times, would have been a Saint Bernard, much greater as a missionary than he was as a writer. His epistle to Falconet on the respect we owe posterity shows him to be a man of lofty feelings and generous convictions. After reading his eloquent words I wish I could wake him from the grave, hold his icy hand, and cry out to him, "Come back to life, Diderot, come back to life so you can believe! You were made to know and to spread the truth!"

But God knows better than I what he is doing. He places men and things in their time to accomplish his purpose, most of the time without them knowing what it is. And yet, if our century can uncover a corner of the thick veil that covers truth, it is because the intrepid jousters of the eighteenth century helped. Like Tasso's or Ariosto's paladins, they have conquered the monsters at the entrance to the sanctuary. It would be ungrateful not to recognize what we owe them.

While I was reading Diderot, I was also rereading, or rather truly reading for the first time, Bossuet. And in my admiration for these two such opposite fanatics I realized how much is missed by the single-minded, those who accept only that which flies under their flag. What does the color or the name matter? To admire the beautiful wherever it is found, to separate it from the errors among which it is often found and to pay homage to it, that is what I call enjoyment, a wise kind of enjoyment. But isn't it the mark of a narrow and selfish mind to look only for that which reflects you and your own opinions? It seems to me that such tolerance in literary matters should also be the rule in private life.

December 3, 1836

In general, I do not like to see a woman, single or married, abandon usefulness without which there is no *dignity,* unless she is obliged by material obstacles. It is agreed, indeed recognized, that she should not be content with being simply an object that pleases the eye. I would prefer she aim higher than simply providing relaxation and amusement to the mind. Gracefulness is a beautiful thing, but it is insufficient to establish equality. If a woman of high social standing can do the honors in a home where good taste and elegant customs reign, at the same time that she supervises the education of her children, that is all that can be asked of her. But, if at the other end of the social ladder, the artisan knows that she must also be an artisan in order to ease the burdens of daily life, why should a woman of the middle class cross her arms, watch others work and reap the fruits of their labor without contributing her share?

. . . Ah! How cruel these people are! They rob me of my Saturdays, of the hour I could have devoted to you. For the last two hours the most insipid visitors tear me away from you. Without wishing to sound biased, our co-religionists are sometimes quite absurd. It would seem that having the same beliefs is enough to establish a feeling of intimacy. We owe it to our brothers, who have been oppressed for so long, to defend them through our own behavior. Most of all we must encourage them to do good, to open the doors of honest occupations to them, to protect them, to use our influence, our talent, our fortune to push them forward as much as possible. But the greatest good will, the most tender pity, the most constant protection are not the same thing as intimacy. For it is not enough to be equally scorned by the Christians. That is what our brothers from Judea still have trouble understanding.

April 17, 1837

I was more touched by the consistoire's offer than by your election to the Academy and I am sorry you reject it on the grounds of your age and your tastes. I understand that it would be a sacrifice, but it is also an opportunity to do good, and this motive should be sufficient to overcome your reluctance. Our current forms of worship lack dignity and I think it would be a good thing to rehabilitate them if possible. Like you, I am pleased with the Jews' moral progress of which this offer is an example. It seems to me that one can be that much more useful to a consistoire because few thorough reforms have been undertaken so far. Besides, if we give up on ourselves, who will have the courage to support us? I don't know if my words will seem to contradict what I wrote to you in the past concerning our brethren, but my opinions in this matter have not changed at all. I do not like the Jewish mindset any more than I like any other sectarian mindset. I cannot stand the insolent familiarity of those who feel entitled to intimacy on no other grounds than a supposed commonality of beliefs. But I also do not like it when, quick to put on another's garment, we affect toward each other today a desperate scorn that aggravates the illness, when we could attempt to cure it with indulgence and pity.

July 1864

Couldn't the Paris journalists cast aside their foolishness and have a little more respect for their Jewish readers? These words of scorn, reproduced with a certain pleasure, cause a painful shock and evoke a feeling of humiliation that is both cruel and dangerous to honest and proud young minds. We feel that we are merely *tolerated* but in reality we are hated, and that racial differences play a part here, as elsewhere! We do not tear each other to pieces, like these sweet lambs the Druze and the Maronites,* but when souls have been developed by culture, by the appearance of equality, how a term of abuse can wound! Indeed, it is difficult to be liberal, unless one is very high-minded . . . or among the injured.

— **Translated by Eva Martin Sartori**

---

*During most of the nineteenth century, the Druze (a schismatic Muslim sect associated with Shi'ism), were in conflict with the Maronite Christians.

Julienne Bloch
(1833–1868)

The daughter of the founder and editor of *L'Univers Israélite,* Julienne Bloch was a teacher while her sister Pauline was the administrator of schools for Jewish girls in Lyons and Paris. Very much involved in Jewish affairs, Bloch was dedicated to providing a religious education for the young, especially for girls. She believed a Jewish education was vital to resist the pressure of religious assimilation. As part of the movement of *régénération,* prominent lay leaders were exerting pressure on the Jewish community to alter religious practices to resemble those of Christianity. For instance, Jewish girls had begun wearing white dresses at the confirmation ceremony that marked their entrance into the adult community, a practice that, according to Bloch, made these ceremonies too much like Christian communions and would ultimately set these girls on the road to conversion. She also criticized parents for sending their children to Christian schools, where they were exposed to slurs and pressured to convert.

In keeping with her pedagogical bent, during the Jewish holidays Bloch took the opportunity to comment on biblical stories, stressing their moral content and the prestige these moral principles conferred on the Jews. In her commentary, she tended to highlight stories in which women were the heroines, among them Esther, Ruth, Sarah, Deborah, and Judith. Bloch wrote, "I salute you lovingly, blessed religion of Israel, that has truly emancipated woman, has assured her a glorious place in the history of our people and the sanctuary of our families." A year later, in March 1858, she reiterated the link between emancipation and the liberation of women: "In this great sublime mission of emancipation and liberation, the Jewish woman has a great role and noble duties." Her columns, peppered with quotations from the Old Testament and commentaries on biblical stories, stress Judaism's moral values, chiefly the love of liberty and the practice of charity, values that made Judaism consonant with those of the French Republic. Ever watchful, she fiercely attacked the stereotyping of Jews in the press and in books as greedy and cowardly. She took every opportunity to praise Jews who had distinguished themselves in government and in the arts and to publicize the misery of the Eastern European Jews.

Julienne Bloch's "Lettres parisiennes," published in *L'Univers Israélite* between 1854 and 1868, are animated by a dedication to community, a strong belief in Judaism, and a conviction that women have a central role to play in Jewish life.

— **Eva Martin Sartori**

Julienne Bloch

Selected Works

"Lettres d'une Parisienne," *L'Univers Israélite de France*. Vol. 9, 1853–54, pp 481–86; vol. 10, 1854–55, pp. 26–29, 124–29, 193–97, 270–73, 374–77, 523–27; vol. 11, 1855–56, pp. 37–41, 137–41, 231–34, 322–27, 519–23; vol. 12, 1856–57, pp. 84–89, 289–96, 433–38; vol. 13, 1857–58, pp. 1–7, 289–94; vol. 14, 1858–59, pp. 40–46, 339–44; vol. 15, 1859, pp. 47–53, 349–56, vol. 17, 1861–62, pp. 37–42.

Secondary Works

Michèle Bitton. *Présences féminines juives en France, XIXe-XIXe siècles*. [Pertuis]: 2M Editions, 2002, pp. 190–192.
Maurice Bloch. "Une journaliste juive," *L'Univers Israélite de France*, vol. 51, 1895–96, pp. 32–34.
"Julienne Bloch, In memoriam." *L'Univers Israélite de France*, vol. 24, 1868–69, pp. 149–51.
"Institution de jeunes demoiselles dirigée par Melles Julienne et Pauline Bloch." *L'Univers Israélite de France*, vol. 17, 1861–62, pp. 47–48.

Letter to Monsieur Eugène de Mirecourt

Sir, you recently honored me with a charming little letter protesting the hostility toward my fellow Jews which I noted in your biography of Meyerbeer. In your reply you wrote that, "Certainly all religions can claim some very worthy people. You and your family are living proof of this. But you don't have the right to judge others on the basis of yourself."

Allow me, sir, to believe that I have the right to reject with all my strength the odious meaning that fanaticism has assigned and continues to assign to the word "Jew." Not so long ago the word "Christian" in Turkey was synonymous with "dog." It is true that the Greeks of Constantinople were not always models of evangelical virtue. You are right to be angry at Muslims' attempt to smear all Christians with this injurious epithet, and yet you think it right to use the word "Jew" when you want to call someone a miser or a rogue or an extortionist, etc.!

If vulgar and brutal people spit at us and insult us with the word "Jew," superior minds and independent and straight-thinking writers have the obligation to protect us against these abuses, and to fight prejudice, to enlighten people, and to promote the cause of emancipation, brotherhood, and love, so that our beneficent country can become the new Palestine. Well, sir, I am sorry to tell you that it seems to me you have done just the opposite.

You speak of Hermione. I urge you to read two passages in the *L'Univers Israélite* (pages 188 and 201, 1854) to discover the editor-in-chief's opinion of the famous actress and to be convinced that we are not at all victims of sectarian opinions. On the other hand, your biography of Mlle Rachel is unworthy of your character and high principles.

On page 7, you say that the Felix family sold "these thousands of indescribable objects which make up the nomadic Jew's bundle." Are the objects sold by Jewish nomads different from those sold by Christian nomads? And among the innumerable stalls that at this moment clutter our streets, can you distinguish a Jewish doll from a Catholic puppet?

Further on you write: "In any case, the Jews have invaded many other professions and careers. The other day a very witty man exclaimed, 'I am only surprised that a Jew is not archbishop of Paris!'"

And should he not be? Was the Christian God anything other than a Jew? You reproach Jews with invading all the professions. Would you prefer that they still be locked in a ghetto, excluded from all social life, prohibited from exercising all public functions, condemned to make a living from usury and

From: *L'Univers Israélite,* January 11, 1855.

peddling, in order to obtain by any means whatever the large sums that would satisfy the greed of their oppressors and feed the shameful vices of princes?

If Jews attain high positions, what does it prove? It proves that they are capable, that they are intelligent and deserving, and that secular persecutions have been unable to grind them down, nor to extinguish the divine fire and moral freedom that characterize the true man created in the image of the Eternal. But what can they be accused of when they occupy positions they have attained through their work and our country's trust? You are right to object to the love of gold that motivates a Jewish actress by the name of Rachel. But why don't you also mention the Jewish minister of finance who in 1848 refused a salary and sacrificed his time and fortune for the state? Why don't you also write in your biography of Théophile Gautier that M. Mirès, who made a considerable sacrifice to come to the writer's aid, also practiced the Jewish religion?

On page 44, you write further that "Hermione was Jewish in the magnitude of her greed for gold usually associated with that word." Who makes such a judgment? It is the product of a clumsy and vulgar ill will, the same ignoble intolerance that in old times trampled our sacred books and that today seeks to sully our name. But you, sir, you must know that in no human race is charity as prevalent as among Jews and that Jews are the most generous people in the world, for they always remember that they are the sons of kings, the descendants of the royal dynasty of David and Solomon. Noblesse oblige, after all.

Finally you tell this delicious anecdote. The famous actress is languishing. Doctors can find no cure for it, but M. Felix, inspired by fatherly love, has a marvelous idea. He places a box filled with gold and jewelry in front of his daughter. The sight of it makes the sick woman tremble with pleasure and brings back color to her cheeks. "Her joy comes from feminine coquetry; but above all it is the Jewess, the Jewess who is overjoyed."

But do you know, sir, what is a Jewess? A Jewess is the charitable and virtuous woman whose praises were sung by the royal poet. She embodies the sweet and saintly charity "whose arm is extended to the poor and whose hand is open to the miserable." The Jewess is the pious and devoted woman who responds to Moses' call by happily relinquishing her gold and her jewels to decorate the sanctuary of the Almighty. The Jewess is the divine prophetess Deborah, this Jewish Joan of Arc, who inspires her brothers with noble fervor and leads them to combat and to glory. The Jewess is the heroic martyr who witnesses the suffering of her sons and willingly accepts a degrading death in honor of her God and her faith. The Jewess is the fearless queen who, defying the terrible law threatening her, confronts the wrath of the king to save Israel from the homicidal furor of Haman. Judith took the life and not the gold of her people's enemy. . . . You can see that you were wrong to give the sublime title of "Jewess" to the heroine of your story.

For you, sir, *Jew* signifies greed and avarice, a thirst for gold, a heart of copper and bronze. How wrong you are! A Jew is the man who first recognized and worshipped God, creator of the universe, who is the first-born of civilization and the teacher of all humanity, the man who has suffered all manners of martyrdom and oppression for the sake of truth, who continues to be persecuted for his convictions, and who can avoid all misfortunes and find all that money and gold that, according to you, constitute his soul and his life by simply accepting a few drops of water!

It behooves you, sir, to mend the ill that your remarks may have caused. Calumnies and attacks against *Jews* do not reach the Rothschilds and the Foulds, the Meyerbeers, and the Rachels, but they do cruelly affect the poor and the weak who must pay for the good fortune of some happy co-religionists. Do you understand now why I was, as you say, angry with you?

I will stop being angry when, loyal and scrupulous as I know you to be, you will recognize the merit of my protest and, disdaining the rewards of popularity, courageously crush the head of the snake and combat religious intolerance in the same way you combat duplicity in the arts and letters.

— **Translated by Eva Martin Sartori**

Elissa Rhaïs
(1876–1940)

Elissa Rhaïs's literary fortune was an unusual one. Her novels and short stories, set in exotic Algerian harems, were a big success among fashionable readers of the *années folles* [Roaring Twenties] and were also praised by critics who admired her "Muslim sensitivity" and her "acute perception of the Muslim soul."[1] By the 1930s, however, an anti-Semitic pamphlet entitled *Le Péril Juif* exposed her as an impostor who was "passing for" Muslim. The pamphlet also sharply criticized her writing. Rhaïs vanished from the literary world for four decades. In 1982, her name resurfaced when Paul Tabet, her step-nephew's son, published a book that purported to be a biography in which he denied her the authorship of all the fiction that had been published under her name. He attributed it instead to his own father, who he claimed had been her captive lover and ghost-writer. Most critics of literature from the Maghreb do not support Tabet's allegation.

Elissa Rhaïs was born Rosine Boumendil, in Blidah, Algeria. Although poor, the family sent her to *école communale,* the local school, until the age of twelve, a decision that illustrates the fact that schooling among Jews in French-occupied Algeria was widespread. In 1845, years before the Crémieux decree gave French citizenship to all Algerian Jews, the ordinance of Saint-Cloud had established that the French state would assume responsibility for the education of Jewish children. The opportunity to benefit from a secular education was one of the main reasons why Jewish communities of the Maghreb generally rejoiced at the arrival of the colonizers. They welcomed the chance to be exposed to Western culture, applauded French Republican values, and were also grateful for this providential way of escaping the status of the *dhimmi*.[*] French was perceived as a valuable tool of emancipation. Indeed, for Sephardic Jews like Rhaïs whose identity had been elaborated through a double diaspora, both polylinguism and assimilation were familiar experiences. They were not associated with a "loss of soul," as they were for Muslim Maghrebine writers.

At the age of eighteen, Rosine Boumendil married a rabbi and moved to Algiers. By the age of thirty-eight, divorced and remarried to a wealthy businessman, she opened a literary salon and soon developed a reputation as a skillful and entertaining storyteller. She began writing down her stories and sent them to literary reviews. In 1919, Boumendil decided to try her luck in Paris where she settled with her son, her daughter, and her adopted son,

---

[*]Dhimmi is a non-Muslim monotheist, Christian or Jew, who can be tolerated according to Muslim law, with the condition that his inferiority and humiliation be made clear and his legal and social status be a subservient one.

Elissa Rhaïs

Raoul-Robert Tabet, a nephew of her second husband. Before the end of the year, she had signed a five-year contract with the publisher Plon and her first novel, *Saâda la Marocaine* [Saâda the Moroccan] (1919), was published under the pen name of Elissa Rhaïs. Her publishers preferred to conceal her Jewish background and, with her consent, advertised her novel as the work of a Muslim woman who had learned French at a public French school, then lived cloistered in a harem, and was now "burning with the desire" to "tell her country" in French.[2] They hoped this deception would attract readers. Novels by an "oriental" woman, and a cloistered one at that, would be sure to contain genuine and exciting insights about mysterious Algeria. Furthermore, the fact that she had chosen to write in the language she had learned in school was living proof of the success of the colonial enterprise. Readers were obviously unaware of the fact that Muslim women, unlike Jewish women, had no access to a French education at that time.

In 1922, Rhaïs returned to Algeria. By then it was widely known that her step-nephew/adopted son, who worked as her secretary, had become her lover. In 1930, her daughter died of typhoid fever during a trip she and her daughter took to Morocco. Perhaps due to grief, or perhaps because the fashion for exotic tales was waning, she never published another book. She died in Blidah on August 18, 1940.

Eager to comply with her publisher's wish that she produce heartbreaking romances in exotic North African settings, Rhaïs had devoted much of her fiction to a description of domestic life in the Maghreb. Most of her narratives are sentimental tales with female heroines. With few exceptions, they depict various Muslim milieux of the two decades preceding World War I. Though her characterizations are sketchy and her plots melodramatic, her portraits of women go beyond the two prevailing stereotypes of colonial times, the odalisque and the *fatma* or maid. She favored strong, passionate, independent, pleasure-loving heroines and described their daily lives, customs, dress, interiors, religious celebrations, family relationships, and forbidden loves with great care and evident delight.

Two of her novels, *Les Juifs ou la fille d'Eléazar* [The Jews, or Eleazer's Daughter] and *Le Sein blanc* [White Bosom] focus on Jewish families. At a time when Jews were invariably represented as backward, grabbing parasites by the notoriously anti-Semitic Algerianists,* Rhaïs's sympathetic portrait of middle-class Jewish characters dealing with conflicts of love and tradition and

---

*Algerianists were a group of writers active in the 1920s who thought of the Maghreb as fundamentally "Latin." They felt their mission was to describe and exalt the life of the colonizer. In general, they were racist and anti-Semitic.

proud of their Jewishness was a courageous project. Both novels idealize the characters that cling to the "old life," but they also stress the fact that the conflict between the old and the new ways of life was creating a new identity for North African Jews. However, neither the adoption of Western values nor the use of the French language is represented as alienating or traumatic.

In the short story "Enfants de Palestine" [Children of Palestine], Rhaïs abandons her usual protagonists and steps outside the domestic sphere. Her choice of plot and setting testifies to the importance that the question of Zionism had acquired for French Jews with the rise of Fascism in Europe. Although her characters are largely stereotypical (the "pleasure-loving Arab" and the "hard-working Jew"), she does not side with one or the other. She includes the familiar clichés: oriental beauty, Arab pride and sensuality, Jewish sense of duty and love of justice. Her text presents the usual powdering of Arab words and titillating descriptions of harem life which keep it within the parameters of the exotic genre. Yet she also gives voice to a longing for goodwill between Arabs and Jews that resonates today.

— Sonia Assa

Notes

[1] Jean Déjeux, *Femmes d'Algérie* (Paris: La Boîte à Documents, 1987), pp. 265-66.
[2] Guy Dugas. *La littérature judéo-maghrébine d'expression française: Entre Djéha et Cagayous* (Paris: Editions l'Harmattan, 1992), p. 42.

Selected Works

Saâda la Marocaine. Paris: Plon, 1919.
Le Café chantant. Paris: Plon, 1920.
Les Juifs ou la fille d'Eléazar. Paris: Plon, 1921.
La Fille des pachas. Paris: Plon, 1922.
La Fille du douar. Paris: Plon, 1924.
La Chemise qui porte bonheur. Paris: Plon, 1925.
L'Andalouse. Paris: Fayard, 1925.
Le Mariage de Hanifa. Paris: Plon, 1926.
Par la voix de la musique. Paris: Plon, 1927.

Elissa Rhaïs

Le Sein blanc. Paris: Flammarion, 1928.
La Riffaine, suivi de Petits Pachas en exil. Paris: Flammarion, 1929.
La Convertie. Paris: Flammarion, 1930.
"Enfants de Palestine," in *Revue Hebdomadaire,* August, 1931. Reprinted in *Israel, rêve d'une terre nouvelle.* Guy Dugas and Michel Abitbol, eds. Paris: Omnibus, 1989, pp. 531–53.

Secondary Works

Denise Brahimi. *Femmes arabes et soeurs musulmanes.* Paris: Editions l'Harmattan, 1984.
Jean Déjeux. "Elissa Rhaïs, conteuse algérienne (1876–1940)." *Le Maghreb dans l'imaginaire français.* Aix-en-Provence: Edisud, 1985, pp. 47–79.
Femmes d'Algérie. Paris: La Boîte à Documents, 1987.
Guy Dugas. "Une expression minoritaire: La littérature judéo-maghrébine d'expression française." In *Littératures maghrébines: Colloque Jacqueline Arnaud.* Paris: Editions l'Harmattan, 1990, pp. 135–43.
———. *La Littérature judéo-maghrébine d'expression française: Entre Djéha et Cagayous.* Paris: Editions l'Harmattan, 1992.

Children of Palestine

On the road to Bethany, near Jerusalem, in the middle of a humble orchard where pistachio and lentisk trees grew, lived a friendly Muslim called Si Mohammed el Djezzari. He was a fine-looking young man of about thirty, a devout, peaceful and pleasure-loving soul. His lively mind, accustomed to solitary meditation, shone through his reserved and unassuming manner.

Though he did wish for a wife, Si Mohammed was not yet married. What could he do? Times were hard! To obey the words of the Koran and pay the price of a woman to his liking, he needed diamonds in his safe or his own house in town. For in the new Palestine, one did not hear of *medjidies or bechliks* any more, but of crowns and pounds sterling.

Si Mohammed's inheritance consisted only of a small plot of land, one league from the Zion gate, a few lentisk trees on which his sustenance depended in the fall, and an old *gourbi** near a pond which sheltered a flock of turtles among its slimy pebbles. In summer, clusters of children stormed this pond. They dived naked into the water and pulled out the sacred turtles that they hoped to sell to tourists.

Si Mohammed's occupations were rather unspecified. He tilled his land and, if necessity became pressing, he hired himself to neighbors. What he loved above all was to play his recorder, which he did delightfully. His skill had won him a small circle of friends and admirers who gathered in his garden in the evening. They enjoyed the cool breeze and listened to the dreamy melody of his reed, while the moon shone with all its splendor on the crumbling walls of the great Holy City. . . .

One spring night, the little gathering was disturbed by the arrival of an elderly lady. A former singer, Zeineb had been famous for a while among the rich households of Jerusalem as well as in certain clandestine haunts on Mount Moriah. At sixty, having lost her voice and her looks, but not her connections with well-to-do families, she earned a living arranging marriages. . . .

The fact was that Zeineb's business was flagging. Springtime had not succeeded in arousing anyone that year: only the almond trees were blooming! A wind of celibacy was blowing over Jerusalem. Thus the former singer was eager to start some matchmaking.

---

*a thatch hut

From: "Enfants de Palestine" in *Israél: rêve d'une terre nouvelle*. Michel Abitbol and Guy Dugas, eds. (Paris: Omnibus, 1998), pp. 531–53.

"Well, gentlemen" she exclaimed, breaking the wake-like silence of the gathering, "what are you waiting for? When will you confide your heart's secret to this old nanny and fill these gardens with the happy sounds of feasts and merrymaking?"

One sigh, then another, answered her invitation. She continued: "What's happened to you, by Allah! Here you are, grown men! Your moustaches are longer than your fathers' and yet not one of you unseals his lips! Oh God, if only you knew what ravishing beauties are ripening in secluded harems, how many lovely plants are waiting for a drop of dew to bloom! I know a certain Moina who is only thirteen, but in three years, mark my words, she will be fit for a king! And I could also mention other beauties who are dreaming at this very moment of a supple and powerful male while they doze under their vine arbors. . . ."

"What can we tell you about us, mother?" answered one of the men. "Earning our daily bread is a torment that leaves us neither respite nor hope for the joys you offer! Not long ago, indeed, as our elders tell us, one *boumedfa** was sufficient to stock a house for a whole week and the errand boy still had enough left to get drunk at the Jews' tavern!"

"It was paradise on earth in those days," muttered the youngest.

"We are the new poor," added Mohammed. "Does any land remain in Arab hands in Palestine? No, these gourbis among stones are all we have left. To hold on to this world, we have nothing but our beards and the tender shoots that spring brings forth."

"It's our own fault," said the eldest. "We sell our properties to the Jews who come to settle here. They multiply like locusts on our plains and mountains. And while they work and strike splendors from the bosom of the earth, we sleep on this unblessed money. Or we travel to nearby towns, we go to Cairo, we party and come back with empty hands hanging by our skinny sides. . . ."

"You're right! Only upon returning do we realize our mistake and the remorse that fills us is as sharp as a burn!"

"What are you saying?" yelped the procuress. "Who is talking about remorse? You regret having enjoyed women's love? You think you have wasted your time when you have satisfied your whole being, when you have tasted the ecstasy of hashish or indulged in blue and green liqueurs? Never regret happy days! They're what you steal from this dog's life. The rest is but smoke in the wind!"

"Maybe," retorted the eldest, "but I can't help feeling heartsick when I see what Jews have done with our land. Seeing those trees bending under flowers

---

*Turkish currency

or fruits and those vast vineyards and fields of wheat, I feel like reclaiming the lands we have sold. . . ."

"Oh my friends, you forget the efforts those accomplishments have cost! Sickness, poisoned lives, despair at the bedside of dying loved ones. . . . I heard each farm cost Jews dozens of men. Is it sensible to sacrifice oneself for the sake of a tree or a house? Life is worth infinitely more. Live like a fly, our forefathers used to say, rather than sleep in the cemetery. May the sea wash away worldly goods! Besides, remember that you are the princes of this earth. Allah has assigned toil without rest or respite to Jews and other unbelievers till the end of their days. What are their possessions good for? Do they enjoy them? They don't know that happiness is enjoying five or six women in the cool shade of a harem, as our men do."

"Allah!" sighed the young pleasure seekers. "Your words are wise, Zeineb, but we are poor. How are we to get all the things that make life enjoyable? There is nothing for us to do but work, struggle, and break our bodies and limbs to wrench the coins that cling to stone."

"No, no," continued Zeineb, whose conviction was beginning to falter. "It is not the one who struggles and works the hardest who becomes rich. To each his own luck. As the proverb says, if Allah means to give to me, he will pierce open the roof and pour down a fortune."

The former singer ran a discouraged look over her audience. She could see that those young men had nothing but charming eyes and fresh complexions. The most persuasive eloquence would not wrest a bride price from a single one of them. She shook her head, got up, threw her cigarette butt in the turtle pond, and walked away from that beggarly gathering, muttering under her breath. . . .

At daybreak, after his companions had left, Si Mohammed put away his recorder, blew out his candle, and lay down on his bed of corn husks. With one arm tucked under his head, he pondered the old singer's words: "I know a certain Moina who is only thirteen, but in three years, mark my words, she will be fit for a king!"

His imagination was fired and from that day on he had only one thought: to amass the money he needed to obtain Moina, the queen of his dreams.

After thinking it over for a week and having gathered information from city folks, he made up his mind to go to Haifa. There, he was told, Jewish farmers required a skilled labor force. They paid very well and work was guaranteed for long periods of time. Although he had hitherto led an idle life, Mohammed, who belonged to a family of land-owning farmers, knew everything about farming, including the latest improvements in modern equipment. He was determined to work hard, to save every penny and persevere doggedly, until he won the object of his dreams and put an end to his loneliness.

He inquired after the dowry. It was one hundred English pounds.

He also found out where the beautiful captive lived. Many an evening, with his tarboosh over his ear and his hands behind his back, he would walk along a certain muddy lane neighboring the Mosque of Omar. Neither the high walls crowned with lookout turrets nor the steel-clad door revealed anything about the life inside. And the mystery of it excited his love. . . .

One morning in July, Si Mohammed called at a large estate in the suburbs of Haifa. Isaac Reboux, the owner, known to everyone as Master Isaac, was an Algerian of about sixty, still vigorous, who put his whole heart in the management of his farm. He was stern but fair to his personnel, and he showed gratitude and generosity to those who exerted themselves sincerely. He was an ardent Zionist. Not long before, in the hardware store of the Rue de la Lyre in Algiers where he had made his fortune among his co-religionists, he was haunted by the dream of returning to the Holy Land. As soon as circumstances allowed, he sold off his shop, summoned his large family—his wife, four pretty, dark-eyed girls, three boys bursting with health, his son-in-law, his two sisters and their husbands, three servants whom he considered his own children—and wrested them from the modern capital's dissolute life.

He had also tried to urge along some friends, but only met with inertia or selfishness. To go back to Palestine, how wonderful, but so complicated! Some alleged self-interest, others emotional attachments. Most preferred the easy life of Algiers, the incomparable mildness of her climate, her clubs and casinos, over the prospect of the unknown and arduous exertion. Isaac's children, who had resisted at first, were soon won over by the ambiance of the Jewish colonies and the fearless example of the Russian and Polish immigrants. And they set to work wholeheartedly for the reconstruction of the homeland. . . .

On Sabbath, men and women flocked to the city's synagogue. There, among Jews from all corners of the world, opulent or poor, uneducated or well-read, the Algerian family was delighted to share the same fervent ideal, the same deep conviction in the destiny of Eretz Yisrael.

Hardly ten years had elapsed since the Reboux family had settled in Haifa and the Arabs, who had known that land as rutted and arid, gazed round-eyed at the new Eden: vineyards on the hillsides, verdant orange groves in the dells and—set in the middle of fields of wheat swelling as far as the eye could see—the neat, comfortable dwelling, almost a mansion, which had replaced the wooden shed of bygone days.

Harvest was approaching and the farm was shorthanded. Needless to say, Si Mohammed was kindly welcomed. . . .

The master's eye was not long in noticing the new employee's skill, his knowledge, and his methods. Si Mohammed operated the sheaf-binding harvester with almost artistic ease and dexterity. He had no equal on the entire farm for tracing firm and straight furrows. He was also good at winning the affection of his companions, particularly intellectual Jews who had come to Palestine in the hope of renewing their race by working the land. These men admired the endurance, patience, and friendliness of the Muslim. They loved to sit with him at recess and hear his chats peppered with lively images and wise sayings. . . .

One evening, having admired the rows of furrows freshly traced under the autumn sky, Master Isaac said to Si Mohammed, "How perfect! I am very pleased with you. Tomorrow I will put you at the head of the ploughmen team and I'll double your salary. Also, you won't need to worry about breakfast or lunch. I'll have them served to you near the well where you like to sit."

A mischievous satisfaction flashed in Si Mohammed's slightly slanted eyes, "May Allah favor you, Master Isaac," he said to his boss. "I see that your religion does not exclude fairness."

The Haifa notables, and not just the greybeards, did not fail to scold Isaac Reboux. Employing another non-Jew, and making him a foreman! What about the children of Israel? How could he, a Jew, let an enemy of his race lord it over his own brothers?

Master Isaac calmed everyone down with a few straightforward words, "My friends," he said, "I have no intention of allying this goy to my family or allowing him into my house, let alone sharing his faith. I employ his hands and his intelligence, because they are useful to me. And let me tell you that we must make friends with our neighbors, if we want to continue our work and achieve our ideals. Without union with the Arabs, there is no national Jewish homeland in Palestine and we are simply spinning our wheels. We Jews are a weakly plant, an "aachba dlila," a few beans in the middle of a field of oats. Remember we are only tolerated here. We must establish good relations with those you consider our enemies, associate with them, make them love us or at least appreciate us. If we cannot win their affection, let us at least ensure they acknowledge our goodwill and our wish to get along with them!"

At sunset, when all was quiet . . . Master Isaac liked to drop in on Si Mohammed. He would find him sitting on the rim of the well under a jasmine vine, holding a little cup of steaming coffee where a white flower was floating. Judith, a servant in the master's house, had just served it to him. Si Mohammed admired the young woman and with increasing lust, devoured her with his eyes. As soon as the farm bell rang, she appeared behind the leafy branches holding the tiny tray with one hand and walked up to him with measured steps. She was a picture of hieratic grace with her blond braids over her shoulders, her blue eyes rimmed with long black lashes, her proud nose, her mouth as red as glowing embers, her slender body barely covered by a flannelette dress that revealed her white legs, and her bare feet shod in sandals. It was more than enough to arouse Si Mohammed's sensual temperament. What would he have given at that moment for one smile, one glance from the fair Judith! But Judith put down the coffee cup abruptly and, recoiling disdainfully, walked away with a rhythmic step. Being only thirteen, she followed literally the recommendations the mistress of the house repeated constantly to the women and young girls: "Turn away from Arabs as from the plague. Never smile at them, never speak to them, so they won't be able to think you are flirting with them. Arabs work and live for love."

After she left, Si Mohammed fell back to brooding. He never tired of admiring the countryside. His thoughts went to his little garden in Bethany but most of all to Moina. The blond Jewess had not dimmed the vision of the dark Muslim. . . . He imagined Moina dressed in a gold caftan, decked out in her finery. She was sitting at his side, her head on his shoulder, and drawing him to her arms, she fired his senses with the heady perfume of her flesh, as smooth and sensuous as jasmine petals. . . .

How much longer could he suffer the monotonous and disheartening rule of work? Sometimes he was overcome with despair . . . Then hope would dawn again in his heart. The vision of the regal stranger infused him with renewed vigor. However, his decision was made: "As soon as I have amassed the price of my beloved, I will throw down my pick, forget tractors and Jewish lands, and never set my feet in this place again. What is the use of earning money, if we are not to enjoy it? Life is short; we smile at it, but death is there, laughing behind our ears."

One afternoon, Master Isaac found Si Mohammed with an angry look on his face, his *chechia*[*] all askew, his coffee cup knocked over at his feet.

"What's the matter?" he asked, trying to sound lighthearted. "Have you had bad news from home?"

Evidently agitated, the ordinarily calm Si Mohammed was restlessly pacing the strip of flat ground around the well. He made a visible effort to take hold of himself and stopped in front of his boss.

"Listen, Master. You know a fly will not kill, but it will torment the wisest ones. Yes, I am furious because you make me feel like an outsider, an exile, a slave who is only entitled to his ration and with whom no one will consent to have friendly ties, on whom no one bestows the merest smile! Yes, I am kept apart, like an alcohol drinker. There is an iron wall between you and me!"

---

[*] cylindrical hat, generally red

Master Isaac threw a surprised glance at Si Mohammed.

"How can you think that?" he said. "You underrate my friendship! Do you forget the cordial chats we have had together in the evening, every time the weather has allowed? Don't we always part with an affectionate word? Aren't you served the same food we eat at the house, as you have wished? When your friends come to see you, no matter how many, aren't they offered hospitality? We treat them liberally to coffees and meals! If you are complaining about the amount of work, remember that we all work hard. Have you ever seen me, your boss, stop for a single day? At night I am still working. Believe me, the little sleep I grant myself is less peaceful than yours."

"Yes, master," agreed Mohammed, his hand on his heart, "all that is true. I admit it and I do my best to thank you by working as conscientiously as I can. Still what hurts me and angers me is that, in spite of the friendly feelings you show me, you have never asked me to cross your threshold. I cannot tell your wife from your daughters or your sisters. I do not know the color of their eyes. Have you ever asked me to dinner on Friday night, when you invite those of your employees who have no family? Why do you exclude me? Am I not lonely like them? Am I unworthy of you? Have I been disrespectful to you or your family? Am I a criminal? Even your little maid, when she sets down my meals here, averts her eyes and does not even acknowledge my thanks with a glance. If I have to be like the donkey that works all day and returns to its litter at night, I prefer to leave. May Allah curse me, for I have forsaken the life I used to live for this filth called money!"

The Arab drew out of his belt the pay he had received an hour before and threw it contemptuously on the ground. Master Isaac had heard his recriminations without interrupting. "Pick up your money," he commanded now. And when the Arab, subjugated by his firm and quiet gaze, had obeyed, he added: "You reproach me for not introducing you to the women in my house. You complain that our young servant does not linger long enough for you to express your satisfaction. Have I created a family for the pleasure of a stranger's eyes or to provoke lust? Do you and your friends and co-religionists expose your harems to outside dangers? Aren't your women cloistered like princesses? Don't you carefully protect your young girls from any contact with men? You mistrust your brothers and your own selves! If I invite some of my workers to share a meal once a week, it's because they are Jewish like me. They come to say their prayers with us. Our hearts are filled with the same sorrows and the same hopes."

The Arab dropped his head, blood rushed to his face. Silence blew in the fragrant breeze. Si Mohammed waited for more explanations, but none came.

"Master Isaac" he said at last, "you speak like a book. I will not press my point. Let me only ask you one last question. The other night, when I felt like remembering the good old days and started playing my recorder to cheer myself up, you forbade it categorically. You sent word that should I wish to revel in amorous tunes, I had better step out of your property. But your property extends over several kilometers! How can I do that after a long day's work? I would have liked to play my instrument here, under this jasmine, before these flowers and trees."

Master Isaac smiled. "If I have not allowed you to play the recorder on my property, it's because our religion forbids it. Have you ever seen a Jew with a recorder in his hands? Have you ever seen one whistle?"

"No—so why is that?"

"Well, superstitious people say that anything that sounds like whistling scares happiness and prosperity away and plays the devil's game. Our wise men, on the other hand, hold that the recorder is a cajoler that makes us forget work and prayer. It is too good at expressing love, lust, and women's charms. You can well imagine, Si Mohammed, that in this Holy Land, we have other things to do!"

The Arab kept silent, but he thought: "So then, why do we live, if we must not taste either of music or of women's charms?" Neither the daily uphill struggle, nor the sacrifices for the sake of the future, nor the devotion to a collective ideal appealed to Si Mohammed's mind and heart. The austerity of that life of unceasing labor and abstinence exasperated him. As Judith brought the foreman his evening meal, Master Isaac wished him a good night and left. The young servant spread a red napkin on the rim of the well, set down the spiced soup, the olives, the roast lamb, the anise bread and departed, not having said a word, not having even lifted her eyes toward the goy. . . .

Si Mohammed had been worried for some days. The Jewish workers seemed upset. Contrary to usual, they were slow to complete their tasks and needed to be urged along. . . . On that Sunday morning, at six, not one Jewish worker was in the field. Gathered in small groups in front of the machinery sheds, they gestured and argued passionately.

"What's the matter?" asked Si Mohammed. "Are your clothes on fire?"

"Your brothers threaten us!" exclaimed one of them, turning a convulsed face toward the Arab. "They are planning to fall upon us. A murderous rage has taken hold of them again. They want to seize this land we have fertilized with our work, our money, and our blood, after first slaughtering us."

"But we will not be passive victims!" retorted another. "We will defend ourselves against injustice and savagery, do you hear, all of us, to the last!"

"You are perfectly right," answered Si Mohammed calmly. "Your rights are unquestionable and you lead a fine life. What have I known among you? Only work, frugality and prayer. Having worked at your side for two years, I value your merits and I admire you. You can be men, when you are not in bondage."

"Alas, Si Mohammed," added Isaac Reboux, holding back his sadness. "For some time now we have been receiving threatening letters. At this very moment, in the city's synagogue, prayers are being offered to the Lord so He dispels your distracted brothers' fury. The news reached us last night that on the road to Hebron, some Arabs attacked a Jewish peddler and his young son. They murdered them and fled with everything: cart, horse, goods, and a sum of money."

Isaac threw a tender glance over the beautiful land, the vast wheat fields, the blossoming trees swaying in the grey morning air. "I truly fear that all our efforts, all our sacrifices have been in vain."

Si Mohammed was visibly upset; confused thoughts jostled in his mind.

"Listen, master," he said at last. "I am indebted to you. Thanks to your fairness and generosity, I will soon be in possession of a sum of money that is a fortune to me. Among you I have become a persevering and sober man. And most of all, your admirable work is worthy of respect. Tell me what I can do to help. I am at your disposal, body and soul."

A brilliant idea crossed Isaac's mind. "Certainly, Si Mohammed, you could do something. In fact you could do muxh. You are such a brave heart. You speak so persuasively and receive so much esteem and affection! So many friends come to visit you. Such is your fame in the region that they travel for miles just to spend an hour with you."

"That's for certain, Master Isaac. One of my uncles was a barber in Hebron. Besides honey pastries, he sold or rather gave away medicine. Furthermore, he bled sick people for free, which was considered a good deed at the time. People still talk about him with veneration in Hebron."

"Well, Si Mohammed, I am not about to ask you to commit treason. On the contrary, I would like you to convince your co-religionists, the Beni-Metmora, to listen to reason. I entreat you to lay our lives out to them so that were they to attack us, they would be severely judged by Allah. Make them understand that they have only to gain by our presence, that we are ready to collaborate with them and help them with advice, services, and even money. We want to be brothers or at least friends."

"I am ready, Master Isaac. As of today, if you wish, I will set aside my knapsack and my pickax and take my walking stick. I will go from one tribe to another and spread the good word about you. I'll talk about your virtues and your faith which have had no equal since Job."

A hopeful smile lit the old man's face. "I'll arrange a collection in the synagogue to cover the cost of your mission. I know that vinegar does not trap flies and honey is expensive. You will have to treat your friends to succulent couscous with lamb, thick coffees, and good pipes. I entreat you not to worry about the expense. And if you reach an understanding with them, I promise you won't have to wait until you go to heaven to receive your reward."

On the following Saturday, in the new temple built of concrete with stained glass windows and black and white flagstones, Isaac Reboux presented his plan to an assembly of older men in caftans and resolute young men.

There was an immediate outcry among the graybeards: "What, Master Isaac, is it possible that you have come to this? You believe in the good faith of an Arab! Hasn't your experience taught you anything? As for us, we have been living among Arabs for close to a century now and we know what Israel's *galut* has been under them! But you, an Algerian, don't you remember the recent massacres in your ancient cities? Aren't you aware of the fate of your Moroccan brothers? Every five years, in the *mellahs*[*] of Marrakech, the Arabs swoop down on poor Jews. They plunder and massacre, rape the women and brutalize the children. Only yesterday the Sultan of Morocco protested to the French government that Jews were donning European dress and were seen in the vicinity of mosques. May God bless the French! If the French were in charge here, as they are in Morocco, we would not know this anguish. A curse on the Arabs! We will never believe in their friendship!"

The college graduates and other young people took Si Mohammed's side. One of them, a mechanic for Master Isaac, who held a bachelor's degree in literature, declared firmly:

"Times and minds have changed. Should we persist in hating, we will never accomplish anything. Granted, there have been and there still are barbarians and murderers among the Arabs. But there are also healthy, clear minds, who understand that peace is a blessing for all and that the future of Palestine lies in the union of Arabs and Jews. Let us trust this man. After all, what could possibly happen? If he does not do us any good, he cannot harm us either."

So it was settled. The collection, to which Master Isaac contributed the largest share, brought in one hundred and ten pounds sterling. And the next day at dawn, Mohammed was on his way.

A fortnight later, Isaac received a letter from his ambassador. Mohammed recounted the ups and downs of his trip: the difficulties he had to overcome, the ruses he had to invent in order to penetrate among the tribes, the irate "greeting" he had received from his co-religionists. The Beni-Metmora envied

---

[*] Jewish neighborhood

the wealth of the Jews and spoke only of Holy War. "The situation is much more critical than I thought," he said. However, Si Mohammed had not lost hope. He had made friends among the older men, heads of *djemaas*[*] and, through them, he intended to work on the angry mob. "Sweet talk will melt iron," he concluded.

A happy event at the farm dispelled the anxiety for a while. Young Judith married Saul, a handsome lad of eighteen who had fallen in love with her when he entered Master Isaac's service. He had asked for her hand in marriage and three weeks later everything was settled according to the Torah's commandments. The wedding feast was short and the banquet sober, but fellowship and love were in every heart.

Having fulfilled his duties toward the newlyweds, Master Isaac went back to his regular activities and his worries. He waited in vain for more news from Si Mohammed. What had happened to the Arab of goodwill? Had he betrayed them? Had he been won back by his brothers? Master Isaac refused to believe it. Perhaps he had been stabbed by fanatics who would not forgive him for defending the Jewish cause? Or perhaps he had simply been attacked by highway robbers who knew he carried money.

Isaac's torment was made even more grievous by the ceaseless pestering, the recriminations and reproaches of Haifa's graybeards. In his mind, the thought that Si Mohammed had been the victim of his own selflessness became clearer and stronger. He finally resolved to go to Jerusalem. He was sure to gather some information about the unfortunate man's fate in his former employee's native town, where he knew that Si Mohammed owned a small property. And one fine morning, the rich farmer's car, a simple Ford, stopped before the walls of Jerusalem, at the Mughrabi gate.

Having had a drink with his driver at the counter of a humble tavern, Master Isaac proceeded alone on foot through the Arab neighborhoods. After painstaking enquiries, he met an old dervish who pointed to a young man sitting on a stool in front of his shop, working on a copper vase with his hammer. Master Isaac was overjoyed to recognize an excellent fellow who had frequently visited Si Mohammed at the farm. He pressed him with anxious questions.

"Praise Allah," said the craftsman, "Si Mohammed is safe and sound. He got married last month and invited us to a wedding the likes of which haven't been seen in a long time. He married a girl from a good family who is also the most beautiful in the country. Let's go see him at his shop."

---

[*] local village council

The Arab took off his smock flecked with chips of copper, slipped on his *babouches** and put his arm around Master Isaac's shoulders. The two men walked up steep narrow streets, one telling stories of his friend's good fortune, the other feeling disappointed and broken-hearted, and unsure what to think of his former employee's betrayal.

"We must pay homage to Si Mohammed," said the Arab. "He has not forgotten his friends now that he has gone up in the world. We are proud of him. On his wedding night, his thoughts flew to you. He had the courage to tell his guests loud and clear: 'Brothers, you must know that we owe this sumptuous wedding to a Jew's fairness and generosity. In the name of Sidna Moussa and for the sake of this gathering, I beg you to forget your quarrels and come together. Those sons of God only ask to live in peace next to us. Aren't we first cousins? Weren't our fathers brothers? Let's try to emulate their energy and perseverance. May Allah's blessing be upon us all. And may their share of these festivities be kept for them in heaven!'"

When they arrived in the fabric souk the young man stopped in front of one of the nicest shops which was filled with rolls of silk, shimmering belts and *babouches* embroidered with gold thread. In the semi-darkness, Master Isaac saw Si Mohammed sitting crosslegged on a mat, looking radiant. Wrapped in a pink *gandourah*,** his *chechia* tilted on his ear, he was smoking his pipe.

"Hey, Si Mohammed, you have risen in the world, old chap, how are you? And how about the mission I had entrusted to you?"

"I accomplished it, Master, in good conscience. I visited many tribes. I treated them to succulent couscous, thick coffees, and pipes that would make Indian smokers die with envy. But once those dogs had drunk and eaten their fill, they wiped their mouths, closed their eyes, and went back on all their oaths."

Si Mohammed looked straight at Master Isaac. "We must wait for the miracle that will come from Allah the All-Powerful, not from men! As for me, I was discouraged. An irresistible desire to see the place where I was born, to rejoin my friends and our quiet life under the protective wing of Islam, took hold of me. I decided to renounce the austere and grinding life I was living with you. Meanwhile, I received a small inheritance. I bought this shop and I earn my bread as God willed. . . . But do you know what kept me prisoner on your farm for so long, what gave me patience, and held me better than chains could have? It was the sight of your negro-woman walking between the blossoming orange trees, against the evening sky . . ."

---

*leather slippers

**sleeveless tunic

"My negro-woman?" asked Master Isaac, astounded. "I have no negro-woman in my service."

"I mean your servant."

"My servant? Judith? But she's blond . . ."

"No matter. I cannot erase from my memory the vision of that slave bringing me manna in her splendid arms. Were she not to be your future wife, Master Isaac, I would have bought her from you."

Isaac sank down on the mat he had at first declined. He felt crushed under those revelations. So the Arab thought that he, a white-haired man, four times grandfather, would remarry and add to his household a woman who was younger than his last daughter. . . . The Jew kept on passing his hand over his damp forehead. Decidedly, he thought, the old people were right. We will never be friends, we will never understand each other. Their soul is as far from ours as the unfortunate man is from happiness . . . .

He hastened to reassure Mohammed, "Judith just got married!"

The Arab winced slightly. "Was she your daughter?"

"No, she was an orphan."

"So why did you raise her, to give her away?"

Isaac declared firmly, "When we have taken our share, Si Mohammed, we close our eyes!"

"I cannot say the same about us, Master Isaac. Our God-given nature is at peace about everything; money, food, work, self-interest. . . . But we never have our fill of women. If I had your means, Master Isaac, what a bouquet of flowers my harem would be. . . !"

Isaac shuddered at the thought of the drama that could have unfolded had Mohammed's desire for Judith degenerated into passion. Who would have been able to tear the Arab away from his love? War would have broken out on the farm, before the hostile tribes attacked. Everything had ended for the best with the Arab's departure. The community would have held Isaac responsible for this terrible sin: a daughter of Israel marrying a non-Jew, perhaps conceiving from him. It would have weighed on the farmer's shoulders until Judgment Day!

And Master Isaac, who was not superstitious, thought he recognized Yahweh's hand in the Arab's betrayal. "The remedy was prepared before the ailment," he said to himself.

— **Translated by Sonia Assa**

Irène Némirovsky
(1903–1942)

Irène Némirovsky was born in Kiev, Russia, to wealthy Jewish parents. The family fled during the Russian Revolution and settled in France in 1919. For the entire family, but especially for Irène, immigration to France meant coming home. Like many wealthy Russians, they had great admiration for French culture and in their speech and social behavior modeled themselves on the French. Irène had a French governess and spoke French from infancy, so that she could truthfully claim that French was her native language.

Némirovsky achieved literary success at a very early age. Her first novel, *David Golder*, published in 1929, was both a commercial and a critical success; it was adapted for the screen and stage. A steady succession of novels and short stories followed. Though she explored a number of subjects in her fiction as disparate as family relationships and the psychology of the terrorist, the question of Jewish identity preoccupied her throughout her all too brief career.

As a Jew, in spite of her literary success, Némirovsky had trouble getting published during the Nazi occupation, although her work continued to appear, sometimes under pseudonyms. In 1942 she was arrested and sent to Auschwitz. She never returned. Her husband, Michel Epstein, also perished in Auschwitz, but her two daughters survived.

Minority groups in all settings experience the psychological tension between the characteristics of the minority and the demands of the majority culture. The tension is particularly strong when the minority culture is devalued, as the Jewish culture has been throughout history. In the story "Fraternité," Christian Rabinovitch, confronted by his "double," is intent on differentiating himself from his unfortunate foreign namesake. But his interaction with the "other" and the narrator's observations do not allow him to perform this surgery. Némirovsky forces the reader to examine what the "brothers" have in common. But there is also a specific historical dimension to the story. "Fraternité," with its echo of the revolutionary slogan "liberté, égalité, fraternité," reflects the special circumstances of French Jews on the eve of the Holocaust.

By virtue of her wealth, education, and professional success, Némirovsky belonged to the assimilated class, and yet her origins were Eastern European. Many of her works—*David Golder, Le Bal, Le Vin de Solitude, Les Chiens et les Loups*—deal with the question of Jewish identity. Némirovsky's portrayal of Jews in her early novels and plays is savage. David Golder is a Jewish financier willing to sacrifice business associates for the sake of money. In *Le Bal*, the two main characters, a Jewish husband and his non-Jewish wife, are social climbers eager to forget their lowly origins. In her early novels, Jewish characters are always described as obsessed with money. In her later works, however, her portraits of Jews are more nuanced. In *Les Chiens et les loups,* she renders sympathetically the struggles of immigrant Eastern European Jews to assimilate, though they remain physically and psychologically a group apart.

Her short story "Fraternité" reflects the tension between the need felt by assimilated Jews to distance themselves from the class of "Jews" as viewed by the majority culture, and the need to define the ways in which they nevertheless remain Jews. In 1937, when "Fraternité" was published, the question still seemed theoretical. It soon became clear that it was a pragmatic one. In 1939, Némirovsky was baptized. Whether this was an act of conviction, as her biographer Jonathan Weiss claims, or a final attempt to save herself and her family we cannot know.

Many of Némirovsky's works have been republished during the last fifteen years. In 2004, an unfinished two-volume novel written in 1942 and conserved by her daughter Denise Epstein was published and, exceptionally for a posthumous novel, was awarded the prestigious Prix Renaudot. Her sensitivity to emotional coloration, the art with which she was able to convey both private pain and the tragic temper of her time, have won her the admiration of a new generation of readers.

— Eva Martin Sartori

Selected Works

David Golder. Paris: Grasset, 1929, 1992.
Le Bal. Paris: Grasset, 1930.
Les Mouches d'Automne. Paris: Grasset, 1931, 1998.
L'Affaire Courilof. Paris: Grasset, 1932, 1990.
Le Vin de Solitude. Paris: Albin Michel, 1935, 1988.
Jézabel. Paris: Albin Michel, 1936.
Les Chiens et les loups. Paris: Albin Michel, 1940, 1988.
La Vie de Tchekhov. Paris: Albin Michel, 1946, 1989.
Les Feux d'automne. Paris: Albin Michel, 1957.
Dimanche et autres nouvelles. Paris: Stock, 2000.
Suite française. Paris: Denoël, 2004.

Translations Into English

David Golder. Trans. Sylvia Stuart. New York: Horace Liveright, 1930.
A Modern Jezebel. Trans. Barre Dunbar. New York: Henry Holt and Company, 1937.
A Life of Chekhov. London: Grey Walls Press, 1950.

Secondary Works

Alan Astro. "Two Best-Selling French Jewish Women's Novels from 1929." *Symposium.* Winter 1999: 241–54.
Elisabeth Gille. *Le Mirador: mémoires rêvés.* Paris: Presses de la Renaissance, 1992.
Paul Renard. "Irène Némirovsky (1903–1942): Une Romancière face à la tragédie." *Roman 20–50: Revue du Roman du XXe Siècle.* (Dec. 1993) 16:165–74.
Jonathan Weiss. *Irène Némirovsky.* Paris: Félin, 2005.

Fraternité

He went into the empty first-class waiting room for a moment. Though the radiators were on, a cold wind rose from the ground through the thin floorboards. He went out. The train station was very small and was surrounded by barren fields. It was an icy October day, still rosy, radiant but short, because standard time had come into effect the day before. He walked up to a covered bench, hesitated, then sat down. He regretted now that he had not listened to his chauffeur, Florent, who had advised him to spend the night in town. The hotel was not so dirty. To wait on this deserted platform, to be dragged around until nightfall on some disgusting local train that snaked its way through the countryside. . . . He would arrive at the Sestres' house after eight o'clock. The car wasn't drivable; it had smashed into a pylon. He shouldn't be driving. He was too tired. His reflexes were poor. It was a miracle that he had escaped injury. He hadn't had time to see the danger, to even consider death. Afterward, he had tried so hard to hide his fear, which he was ashamed to show Florent, that he had managed successfully to control all outward manifestations of his nervousness. Or so he hoped! Now he was shivering . . . maybe from the cold. He feared the open air, the wind. He was a thin man—frail, bent, with silver hair and a somewhat sallow narrow face. His dry skin seemed deprived of nourishment. His nose was extremely long and pointed. His lips, always dry, seemed wilted by a millennial thirst, a fever transmitted from generation to generation. "My nose, my mouth—the only specifically Jewish traits I have retained." Gently, his hands pressed his diaphanous ears, thin, trembling like those of a cat; they were particularly sensitive to cold. He pulled up the collar of his overcoat made of a fine English wool, dark, thick, and soft. But he didn't move. This deserted train station, the lights along the rails, still pale, hardly visible against the brilliant fawn of the evening, this solitude, this sadness were inexpressibly attractive to him. He was one of those men who have a profound and perverse tendency toward melancholia, regret, bitterness, too lucid—"self-conscious," he said to himself in English—to believe in happiness. Impatiently, he looked at his watch. Hardly five o'clock. . . . He felt his chest for his cigarette case and immediately dropped his hand: he smoked too much; he had palpitations, insomnia. He sighed. He was rarely sick, but his heightened senses, marvelously suited to pain, were in wait for the slightest discomfort, attentive to each movement of his body, to the flow of his blood. Rarely ill, but with a

---

This translation of "Fraternité" and the introduction to Némirovsky were first published with minor variations in *Prairie Schooner,* Summer 2002. The translation received the Jane Geske Award in 2003.

fragile throat, a delicate liver, a tired heart, a poor circulation. Why? He had always been sober, careful, measured in all things. Ah! So prudent that even in his youth, even in his period of blindness, of unforgettable madness . . . he didn't regret his youth. And yet it had been easy. Then he had experienced only natural griefs, those inherent in the human condition—the death of his parents, disappointments in love or in his career. Nothing to compare with the pain he felt at the death of his wife, ten years ago. He knew that those near him wondered at this persistent sadness. And, in fact, he had married Blanche without being in love and their union had been calm and tepid. But he belonged to the race of the faithful: He had sought the warmth of a house, the light of a lamp, the feeling of stability, of peace, within himself and around him. That is what he had loved, that is what he had lost when he lost Blanche. There would never be another woman. He was not easy prey for love, too reticent, too easily offended, too timid. "Coward," he thought. He lived as if everything conspired to rob him of life, of happiness. A contrite heart, humiliated, perpetually trembling, the heart of a rabbit. An hour earlier, on the road, another minute and all his worries would have ended. "I always said that car was worth nothing. And the lunch was heavy. I was sleepy, sluggish. I didn't react." What had he eaten, in fact? Some pheasant, a mushroom omelet . . . what else? A slice of brie. "That's too heavy for me. Eggs are not good for me. Oh! This sedentary existence, at my age! I'm fifty years old. From the beginning of the year to the end, no more than a month of fresh air. And the rest of the time I'm in the bank, at home, or at the club." He thought again that, as soon as he could, he would leave his business. He would spend more time in the country. Gardening, golf . . . golf? It seemed to him that he felt the wind cutting across his cheeks on the golf course on a day such as this. He knew that he hated it! He also knew that he hated walks in the country, sports, horseback riding, cars, hunting. . . . He was happy only at home, alone or with his children, protected by a roof, protected from human beings. He didn't like people; he didn't like society. And yet he had always been well received everywhere, with friendship, with kindness. In his youth, charming women had loved him. Why? Then why? It always seemed to him that people weren't affectionate enough, tender enough toward him. How he had made Blanche suffer at the beginning of their marriage! "Are you happy here? Not only in your heart, but in your senses? Am I making you happy? Completely happy? Am I the only one who can make you happy?" A shaky heart, unsatisfied. And the oddest thing was that others thought him so cold, so calm. He sometimes thought that only extraordinary beauty, glory, or genius would have satisfied him, quenched this thirst for love. But he had no unusual gifts. And yet he was rich, well established in life, happy. Happy? But how can you be happy without absolute calm? And who could be calm these days? The world was so unstable. Tomorrow he might know disaster, ruin, poverty. He had never been poor. His father had been comfortable; he himself was rich. He had never needed anything, nor feared what tomorrow would bring. And yet this fear, this anxiety had always been part of him, always, always, taking the most outlandish forms, the most . . . grotesque. He would awaken in the middle of the night, trembling, fearing that something would happen, had happened, that everything would be taken from him, that life was as unpredictable, as shaky as a stage set ready to collapse, revealing he knew not what abyss. When war had broken out, he thought that this was what he had been waiting for, what he had been expecting. He had been a soldier, a conscientious soldier, performing his duties punctually and with patience, as in everything he did. After several months, he had been sent to the rear; he had a weak heart. After the war, life was easy, business was very good. But always this apprehension, this latent worry that poisoned his life. This anxiety. First poor health, then the children. Ah! The children. His oldest daughter was married. Was she happy? He didn't know. Nobody ever told him anything. And the crisis, the taxes that were continually rising; business was becoming more difficult, soon it would probably be disastrous. The political uncertainty. . . . He was one of those who, every time he heard a talk by one dictator or another, expected war, not next month or next year, but tomorrow, right away. And yet his speech never betrayed panic, unlike the rich bourgeois, his brothers. But again, it was strange: the others, while prophesizing the worst disasters, nevertheless seemed healthy, in good spirits, did not lose an hour of sleep or miss a good meal. Only he was consumed internally, drinking his own blood as the popular saying goes. Only he seemed to think that misfortune could reach him personally, while others thought of misfortune as amorphous, as only a shadow. They talked about it continually, but didn't believe in it. Only he! And all around him people said, "Christian Rabinovitch? The most sensible of men, the most poised, the calmest."

The wind was icy at times. From the beginning, the hunting party at the Sestres' seemed hateful to him. But he had to . . . he had to see with his own eyes his son Jean-Claude and the Sestres' young daughter. He sighed deeply. It was characteristic of him that he never admitted right away the real sickness, the real wound. Thus, during his long periods of insomnia, when he was preoccupied with a business matter, he remained awake for hours, his heart pounding, thinking about an unpleasant meeting, a boring trip. He hated train stations, ports, boats. To remain still, to live and die in the same place. Then toward morning finally an invisible barrier in the depth of his heart seemed to give way, and the real flood of distress broke, came up to the surface, smothered him.

Thus . . . now . . . everything began with his son and everything went back to him. How he loved him! He loved his two daughters: the older one married, a mother, the young one still in short skirts. But this son. . . . And yet, he had been the source of more pain than joy: so light, so worried, so unsatisfied. He had been a brilliant student but had abandoned his studies early. Frivolous? No. Unsatisfied, that was it . . . unsatisfied. Now he was in love. He wanted to marry the daughter of Count Sestres. Oh! It was hard. His race. . . . "He won't be happy, I feel it, he won't be happy." And, most importantly, would Sestres agree? Would he insult Jean-Claude, himself? His heart was bleeding already, and yet he would cut off both his hands to stop this marriage! They won't be happy, Jean-Claude and this young woman. They would never truly understand each other, not really. They would be one in body, but each would remain solitary, unsatisfied at heart. But he, what could he do? He knew very well that they wouldn't listen to him. Already his children saw him as a man of another era, an old fogey. Already he belonged to the race of men who age quickly. No, who are born old, loaded with experience. Oh, why did Jean-Claude want to marry? Wasn't he happy? There wasn't a moment of peace on this earth!

He looked at his watch. He had thought so much, had daydreamed, and yet only twenty minutes had gone by. A sad autumn, a sad evening. . . . It was then that he saw for the first time a man sitting near him on the same bench, a poorly dressed man, thin, unshaven, with dirty hands. He was watching a child. The child was repeatedly going toward the rail tracks, fascinated by them. He was wearing a drab worn little coat, a cap, and you could see his horn-shaped ears sticking out on both sides. His wrists and his red hands hung from sleeves that were too short. The child's movements were lively. He would turn his head toward the bench; his very large eyes, of a liquid black, swallowed up his face, seemed to jump from one object to another. He took a step forward and, even though the track was entirely clear, the man who was watching him anxiously leapt from his seat, scooped him up in his arms and sat down again, holding him tightly against his heart. He saw that the eyes of his richly dressed neighbor looked down on the child, and right away he smiled timidly.

"May I ask you what time it is?" He spoke with a foreign accent, in a hoarse voice that distorted his words.

Rabinovitch, without saying anything, pointed to the clock above their heads.

"Ah, yes! I'm sorry. It's only five twenty? My God, my God! The train doesn't come until six thirty-eight. Forgive me . . . are you also waiting for the Paris train?"

"No."

Christian rose; the man immediately murmured.

"Sir, if you would be so kind . . . it's for the child. He has just been ill and the third-class waiting room is not heated. Allow us to follow you into the first-class waiting room. If we go in with you, we will be allowed to stay."

His facial expressions changed very quickly; they were almost simian. Not only did his lips move, but so did his hands, the creases on his face and his shoulders. His black eyes, feverish, bursting like those of the child, seemed to run from one thing to another, turn away, anxiously looking for something they didn't see, would never see.

"If you like," said Rabinovitch with effort.

"Oh! Thank you, sir, thank you. . . . Come Jascha." He took the child by one hand, and with the other took Christian's overnight bag, even though the latter, uncomfortable, tried to stop him.

"Leave it, please."

"I insist, sir, why not?"

They entered the first-class waiting room where a three-pronged chandelier spread a thin pale light. Christian sat down in one of the velvet armchairs and the man, fearfully, sat on the edge of a bench. He kept the child on his lap.

A sad little bell tinkled interminably in the silence.

"Your son has been ill?" Christian finally asked, distractedly.

"He's my grandson, sir," said the man looking at the child. "My son has just left. He's going to live in England, Liverpool. He's been promised a job, but in the meantime he left the child with me."

He sighed deeply.

"He was living in Germany. Then for four years I was able to have him with me in Paris. Now, again, separation. . . ."

"England," said Christian, smiling, "that's not very far."

"For us, sir, England, America, it's all the same. You need money to travel, you need a passport, a visa, a work permit. It's a long separation.'"

He stopped speaking, but it was clear that speaking made him feel better. He started again, "You asked if the child has been ill? Oh! He's sturdy, but he catches colds easily and then he coughs for months. But he is strong. All the Rabinovitches are strong."

Christian was startled. "What is your name?"

"Rabinovitch, sir."

Christian said in a low voice, in spite of himself, "I have the same name as you."

"Ah! . . . *Yid?*" said the man slowly.

He added a few other words in Yiddish. Christian recovered. He murmured dryly, "Don't understand."

The man gently shrugged with an inimitable expression of disbelief, of scoffing, but with affection, almost tenderly, as if he were thinking: "If he wants to show off, let him. . . . With a name like Rabinovitch, not to understand Yiddish!"

"A Jew?" He repeated in French. "Gone a long time?"

"Gone?"

"Well, yes! From Russia? Crimea? Ukraine?"

"I was born here."

"Ah! So it was your father?"

"My father was French."

"Then it was before your father. All the Rabinovitches come from over there."

"That's possible," Christian said coldly.

Now the brief emotion he had felt when he heard his name spoken by this man had subsided. He had a painful feeling. What did he have in common with this poor Jew?

"Do you know England, sir? Yes, of course. And the city where my children will live, Liverpool?"

"I've been through it."

"Is the climate good?"

"Well, yes."

The man sighed, a long modulated sigh that ended in a plaintive oy-oy-oy. . . . He pressed the child between his knees.

Christian looked at him more attentively. How old was he? Between forty and sixty, that was all he could have said! Probably no more than fifty, like himself. His narrow chest seemed compressed, hollowed by a heavy invisible burden that had bent and pulled his shoulders forward. At times, when he heard an unexpected noise, he tried to shrink, pressing his body into the bench. And yet, although so fragile, so thin, he seemed to have an inextinguishable vitality. Like a lit candle in the wind, barely protected by the glass of a lantern. The flame beats against the glass, the light trembles, pales, ready to be extinguished. But the wind dies down, and the light shines again, humble and tenacious.

"I worry so much," said the man softly. "You spend your time worrying. I had seven children, five died. They were all born sturdy, but they had a weakness in the chest. I've brought up two. Two boys. I loved them like my two eyes. You have children, sir? Yes? Ah! See, I look at you and I can't help but compare myself to you. In a way, that consoles me. You are rich, you must have a good business, but if you have children, you understand me! You give them everything and they are never satisfied. That is the nature of Jews. My younger son . . . he already started when he was fifteen: 'Papa, I don't want to be a tailor. Papa, I want to be a student.' You think it was easy at that time in Russia? 'Papa, I want to leave.' And what else do you want, misery of my life?' 'Papa, I want to go to Palestine. Only there can a Jew live in dignity. That's the homeland of Jews.' Eh! I said to him, Salomon, I respect you, you have studied, you are more educated than your father. Go, but here you can have a real occupation, a gentleman's occupation; one day you can be a dentist or a businessman. There you will plow the earth like a peasant. I told him that for Palestine, you won't be able to take all the herrings that swim in the ocean, and put them back in their mother's belly. The day you can do that, then you'll be able to call Palestine the Jews' homeland. Until then. . . . But go ahead, go ahead, if you think it will make you happy.' Finally he left. He got married. 'Papa, send money for the wedding. . . . Papa, send money for the birth of the child. . . . Daddy, send money to pay the doctor, the debts, the rent.' One day, he began to spit blood. The work was too hard. Then he died. Now only the older one is left, the father of this one. He too left me, hardly a man. He went to Constantinople, then to Germany. He began to earn a living. He was a photographer. Then Hitler comes! I had left Russia because I had begun to earn a living for the first time in my life when the Revolution came. Jewish luck! I became frightened. I left. Life is worth more than money. For the last fifteen years, I've been living in Paris. It will last as long as it will last. . . . Now my son is in England! Where doesn't God plunk down the Jew? Lord, if only one could live in peace! But one is never ever at peace! One has hardly earned one's bread, four walls, a roof over one's head by the sweat of one's brow, when a war, a revolution, a pogrom, or some other disaster happens, and it's good-bye. Pick up your packages, run. Go live in another town, in another country. Learn a new language—at your age, you're not discouraged, are you? No, but you're tired. Sometimes I say to myself: You'll rest after you die. Until then, it's a dog's life! Later you will rest. God is the master in the end!"

"What is your occupation?"

"My occupation? Naturally, I do a little of everything. At the moment, I'm working in hat-making. As long as I have working papers, right? When they take them away, I'll start selling again. Selling this or that—furs wholesale, mechanical objects, whatever comes up. I am able to make a living, because my markup is very low. Happy are the native born. Why, looking at you, one can see what wealth you can acquire! And no doubt, your grandfather came from Odessa or from Berdichev, like me. He must have been a poor man. The rich, the happy, they didn't leave! Yes, he was a poor man. And you . . . one day maybe, this little one.

He looked tenderly at the child who was listening without saying anything, his face a knot of nervous tics, his eyes shining.

Uneasily, Christian said, "I think I hear my train."

The man immediately rose. "Yes, sir. Allow me to help you. Don't call a porter. Why bother! Allow me, please, it's nothing! Come, Jascha. Don't go away! This child is like quicksilver! We have to cross the tracks."

The train didn't come for another ten minutes. Christian was walking silently along the platform, the man behind him carrying his suitcase. They were quiet. In spite of themselves, when they passed the lamplight, Christian and the Jew stole a glance at each other and Christian thought, with a strange painful feeling, that it was in this way that they understood each other best. Yes, like this . . . without words, but through a look, and in the way their shoulders moved, in the nervous strain of the mouth.

"Go ahead and board, sir. Don't worry about the suitcase. I'll hand it to you through the window," said the Jew, lifting the English gun in its suede case.

Christian slipped him a twenty-franc piece. Shamefacedly, the man quickly put it in his pocket and grabbed the child's hand; the train was leaving. Christian turned around immediately and entered his empty compartment. With a sigh, he threw the gun and the overnight case into the overhead bin and sat down. Outside the night was pitch black. The little overhead lamp hardly gave any light; he couldn't read. The train was crossing the now darkened countryside; the sky was cold, almost wintery. It would be almost eight o'clock when he reached the Sestres' house. He thought of the old Jew, standing, holding the child by the hand, on that glacial train platform. Miserable creature! Was it possible that he was of the same blood as this man? Again, he thought: What do I have in common with this man? There is no more resemblance between this Jew and me than between Sestres and his servants! The opposite is inconceivable, grotesque! An abyss, a gulf! I am moved because he is quaint, a witness to bygone times. Yes, that's how, that's why he moves me, because it's far, so far from me. . . . No point of contact, nothing.

He repeated softly, as if he wanted to persuade an invisible companion, "Nothing, right? Nothing."

He now felt astonished and also indignant. To be sure, they had nothing in common, he and this . . . this Rabinovitch (in spite of himself, he made an irritated gesture).

By virtue of my education, my culture, I am closer to a man like Sestres; by my habits, my tastes, my life, I am further from this Jew than from a Levantine lens grinder. Three, four generations have gone by. I am a different man. Not only morally but physically. My nose, my mouth, that's nothing. Only the soul is important!

He did not know it, but deep in thought, he was rocking softly in his seat, with a strange slow movement, front to back, to the rhythm of the train. In this manner, his body rediscovered, when he was tired or uncomfortable, the swaying that had earlier rocked generations of rabbis bent over the sacred Book, of money changers over their piles of gold, of tailors at their workbenches.

He looked up and saw himself in the mirror. He sighed and slowly passed his hand over his brow. In a flash, he thought: "That's what I suffer from. . . . That's what I pay for in my body, my soul. Centuries of misery, illness, oppression. . . .Thousands of poor weak tired bones have formed mine."

Suddenly he remembered some of his friends who died for no obvious reason, when they retired to golf and a life in the country. They were uncomfortable with their riches, their leisure. The old bundle of worries fermented in his blood and poisoned him. Yes, he himself was free, at least for the moment, of exile, poverty, need. But the mark remained—it couldn't be erased. And yet, no, no! It was insulting, impossible. He was a rich French bourgeois, nothing else! And his children? Ah! His children. . . . "They'll be happier than I," he said to himself, with a deep, fervent hope. "They will be happy!"

He heard the train wheels pounding through the sleeping countryside. He dozed off. Finally, he arrived.

The train stopped at the small station of Texin near the Sestres chateau. He had instructed his chauffeur to send a telegram announcing his arrival. Three of his friends were there: Louis Geoffroy, Robert de Sestres, and Jean Sicard. They gathered around him.

"My poor friend! But that's awful! You could have died!"

He was walking between them, answering them with a smile. They spoke the same language, they were dressed in the same way, they had the same habits, the same tastes. As he walked toward the waiting car, framed by them, he felt more confident, happier. The painful impression created by his meeting with this Jew faded. Only his body, trembling with cold in spite of the warm English clothes, his painful nerves, acknowledged the ancient legacy.

Robert de Sestres breathed deeply. "What wonderful weather!"

"Yes," said Christian Rabinovitch, it's true. A little cold, but so healthy. He furtively pressed his freezing ears with his hand and got into the car.

— **Translated by Eva Martin Sartori**

Sarah Lévy
(?–?)

We know nothing about Sarah Lévy, the author of two novels, *O Mon Goye* published in 1929, and *Ma Chère France* published a year later. The first novel was promptly translated into English in 1930 as *Beloved* and into German in 1931 as *Geliebter.* The second, less popular, was translated that same year into German as *Henri und Sarah*. While the US publisher asserts that *O Mon Goye* is autobiographical, he slyly notes that the author's name is so common that it might as well be a pseudonym. Was the author a woman? A Jew? We can only speculate.

O Mon Goye, from which the following passage is excerpted, was reviewed favorably in the mainstream press, which praised it for its novel portrayal of an interfaith romance, and was criticized in the Jewish press for its unfavorable portrayal of Jews. It is the story of a young and wealthy Jewish widow who falls in love with a handsome gentile man. The heroine, also named Sarah Lévy, is emancipated, urban, and lax in the practices of Judaism, even as she continues to assert her allegiance to her religion and to her "people." The young man's milieu is diametrically opposed to hers. He is a true Frenchman who owns land in the French countryside, moves in gentile circles, and has a Jesuit uncle. Sarah and Henri carry out their romance against the background of these two very different environments.

Although she belongs to the Jewish milieu, Sarah distances herself from it early in the novel. An assimilated and emancipated woman, she feels she has transcended her origins and is therefore entitled to make satiric comments. She can ridicule the Jews' obsession with business, money, and power as measures of belonging. But as an outsider, she is also able to satirize the gentiles' less overt devotion to financial gain. This double vision allows her to successfully prosecute her romance with the "other" while claiming her ethnic allegiance. The goal is to create a new environment, a new way of life, however fragile its foundation, from the fused strands of the Jewish and gentile traditions.

The novel offers a fascinating example of the way the Jewish bourgeoisie incorporated anti-Semitic stereotypes into its definition of itself. Unlike the French, grounded in the land and able to live in and for the moment, the Jews in the novel are portrayed as rootless, although they may be citizens of the state. Their rootlessness has physical as well as psychological consequences. In contrast to the French, who are well-built, sensual, self-possessed and who live in harmony with nature, the Jews are sickly, neurotic, analytic, and always worrying about the future. Sarah can bridge the profound chasm that exists between "them" and "us" only by shedding her Jewish characteristics—her urbanity, her Jewish family and friends, her nervous energy—and becoming truly "French" by settling into a rural Christian village and adopting its values and its century-old traditions. This novel is a testimony to the powerful hold that a certain idea of France and of French identity had on the Jewish imagination. With hindsight, we can see all too easily where the anti-Semitic stereotypes uttered by Henri—which Sarah rarely contradicts—will lead.

The following selection describes the first meeting between Sarah and Henri and establishes the differences between "them" and "us."

— **Eva Martin Sartori**

Selected Works

O Mon Goye. Paris: Flammarion, 1929.
Ma Chère France. Paris: Flammarion, 1930.

Translations Into English

Beloved! Trans. William A. Drake. New York: Simon and Schuster, 1930.
Excerpt from *Ma Chère France*. Trans. Glenn Swiadon, in Alan Astro, ed. "Discourses of Jewish Identity in Twentieth Century France." *Yale French Studies* 85, 1994, pp. 67–72.

Secondary Works

Alan Astro. "Two Best-selling French Jewish Women's Novels from 1929." *Symposium*. Winter 1999, pp. 241–254.

Beloved

It was certainly Uncle Alphonse's fault. But it was also the fault of Janie and her crowded receptions. Slightly delirious at the idea of actually having company at her house, company to command and to feed, she thinks only of showing off her admirably white bosom and her diamonds. Her broad face unfolds even more Buddha-like, and her blonde negress's hair is tumbled with excitement. She introduces no one to anybody, or if she does, invariably makes some mistake, names the lady to the gentleman, mangles the names, and if corrected, re-mangles them. She forces food upon people who have already eaten too much and forgets to offer a thing to those who may be famished. Any particularly distinguished guest she is certain to monopolize at the risk of making the rest of us die of jealousy. On these occasions her Robert is utterly neglected.

That evening I was wearing a black and very becoming velvet dress.

It was thus that I perceived a well set-up young fellow, clean-shaven, with a vivid face and light eyes. He was the momentary prey to the questions being hurled at him by Janie's acid voice. Marie Decker and Leonie Sulzbacher, Janie's intimate friends, and Jane Halphen, in a green dress, fearfully decolleté, were clustered about. I learned that Henri—for it was he—had just committed the imprudence of saying that he knew the Minister of Public Works. Already Naomi Maer was recommending her cousin to him: "A most remarkable young chap." A man with a monocle confided to him that a brief of his was even then being examined by the head of the cabinet. Henri answered politely, almost indulgently, as if speaking to greedy children. He resigned himself to his fate, or at least pretended to, for I should be unable to say how vividly his first gesture struck me. It was his shoulders beginning to vacillate, preparing an escape, almost imperceptibly, without violence, but with a rhythm which broke through all resistance. Smiling, he planted Janie and his audience there and with the suppleness of a dancing girl glided off in the direction of the card-room. He patted his forehead lightly with a white silk handkerchief. He must have thought that he had jostled me for he stopped short and excused himself:

"I beg your pardon, Madame! I am fleeing—they are too much for me!"

"To whom do you say that?"

I uttered the words with the most gracious expression; it must have been the first time in my life that I gave evidence of a certain gift for repartee. His smile expanded. His eyes radiated sympathy. From that moment, Janie,

From: *Beloved*. William A. Drake, trans. (New York: Simon and Schuster, 1930), pp. 25–36.

egotistical and indecorous as she was, would have been shrewd enough not to introduce us to each other.

It is not that my nose is unreasonably aquiline, that my hair is kinky; or that my complexion is the least bit oily. On the contrary, it is pink and white. My lips are not at all thick, and if my eyes are large and almond-shaped, they are just pretty black eyes, and that is all.

However, beyond all shadow of doubt, Henri's observing eye did not grasp, spread over my personality, that something which should not have deceived him, and which I thought rendered further advertisement quite unnecessary. As a matter of fact, he seemed to experience a sense of relief and refreshment.

"You don't like Jews?" I asked, smiling.

"Eh? I like Bernheim. That's why I'm here. He's a fine Jew—I defy you to find a better man! Lame since Verdun, pumped for money all day long by all of his old regiment—and do you know what he does for a living? He deals in vegetables at the *Halles*. It's excruciating. How many times we played bridge together in the valley of death, with the chaplain and the professor. How we used to laugh! Would you like me to call him? I don't know a man in France who can say the way he does: 'The Boches*! Filthy Swine!,' looking down at his foot. He can't forgive them for that foot of his—a bad business. He's a good *Yid* with a heart of gold; but that was a bad business, and he just doesn't like it!"

He seemed happy to relax beside one whom he felt to be a sister soul.

"The Jews . . . what a strange, what a contradictory race! During the last twenty minutes at least six noses have hooked me to ask whether I am in finance, building or wool; if Huanchaca is going to go up; what I think about this dreadful event, to wit: that wheat has just closed with a rise of three cents a bushel in New York, whereas the Liverpool market is weak. . . . And the women! Just listen to that cage of parrots! What chattering! A collection of near-sighted nanny-goats. They handle their lorgnettes as if they were instruments for testing metal. They simply can't untangle them from any passing stranger who happens to be reasonably good-looking. I saw one, just now, running to tell her husband that there's a Christian here who said he knew the Minister. Their appetite for profit is disgusting. It disgusts one's eyes and ears. You feel like walking off, grumbling: 'Frightful! Frightful!' And then you recollect: 'Good old Bernheim!' In France there are a hundred thousand Israelites and forty million Christians. As all Frenchmen have their Bernheim, every Jew finds himself provided with four hundred Christian friends. More than

---

*Derogatory term referring to the Germans.

friends—protectors! If I had only a quarter of that number, what a career I should make, Madame! . . ."

"You're staying then?"

"Of course! Except it's just a bit painful."

"Shall we talk, then?"

"With you—till dawn!"

We took possession of a corner. Janie, very pale, regarded us from a distance. My companion's broad shoulders annoyed her.

He continued with animation:

"I ask you, what are they afraid of? They seem to shriek just to stupefy themselves. Look at those hollow cheeks, that complexion; look at those girls green with chlorosis or nervousness, or heavy with useless fat. Did you ever see such sunken shoulders . . . ?"

I too grew animated. I pointed out to him one of our professional beauties.

"That one over there, you mean? Rebecca? Very beautiful, but they tell queer stories about her. A Chaldaean Magian was her ancestor, or some noble of the Pharaohs' court, or simply a Roman senator determined to enjoy his Syrian proconsulate. They're afraid, I tell you; afraid in the past, afraid in the future. They burn up their lives to make up for lost time, to gain quickly, immediately, this very moment. Social gatherings or not, everything must yield a profit. Confound it, I'll bet that these people—I beg your pardon—make love with their minds on their inventories!"

Once more, I was on the point of blurting out: "To whom are you saying all this?" but I stopped myself in time, red with shame.

Janie, at the back of the room, transfixed me with a glance. Around us Marie Decker, Leonie Sulzbacher and Jane Halphen were passing back and forth, darting their lorgnettes at us, trying to overhear snatches of our conversation.

"There they are, at it again," smiled Henri. "Unless they can hear everything you say, you're stealing something from them! Very amusing. Let's stay here, shan't we—unless I'm presuming . . ."

"Not at all."

I revelled in the opportunity which threw in my way this evening the very one all the others desired. My mind had been distracted by my suitors, two of whom were present. Bloch particularly had pursued me with his light assiduities, doing his best to delight me by an expert showing-up of the false pearls of all the ladies present, even of those who wear little ones knowingly proportionate to their financial possibilities. My heart was entirely indifferent to all this.

But beside this gorgeous fellow, who classified ideas and sentiments so rapidly, I experienced a feeling of security which neither marriage nor money nor morals has ever expressed for me. His eyes communicated an assurance I am unable to explain. Hanging on his words I bathed in the rays of his good humor. When it began to dim, I tried with a single word to make it shine once more. Already I was regretting that this interlude would soon be over.

"At bottom you pity them?"

"Yes, I said 'them'! I did not say 'us.'"

"Perhaps. They are neurotics; sick people who struggle for publicity in order to acquire some superiority. They pride themselves on their subtle intelligence because they're fond of burying themselves in an analysis of the morbid. They shout about fraternity, confusing it with the true nobility of the heart. They are poor, homeless people, deluding themselves with Utopian visions. When Jews give themselves the air of teaching us about life, they seem like puppets who cackle and strut. The poor devils would split the world in two, I wager, just to hear one word of love."

"But why do you tell me these things?" I said, my voice full of emotion. "And in the first place, let me interrupt you. They may be a homeless people, but—"

"Permit me to finish, Madame! The atmosphere inspires me. The most advanced Jew I see as a nervous doll to whom we can say: 'We have passed through the cycle of existence better than you. We have built temples more durable than that of Solomon. We have constructed ideas equal to those of Spinoza. Our martyrs remain without peer. And no one can claim to teach us the true meaning of life which is to dream and to seize the moment of happiness. No one knows better than we do that happiness lies in a woman's smile, which promises forgetfulness. Happiness, Madame, does not lie in reflection, in agitation, in playing the busybody avid for profit. Happiness consists in allowing oneself to be carried along like a good-natured animal by the temptations of Nature—to correct them a little, perhaps, and above all to channelize them. Don't you think so?"

I didn't know what to think. At that moment I should have liked him to caress my shoulder with his broad, compact hand. I should have rolled up like a peaceful little cat, unconscious of its peacefulness. I should have drawn in my claws, purred words infinitely stupid, and softened my paws proudly and submissively.

I didn't think at all. In his odour, the odour of health with a touch of lavender, I was content merely to breathe the air which was precisely that of my own health. . . . Was this happiness? Forgetfulness? I did not know.

"You often forget, then?" I said to him.

"As much as I can!"

"How?"

"Six hours in the open fields . . . A wood-cock pasty, and a bottle of Nuits . . . Fairy stories—and the sweet stupidity of love. It is amusing to watch others exhaust themselves in making profit, while one enjoys silently . . ."

Alas, my weak stomach! Alas, my heroes of the will!

"And there, war is incomparable. To die dreaming a great dream—that is life; that . . ."

Oh, my horror of bloodshed! Before me was the complete incarnation of all that I had ignored and wanted to ignore.

I was on the point of crying out: "Assassin!" I came nearer. My whole being rose to his to beg of him: "Protect me!"

"I fancy that they have seen enough of me this evening," he suggested, planning his retreat.

"Won't you see me home?"

He paused for one single second; just enough time to weigh me with a glance.

"With the greatest pleasure!"

How can I describe the gesture his arm made as he wrapped me in my furs?

What an exit! As she pressed my hand, Janie insulted me with her eyes: "Thief! Traitress!"

We walked a few steps from Passy in the direction of Auteuil. I shall never forget the obscure mass of trees on the lawn before La Muette. Although autumn had barely begun, it was cold. A glow caressed the grass. I shivered. The air smelt of ether and wet leaves. The cone-shaped traffic towers at the street intersections illuminated for one moment our merged silhouettes. Then everything fell back into shadow. We were the more alone, and I the more cowardly, the more intoxicated, abandoned myself to an emotion utterly new, whose memory even today tightens my throat deliciously. Henri hailed a taxicab. I was in a complete funk. I tensed, watching to see whether his arm, which had glided to the hollow of my back, would tremble or content itself with waiting. The arm did not tremble. The light of the arc lamps threw his face into chiaroscuro; looking up, I saw it was as immobile as that of a god. Emotion made a tatter of me. I lost my head. I remember, nevertheless, that when the car stopped, I smiled at the dexterity of a man who could support a woman, a mere rag, on his left arm, close the door, pay the chauffeur and ring with his right hand, without the slightest break in the balance of his movements. I still hear that voice which I could not help but obey:

"What floor?"

It is through the mists of a dream that I see him in my boudoir, on the divan. His crisp words were muted as they reached me. He was still laughing at the soirée. I answered him. He held my hands in his. I felt a tender warmth through all my body. For a moment I watched my shoulder glistening, moist. He looked at it too; and suddenly his lips were upon it, hot, possessive, tenacious. They remained there for a long time. In a daze I fastened my eyes on his red neck, a little distended between the white gleam of his collar and the black gleam of his hair. His neck, his blood-coloured eartips, the panting music of his breath—from all these proceeded emanations of a force such as I had never yet experienced. I let myself be carried away as if by a torrent, at the same time that fear, now more specific, re-invaded me. For the first time in my life a man was there in my house, near me, upon me; a man whose gesture crushed me, whose life drank my life. I started to my feet.

"Thank you for having been so kind as to take me home. Now you must go. It is very late."

It was the raucous sound of my voice which, climaxing my terror, marked the moment of my defeat.

Only a little while later did I return to reflection, having, by giving myself clumsily, offered sure proof of my innocence.

Here he was in my bed, resting peacefully at my side. Strange to say, my first thought was one of triumph over Janie, over my friends, over all women. It was I who had him, this *goy!* Then I smiled at the idea of the trickery by which I had just inaugurated my conquest of intense sensations, sensations I had never before imagined, a rich world of pleasure and happiness. Poor Levy's memory flashed through my mind and made me laugh again. Then I began to cry, less from shame than from fear; from fear of tomorrow.

His voice asked me:

"You are unhappy? Why?"

"Listen," I murmured. "You don't know! You didn't give me the time to tell you . . ."

"What?"

"My name is Sarah . . . Sarah Levy! . . ."

"Good God!"

He raised himself and leaned squarely against the pillow. By the faint light from the half-opened bathroom, where for the first time in months the hot bath which makes me sleep was growing cold awaiting me, I saw Henri take a cigarette, light it and blow out the smoke energetically. I saw him laugh.

"Well, my uncle's a Jesuit," he said.

But already he was gathering me up, all naked, asking me, mouth to mouth:

"Do you love me, Sarah?"

"I love you, Henri."

"Then go to sleep, little angel! Jehovah will arrange this matter with the Virgin Mary. We are doing no one any harm. Kiss me, sweetheart!"

Thus, broken, I went to sleep without a bath, without a dream, beside this stranger who did not even fear that the heavens would fall upon his head. They have terrible nerves, sometimes, these *goyim;* and then again, when it serves their purpose, it would seem that they have none at all.

Clara Malraux
(1897–1982)

Clara Malraux, née Goldschmidt, spent much of her life trying to emerge from the shadow of her famous husband, André. However, this association was not the most difficult obstacle in her life. Born in the midst of the Dreyfus era, she was a Franco-German Jew torn between two worlds. When war broke out between France and Germany in 1914, she chose France, only to be persecuted during the Second World War by the country to which she had given her allegiance. Her saga during that dark time was an important stage in her quest to find an identity.

Clara Goldschmidt was born in Paris to wealthy German-Jewish parents and was perfectly bilingual in German and French. She never lost the appreciation for the German literature she had read in her youth with her German governess. When, at the age of twenty-three, she met André Malraux (he was only nineteen), she was fascinated by his intellectual brilliance. With him at her side, she envisioned an exciting life of travel, writing, and scintillating intellectual conversation. They were married in 1921 against the wishes of her family. Only later did she discover his domineering nature and inability to share his life or fame.

She did share André's voyage to Cambodia in 1923 in a search for antiquities whose illegal sale was to finance the couple's luxurious life style and in her memoirs she relates the adventure with considerable bitterness. Except during their extended periods of travel, their marriage grew more and more stormy as Clara struggled to create a space for herself in André's world. Although she was the sounding board for his novels of the 1920s and 1930s, he did nothing to encourage her own desire to write. In fact, she was forced to write in secret, because André could not tolerate competition, especially from his wife. Clara found herself being pushed more and more into the background as André was unwilling to give her credit for her accomplishments. Even the birth of a daughter, Florence, in 1934, did nothing to bring them closer together.

During the 1930s, she worked tirelessly with various anti-Fascist organizations in France, often serving as interpreter. She allied herself with the Communist left in its efforts against Fascism, although she never became a member of the Communist Party. She also finished *Le Livre de Comptes,* a short novel which tells the story of her heroine's progressive disillusionment with her role as the wife of a great man. When the war broke out in 1939, Clara, estranged from her husband, was alone in Paris with her frail young daughter. André asked her for a divorce in 1941 but she refused because her maiden name, Goldschmidt, was all too likely to identify her and her daughter as Jews and made her vulnerable both as a Jew and as a member of the

Clara Malraux

Resistance. When Hitler invaded France in May 1940, Clara and Florence fled to the Free Zone in the south of France where Clara continued her work for the Resistance. This was the beginning of the long journey that Clara would later refer to as her "Exodus." When the Germans annexed the Free Zone in 1942, Clara began the most perilous phase of her saga, wandering from village to village with her small daughter and one suitcase until they reached safety in the Drôme village of Dieulefit.

After the war and her divorce from André, Clara's real career as a writer began. *Portrait de Grisélidis,* another thinly disguised account of her life with André, was published in 1945. Little by little, Clara rebuilt her life as a writer and activist. She wrote fiction, including a novel, *La Lutte inégale* (1958) [The Unequal Struggle] and a collection of short stories, *La Maison ne fait pas crédit* (1947) [No Charge Accounts/ Strictly Cash] both based on her experience as a single Jewish mother during the Nazi Occupation of France. As a reflection of her many intellectual interests, she wrote essays, critical reviews and did numerous translations.

Clara's encounter with her Jewishness filled the void left by her divorce from André. Her last three published works deal with that subject: *Civilisation du Kibboutz, Venus des quatre coins de la terre,* and *Rahel ma grande soeur.* With *Rahel, ma grande soeur* Clara laid claim not only to her Jewish identity but also to her German heritage. The article she wrote for the journal *Eléments,* "De l'appartenance au Judaïsme" is an account of the developing awareness of her place in the Jewish world.

The following excerpt from her six-volume autobiography, *Le Bruit de nos pas* begins with a poignant allusion to the New Testament illustrating Clara's realization that although she received her early education in a parochial school, she is excluded from the Christian tradition. Unlike the Virgin Mary and her child during their flight into Egypt, Clara has neither donkey to ride upon nor companion to protect her. Her journey acquires a larger meaning through numerous references to biblical and mythological wanderings.

— Patricia Le Page

Selected Works

Portrait de Grisélidis. Colbert, 1945.
Contes de la Perse. 1947. Editions G.P. Rouge et Or, 1972.

La Maison ne fait pas crédit. Bibliothèque française, 1947; Messidor, Temps actuels, 1981.
Par de longs chemins. Stock, 1953.
La Lutte inégale. Julliard, 1958.
Java-Bali. Rencontre, 1964.
Venus des quatre coins de la terre. Julliard, 1972.
Le Bruit de nos pas. Grasset, 1963–1979.
    1. *Apprendre à vivre,* 1897–1922.
    2. *Nos vingt ans,* 1922–1924.
    3. *Les Combats et les jeux,* 1924–1925.
    4. *Voici que vient l'été,* 1927–1935.
    5. *La fin et le commencement,* 1936–1940.
    6. *Et pourtant j'étais libre,* 1940–1968.
Rahel ma grande soeur. Ramsay, 1980.

Translations Into English

Memoirs. Patrick O'Brian, trans. New York: Farrar, Straus and Giroux, 1967).
    The first two volumes of *Le Bruit de nos pas.*
A Second Griselda. Hugh Shelley, trans. London: A. Wingate, 1947.

Selected Translations by Clara Malraux

Gustav Janouch. *Kafka m'a dit.* Calmann-Lévy, 1951.
Grete Lainer. *Journal d'une petite fille* (preface by Freud). Gallimard, 1928. (trans. of *Tagebuch eines halbnuschsigen Mädchen*).
Louise Rinser. *Les anneaux transparents.* Seuil, 1956. (trans. of *Die Glasernen Ringe*).
Virginia Woolf. *Une chambre à soi.* Gonthier, 1951. (trans. of *A Room of One's Own*).

Secondary Works

Christian de Bartillat. *Clara Malraux. Biographie-Témoignage.* Perrin, 1985.
Isabelle de Courtivron. *Clara Malraux, Une femme dans le siècle.* Ed. de l'Olivier, 1992.
Isabelle de Courtivron. "Of First Wives and Solitary Heroes: Clara & André Malraux" in *Significant Others.* Thames and Hudson, 1993.
Susan Rubin Suleiman. "Malraux's Women: A Re-vision" in *Witnessing André Malraux, Vision and Re-Visions.* Wesleyan University Press, 1984.
Louise Witherell. "A Modern Woman's Autobiography: Clara Malraux" in *Contemporary Literature* 24, 2 (Summer 1983), pp. 222–232.

And Yet, I Was Free

Was it a flight or a voyage of initiation? Probably both. At each stage, I learned something that I couldn't begin to convey, because in order to understand it, one would have had to be a hunted, defenseless creature, responsible for another life besides one's own. The eternal Jewish mother, holding the child by the hand, without even a companion or a donkey.

Like all voyages of initiation, the beginning was the easiest part: my stopover at the Hamons was almost pleasant. A feeling of real comfort prevailed among friends such as Leo, who was often called away by his Resistance "exploits," Suzanne who was politically active in a number of ways, an old aunt who played the part of grandmother, and the two children who understood the unusual nature of the times. It was best that I not become too accustomed to their marvelous complicity.

So I took advantage of that stopover to risk a trip to Toulouse, taking the train only as far as the first station after Montauban, with a hat pushed down over my eyes and my body deformed by a coat much too big and long. When I got there, Strickler, who represented the movement at that time, told me that I would have to wait a little while—a wonderfully imprecise term—before getting the "real" false papers. In the interim, they could make ordinary false papers and they did but it was immediately obvious that they were fake. As for the "real" false ones, that was another story. They knew how to establish valid identities for the male prisoners on the move, but they hadn't planned anything for women, much less for children. I was forced to be patient—and show myself as little as possible: it seems that the police had a photo of my modest person holding Florence by the hand. That was not a very pleasant thought. Nevertheless there hadn't been any search of the Pâquerettes. Even in the midst of the worst suffering, neither Jean nor Gaby nor anyone from our group had revealed the place where we used to live.

I knew that my hosts were all involved in the Resistance, each in his own way. Staying with them would put them in danger for no reason. I therefore slipped out of their apartment one fine afternoon, with my daughter Florence. Where could we go? Fortunately a garage owner who lived on the outskirts of the city took us in. He was part of our network.

It was a peculiar shelter, where each of us was in danger and was dangerous for the others. My closest neighbors were two English pilots, one of whom was very attractive and caught the eye of the owners' charming adolescent daughter. I felt immediately that I was taking up a room meant for more

From: *Et Pourtant j'étais libre* (Paris: Grasset & Fasquelle, 1979), pp. 159–183.

important guests. Actually the place, which was full of temporary residents, looked more like a train station than a home. We stayed for three days—until the fifth day of our wanderings. Our short stopovers kept me from contemplating more permanent arrangements. Besides, which ones? The most sensible thing seemed to be to stay in contact with Toulouse and circumvent the many different dangers, while waiting for the "real" papers which would eventually reach us. All things considered, it was a wild goose chase where we couldn't get used to the unpredictable.

For the present or for what was then the present, staying in one place was becoming difficult and going back to the Hamons would be much too risky for our hosts and their Resistance activities. I then thought of going to the refuge that had been previously offered by a retired teacher who was the friend of a former town councilor. "I live in a village away from the other houses, you couldn't dream of a safer place." The lady's eyes inspired confidence.

And so I took to the road, my suitcase in one hand, my child in the other.

The route turned out to be longer than I had imagined. On the right, I felt weighed down by Florence's steps. Absorbed in her walking, she had stopped talking. Their cords tied around the poles, the grapevines seemed as monotonous as rice fields. Two or three cars went by, filled with German officers. I knew that the village that was to give us shelter was up on a hill, but I could not see any hills on the horizon.

Tense from her effort, Florence struggled like a boxer against the southern wind that slowed us down.

"Are you tired, darling?"

A soft weary voice answered:

"It's all right, I know that the farther we go the better it is."

It wasn't better because when we finally arrived, the "kindly" hostess turned out to be a shrew. "I can't let you stay—you have become too dangerous—I know that they arrested your whole group." What did she really know? Nothing, probably. She simply deduced that we were searching for refuge because we were in danger. On the other hand, the most disparate and sometimes the most justified rumors followed the arrests of Resistants, the deportations of Jews and the movements of the Maquis. These were followed by the Germans' demands or punishments. I was alone with an exhausted little girl. Outside darkness was falling, it was the end of March and it was cold. The woman allowed us to come inside because we might attract attention standing on the doorstep. In the suffocating heat of the closed room, a stubborn resignation took hold of me. I sat down and had Florence sit down at the rough kitchen table. The idea was for us to look so entrenched that the old shrew would resign herself to putting up with us for a few hours. "I'm going to go talk to—" I don't remember which expert was supposed to come to her aid. "You can spend the night here but tomorrow you have to leave. I may be able to find someone to take you to Toulouse. I think the butcher—-" OK, why not Toulouse? We'd run the risk of being recognized but less of a risk, after all, than getting lost in the crowd. There at least I had some chance of meeting people who could give me advice. "Don't move even if someone knocks. I'm leaving you milk and an egg. You'll have to get along as best as you can. I'll come back as soon as possible."

What was she afraid of when she locked the door behind her pathetic self? I thought of all sorts of things but didn't dwell on any. After all, I had other things to think about, all of them unpleasant.

Later, I was able to reflect on the different stages of our flight. At the time, it was impossible to predict and therefore to alter what was awaiting us, so I took refuge in the vast array of final preparations: trains, stations, routes, shabby inns were transformed into Cartesian stoves. Powerlessness led to thought. But on this particular evening the situation was too new to allow detachment: we hadn't eaten since morning. I knew that the slightest identity check meant danger; that we didn't have much money. We had only a small sum at our disposal and yet we were grateful to have it. What we had, we owed to Jean's foresight. He had said to me one day, "The underground has decided to provide you with a little money, since you incur various expenses in your activities. Its arrival will obviously depend on our liaison with England." Because of problems with the air connections, almost the entire Resistance had found itself without a penny. In order to survive, we had sold our most extravagant things to the newly rich. Watch chains, dancing shoes, sheared fox-skin stoles all disappeared, but not, in my case, the diamond ring that, with the passage of time, had become like a magic wand which would bring me to a mythical America. What value would this jewel have now that Jean could no longer help me flee France? Purely symbolic probably, which only made it more precious.

For the moment, there was no question of crossing the Pyrenees. We would simply have to wait until tomorrow. The place we were in was badly lit, full of clouds of steam from previous meals. Flo was daydreaming, huddled near the fireplace, perhaps imagining the normal lives of little girls who could go to school because their mothers were neither Jewish nor tangled up in dubious activities. She broke her silence to say: "I have to do something. I'm going to make some crêpes because the nasty woman left milk and an egg." She found flour and a rind of bacon in the pantry, mixed the ingredients, beat them and carefully poured them into a frying pan. Entirely absorbed in her work, nothing seemed to interest her except the supple yellowish rounds decorated with brown spots, like beauty marks on the faces of the lovely women of long ago.

Did we have any desire to eat these crêpes? I don't think so, but they seemed proof that we would stay alive on this earth; that a time would come when we wouldn't be hungry; that life wouldn't come to an end in this hostile setting.

The dove from the Ark—somewhere the earth flowered again—-At dawn, we were able to leave our prison, half hidden under the canvas cover of a small truck. Our driver, who knew the checkpoints, called out greetings that served as passwords.

We recognized the outskirts of Toulouse. In a way, like prodigal children, we felt we were going home. But what warm-hearted father would welcome us?

There was one, and he had a wife: it was Strickler. "The apartment is big enough," he told us—"it has three rooms—-to give you shelter until you get your papers." These papers would magically transform us from beggars into princesses. He imposed—on me at least—only one condition: not to go out of the house so as not to attract attention. Of course I accepted without discussion, without realizing that I was thus becoming a sort of shut-in. But did I have a choice? After all, this little apartment near the Esquirol was better than the camps that Jean had told me about. As for Flo, she retained the right to some measure of liberty. The Strickler family had a small child and a boy of ten on whom my child made a great impression: whenever he was available, he and Flo would go for a walk on the Grand Rond; Thursdays they went to the pool. Florence began to smile again. Madame Strickler, who was thrilled by their friendship, saw them as adolescents and friends, if not something more. I was amazed that one could even think about the future.

The news continued to be bad; each day we heard about a new arrest or a new miracle: Gaby had been nabbed on the way to the Hotel Toulier where she was to have dinner with Jean.

A little later we learned that Gaby had been released by the militia thanks to the intervention of her father, a man of some importance, who was the mayor of his region. Perhaps I could take advantage of the good graces of this man who, after his daughter's arrest, warmly welcomed all the Resistance fighters who asked for his help. Strangely enough, after her liberation, Gaby was given lodging by friends in the house next door to the Stricklers. We couldn't resist the temptation to see one another, so one evening we met in the street, disobeying the rules. We didn't cause any problems, even though I didn't heed Strickler's important injunction . . .

In the street, which fortunately was badly lit, we were so overwhelmed at being together after the disappearance of so many in our group that we could neither part nor say what was essential. I knew, however that she had seen Jean bloody, almost blind, after he had been interrogated.

Since the network had broken up, local contacts had become uncertain and mistrust an endemic illness; we had to be content with what we could get. For obvious reasons, we couldn't stay more than a week in the Stricklers' house. The authentic looking papers were taking too long, so we decided to simply fall back on the temporary false papers. Mine turned out to be so bad as to be almost provocative, because they were written in two different colors of ink. I will never know what kept the forgers from being consistent. As for the name Malraux, it became Lamy, André's mother's last name. I gave up my married name not because André's name was dangerous, but because of the danger that I myself represented.

Of course we didn't give up the idea of getting "real" documents. Strickler and my brother knew the mayor of Grenade-sur-Adour in the Pyrenees. But before talking to him we had to wait for a whole series of events to unfold in the region—transfers of members of the Maquis, train derailments, and other such acts of sabotage—about which it was a good idea to remain discreet.

Under these conditions, it was best for Florence and me to proceed in stages, prudently, to the outskirts of the village of Grenade. Then in ten days or so, if we could hold out that long, we would go to Aire-sur-Adour where a member of the network managed a hotel. To these vague instructions, Strickler added that it would be sensible not to stay more than two nights in one place.

The unexpected events at Saint-Gaudens were probably meant to reinforce my vigilance. We had arrived in that lovely city on Saturday and therefore could allow ourselves to stay until Monday. When your soul is at peace, what do you do on Sunday? You go to the cinema. In this case, the theater was located across the street from the railroad station. What secret warning led me to sit near the exit? The same instinct probably that made us wait on a certain platform rather than on another when five minutes later there would be an inspection. Animals, apparently, feel storms coming. Hunted human beings probably do too.

I don't remember anything of the film which unfolded for a half-hour before our eyes, but I can still see the reddish pattern that like a paper cut-out suddenly took shape on the screen. Flo and I were already out of our seats without having even realized the meaning of the reddish design. It quickly became clear: the spectators came out of the flaming building, pushing and trampling on one another, shouting. An attempt was made to put out the fire that wasn't extinguished until the last timber was in flames. For once, we were witnesses to a disaster without being involved. At Saint-Gaudens, only the

And Yet, I Was Free

movie theater burned, but a feeling of peril was linked to the city, a peril that was added to those that seemed to be becoming part of our lives. We sat, huddled together, alert yet resigned. Life is a risk that you have to accept if you want to stay alive. Yesterday's flames only made clearer the images we already carried within of the fires of hell, the fire at the center of the earth, and the fires of the stakes upon which our ancestors writhed.

Once again we were on a train, a short trip this time. Outside, the countryside emerges out of the moving lines that come together to sketch out the hills which, in the distance, become mountains. Perhaps, in the hollows between the valleys, safety isn't such a transitory state. I am thinking of the name of a village, the village of a peasant family where Strickler had guaranteed me hospitality. We are to get off at Lannemezan and walk about five kilometers. Then, who knows, almost safe, we will rest for a few days.

And here we are again, on the road. My left hand in Florence's right, my other hand holding a bundle that gets heavier with every step. What had seemed indispensable now becomes unimportant when the next day will offer neither a glass for a toothbrush nor a bed to lie down on. We walked almost resolutely, Naomi and Ruth for whom no Boaz waited along the road. Ah, what is courage? Death waits for us all. Only courage is left, which consists simply of taking on the difficulties of our condition: the courage and patience of a woman who is trying to protect, without vanity or boasting, the child she loves, the man she loves. The kind of courage that doesn't make a spectacle of strength . . .

The town where we ended up, after an hour's effort, looked like one of those Afghan villages that I had passed through in the course of my travels, whose empty streets and obstructed passages were evidence that they had been abandoned long ago. This particular day, the almost oriental taste of the French for courtyards became apparent. High walls with openings out of which grass and a few yellow dandelions grew against a drab background; doors that stayed closed even when you hit them with a hammer, were also oriental in form. In a tone strident with anguish, we called out repeatedly the names of those who were supposed to be willing to give us shelter. On the second floor, outside a curved door, a man appeared: "What do you want?"

How could I admit to that arrogant creature that we wanted to spend the night at his house?

"They told me . . ."

"They told you nothing. Leave us alone!"

The window closed. In front of the gate a pile of manure was spread out.

Of Kafka's works, I had only read *Metamorphosis*. If I had been better acquainted with the body of his works, this would have been a good time to reflect on it. As it was, I merely made my way along a street that had been devastated by some unknown calamity. A human being finally appeared at the end of the street, a woman wrapped in a black shawl, as was the custom in the Pyrenees region, for women over the age of twenty-five. This woman seemed old, tired, resigned to everything, even to answering me. Why did the village seem empty? It wasn't entirely so; only the young men had fled the region. The reason? Well, the Maquis often came into the village for provisions. The Germans knew it and the previous evening had rounded up all those who seemed suspect. So now they're being wary, right? It wasn't really the right time to ask for anything.

There was no question of going back to Lannemezan and making Flo walk for another hour. This woman should have understood that.

"We can't," she repeated. I will never know what it was that "We can't." Facing one another, we seemed resigned not to make any decision when she said, "Why don't you go to the inn?"

There was an inn. Why didn't she tell me sooner! "You know, they may not be open any more. They have a son."

The door was wide open; the son was supposed to be away in the mountains. They gave us a room, a bed with a nice red down coverlet, and an armoire big enough to hide Bluebeard's wives. Then in a dining room which we had to ourselves, a dinner of bouillon, a stew, cheese and, as the crowning glory, an apple tart. We hadn't seen such marvels for weeks.

The miracle was repeated the next day. It was no use for our hostess to warn us that the Germans would come back, that they always returned after the first round-up, that this time they would clean out all the men, women, and even the animals of the village, and I don't know what else, that it would be better not to stay in a place that had already been marked. We just couldn't leave the desserts. We stayed for three days in this land of milk and honey where terror reigned, then we went off toward Tarbes.

This time I hardly had time to think. We had barely left the Lannemezan railroad station when the Gestapo appeared. "Your papers, please." Flo, sitting huddled between a Catholic sister and old man decked out like Pétain, had a rosier face than usual, a result of the mountain air and the desserts that "stick to the ribs." The inspector gave her back her usual pale complexion. "Your papers, please." In Russia they probably don't say "Please." Here, they behave like polite conquerors, except, of course, if you're Jewish or a member of the Resistance. Flo was becoming smaller and smaller; there seemed to be nothing left of her face but the eyes.

"Your papers?"

I held them out.

The man wasn't even twenty years old; the occupiers seemed younger from day to day. . . . His eyes went from Flo to me, as though he were measuring her. Yes, she's a very little girl who shouldn't be here.

He asked me where I was going. I answered: "To Salies-du-Salat where my child has to go for treatment. She has just been sick."

I know German as well as I know French, but I hardly understood what he said to himself: *"Ein anderer mag es machen.* [Let someone else do it.] And then too, the little girl is sweet."

Even if I live to be one hundred, how will I forget the whispered phrase that allowed us to continue to live. I would have liked to have the strength to look at the fellow but I couldn't find it.

"Here"—his French was rough—"take your identity card." A few seconds later, his voice was heard in the next car: "Your papers, please." "Phew," said the nun. She probably knew. I couldn't even say "phew," but now that the Gestapo—who acted from compassion—was far away, a strange confusion came over me. I imagined I was no longer on a French train, but rather on one in Indochina or in Cambodia, at the time of our arrest.[*] Surrounded by an Asian crowd huddled on a boat, I was perspiring not from fear but because of the heavy heat coming up from the river. A little later I wondered if danger has the same scent, whether it be voluntary or capricious as it was twenty years ago, or imposed and chosen as it is now, for me, on French soil.

At Tarbes, the French militia's visit to the hotel room where we had just gone to bed in a big peasant bed seemed benign.

"No problem, I see that you are with a little girl. Good night, Madame."

Then, there was Pau, a forty-eight hour stopover with my brother who had been part of a network for some time. The recent bombing of a German airfield in which he had been involved had attracted attention and he was getting ready to leave the region quietly with his wife and children. Therefore, the only possibility that was left to me was to get to Aire-sur-Adour before the agreed-upon date. That's what I did.

The hotel was managed by a friend of Strickler who was welcoming, even reassuring. Flo and I began to relax. Not for long. On the second day, a servant standing watch at the corner of the house motioned us discreetly away. An hour later we learned that the Gestapo had just inspected the area. The operation was more or less routine according to my host and it didn't justify my abandoning the place. Thus we were able to stay, happy to be treated with kindness.

---

[*] A reference to when Clara and André were arrested for having taken antiquities from a Cambodian temple without government permission.

Clara Malraux

Aire-sur-Adour has a public garden that in my memory looks like an English park, which it probably did not. Still the spot was charming, welcoming for the wrecks that we were. Under a benevolent sun we slowly recovered a little. Flo even began to play again without ever abandoning her watchfulness. One day I forgot that her assumed name was Claude and I called, "Flo." She replied in a matter-of-fact tone to a friend who asked her, "What did your mama call you?"—"Clo, it's a nickname for Claude."

Sitting on a bench, looking a little like a governess in a good family, I let the time pass.

It had been agreed that Strickler would come to meet me this particular Tuesday. The next day, we were supposed to go to Grenade-sur-Adour where we would be given identity cards authenticated with birth certificates which would allow us to become three-dimensional people once again. Under false names, we would finally have the right to a personal existence.

This particular day we had waited for Strickler in the hotel, we had waited for him in the public garden, we had waited for him during our walk hoping that he would be there when we returned. Like Penelope with no way out except through the return of Ulysses, we had waited like no other fiancée ever awaited her betrothed. The man who didn't come held our lives as one holds a mysterious password. Our wandering couldn't continue any longer without him.

Then the long night began, the only long night I've known, when I struggled with the angel. My child was enclosed by my body, just as before her birth, her breath only came through mine, we were as inseparable as Siamese twins. However between us there was the terrible inequality of my lived-out destiny compared with a life just beginning. It wasn't fair that Flo should die before having known other arms than mine around her; she must not suffer without experiencing some happiness. She wasn't responsible for anything. I was ready to take on everything: my Judaism, my activities with the Resistance, my need—childish perhaps—to assert myself before a man, the wrong I had done to my mother. I was ready to pay for all my deeds as long as she was given her adolescence, the flowering of maturity, middle age, even old age with its paltry joys.

Toward morning, coming out of a half-sleep, she sensed that I had been crying. Her voice was serious when she said to me: "If you couldn't stand it, you shouldn't have started it." How could I make her understand . . . that I hadn't "started" anything, that I had merely "continued," that the Resistance, for me, had only been an option between active and passive death. I searched for the words. Since we were sharing the worst, maybe we could share this way of understanding. I hugged her closer against me. She soon fell asleep again . . . .

When morning came, we got up since we were still alive. We went down to the dining room of the inn and pretended to eat breakfast. "Madame," said a servant while pouring milk into my cup, "Madame, Monsieur Strickler will come for you around noon."

"Monsieur Strickler?" I refrained from saying, "He's not dead, then?" I managed to say: "He's here?"—"He's across the street. When his wife isn't with him, Monsieur Strickler stays with the neighbors, a couple who are his Swiss countrymen." While sponging up a little milk that had spilled on the table, the slightly plump servant—they still ate well in that region—had just given us the gift of our future.

From then everything went as expected—the meeting with Strickler, my brother's arrival, the trip to Grenade-sur-Adour, the kind mayor who modestly assumed the risks of his actions and saved our lives, like the peasants who once would assume the consequences for both rain and good weather.

The papers? They were fabulous: with these papers Flo could have taken the baccalaureate, I could have—God forbid—remarried. We had just been reborn. I was, in fact, who was I? I still have the identity card issued by the town hall in the 16th arrondissement of Paris upon presentation of my birth certificate, where my name is "Marie-Claire Lamy, shopkeeper, resident of Bascons.

And then? Then it was almost peace time. Once again we thought we could sketch out some projects, "next year, when you're grown up, when I'm old." We could laugh without fearing that it would be for the last time. With the immediate danger overcome, I was about to say to myself that although it was awful to be in the center of things, it seemed preferable to me to being only a spectator. In my notebook, my eternal notebook, I had already written: "If it weren't for Flo, I would accept everything easily," which was easy to say because I didn't know the extent of the "everything." While awaiting the terrible discovery, I was recovering, we were recovering. We had crossed Toulouse; once again I had changed my hat. At the time, headcovers played the same role for women as mustaches, beards and dark glasses for men. We had decided to go to Dieulefit, in the Drôme, to rejoin Suzanne Ulmann. The network was born in a stalag, partly around the Ulmanns and for me, it ended with Suzanne.

Along the way, in Avignon I think, there was an alert. They made us leave the train. In spite of difficulties I no longer remember, we managed to get to a hotel and listened with joy to the bombardment, a sign that someone cared about us. But the bombings—on the less pleasant side—transformed our trip into an obstacle course. We got used to it, and one fine day—a really fine day —after passing the sign for Valence we arrived at Dieulefit. Our wanderings, for a while at least, were over.

— **Translated by Patricia Le Page**

Jacqueline Mesnil-Amar
(1909–1987)

Jacqueline Mesnil was born into a bourgeois Jewish family long-established in France. After completing studies in psychology at the Sorbonne, she married André Amar, a philosophy professor. During the war, her husband joined the *Organisation Juive de Combat* [Jewish Resistance Organization]. He was deported in July 1944, in the last convoy to leave Drancy, from which he escaped. She remained in Paris with her daughter, Sylvie, receiving no news from her husband until the liberation of the city. After her husband's return, she organized the *Service Central des Déportés Israélites* (SCDI) [Central Agency for Jewish Deportees] which she headed for the next ten years. From the time of liberation, she devoted herself tirelessly to the dignified treatment of the Jewish prisoners returning from the concentration camps.

Ceux qui ne dormaient pas. Journal des temps tragiques [Those Who Did Not Sleep. A Journal of Tragic Times], the journal she had kept during her husband's deportation, was published in 1946. A new edition, published in 1957, included a new second section, "Des Temps Tragiques aux Temps Difficiles," a collection of articles she had published between October 1944 and June 1946 in the Bulletin of the SCDI.

After the war, Mesnil-Amar published articles in *Nouveaux Cahiers,* the literary and political journal published by the Alliance Israélite Universelle, as well as in *Europe* and *Les Cahiers du Sud*. In an issue of *Nouveaux Cahiers* devoted to Jewish women, she contributed a remarkable autobiographical account, "Nous étions les Juifs de l'oubli" [We Were the Jews Who Had Forgotten] in which she describes her efforts after the war to give content and meaning to her Judaism. She also wrote about meeting the writers Edmond Fleg and André Spire and their families, the musician Léon Algazi, and about her two trips to Israel. The title of this essay refers to the dilemmas of assimilation and denial experienced by Jews before World War II.

Thirty years after the war, Mesnil-Amar still probed her Judaism: "Too Jewish for some, not enough for others, was I Jewish enough for myself?" She and her husband became involved in the study of the Jewish religion and culture.

In her essays, Mesnil-Amar reveals herself as a woman of refinement, generosity, and intellectual honesty, constantly challenging French Jews to define their identity.

— **Michèle Bitton**

Jacqueline Mesnil-Amar

Selected Works

"Le message des enfants perdus". In "Aspects du génie d'Israël." *Cahiers du Sud*, 1950, pp. 293–309.
Ceux qui ne dormaient pas. Fragments de journal, 1944–1946. Paris: Editions de Minuit, 1957.
"Racisme et snobisme chez Marcel Proust." *La Nef. Cahier Trimestriel* 21 (19–20) (1964): 173–182.
"Un Poète . . . un ami." *Europe: Revue Littéraire Mensuelle* 467 (1968): 240–247.
"Marcel Proust, les Juifs et le monde." *Les Nouveaux Cahiers* 19 (1970): 35–45.
"Nous étions les Juifs de l'oubli." *Les Nouveaux Cahiers* 50 (1977): 43–49.

Secondary Works

Michèle Bitton. "Jacqueline Mesnil-Amar." In *Présences féminines juives en France, XIXe-XXe siècles*. 2M Editions, 2002, pp. 238–240.
Gérard Israël. "Jacqueline Mesnil-Amar." *Les Nouveaux Cahiers* 89 (1987): 408.
Sylvie Jessua-Amar. "André et Jacqueline Amar, mes parents." *Sens* 7–8 (1994): 291–299.

Those Who Sleep Through the Night

I can't go to sleep at night thinking that somewhere on earth a man is hungry.

—Charles Péguy, *Jean Coste*

In the tragedy *Macbeth,* there is a passage of rare pathos and grandeur. Macduff, an old friend of Macbeth who has guessed Macbeth's crime and has left Scotland to join the loyalist forces in England, is told that to avenge this desertion. Macbeth has had Lady Macduff and her two children assassinated. The shocked Macduff repeats: "My children also?"

> **Ross** (his cousin): Wife, children, servants, everyone he could find.
>
> **Macduff:** And I was far away! My wife is also dead?
>
> **Ross:** I have already told you.
>
> **Macduff:** Ah! He has no children! All my darlings! Is that what you said? Malediction. All? What? All my sweet lambs and their mother taken away in one stroke?
>
> **Ross:** Avenge yourself like a man.
>
> **Macduff:** And so I will, but I also have to suffer like a man. I can only think of those who were so dear to me. What! Heaven saw that and did not help them?

B. had a wife and two sons. All three were picked up in the Isère in January 1944; they had been denounced by a militiaman. He waited for them, as we all waited. He does not wait for them any longer, as we too no longer wait. In the silence of the night, probably, something absurd and irrational within him still waits. In spite of himself, a portion of his soul still flies off toward the vainest awaiting, the vainest of hopes. And, in those interminable dialogues that a man holds with himself, he probably tells himself incoherent things: "Not both . . . not both . . . That's not possible. Little Jean will come back; he was so full of joy. Surely he will come back. Or maybe my wife and the little one, but then not the older one. The older one will come back. . . ." The boys were tall and hard, with cheerful schoolboy faces. Endlessly tortuous financial arrangements allowed them to take makeshift baccalaureate classes under

From: *Ceux qui ne dormaient pas* (Paris: Editions de Minuit, 1957), pp. 143–160.

assumed names, in secret, in the towns of the free zone. One of them also worked on a farm. Their wonderful young faces expressed their defiance in the face of anxiety, persecution, and arrest—and even hard labor and hunger and cold. And yet they did not come back. Madame B. tired herself out shopping and cooking; she was sweet and modest. I will never forget her resigned smile that was not without courage and that, because of her tragic destiny, has a kind of grandeur in my memory. B. comes and goes, puts on his tie, talks about politics, and no one knows the strands from which his thoughts are woven.

Madame P. was waiting for her daughter, son-in-law and three grandchildren, the oldest eleven years old, all taken away because the father was a victim of his loyalty to his job. Madame P. waits still; she will wait for months and years, deep inside herself. She is one of those women who wait for centuries, the duration of human suffering, because in the longest and most absurd waiting there is still a trace of hope. She will wait until her own death, expecting to see her family emerge all at once out of the shadows, their flesh newly sculpted, standing on their own ashes, solid, alive, and smiling—this charming girl I knew, holding her fragile happiness in her hands, her husband, her children, her house. . . . Madame P. does not want to know the implacable—"Turn to the right! Turn to the left!" screamed out by the SS officers at the Auschwitz train station—or that the mothers themselves led their children to the gas chambers to die together in the glare of the ovens.

Per me si va nella citta dolente
Per me si va nel eterno dolore
Per me si va tra la perduta gente . . .

Through me the way into the woeful city
Through me the way into eternal grief
Through me the way among the lost people

Perhaps she hasn't read Dante? What for? In her mind, she will live her future near the three little beds, the three curly heads, the three young voices, the joy and reward of her old age, leading her life with dignity. When the weather is good, she will go to the park to watch other peoples' children play ball or hopscotch, amid cries of joy, watched over by their young mothers who imprudently give them over for safekeeping to the false guardians of free countries.

Those Who Sleep Through the Night

They took away A.'s father, an admirable man if ever there was one on earth, his sick mother, a very old grandmother, denounced in the Isère in October 1943 and deported to Drancy in November. His brother was picked up in a roundup in February. No one came back. He stopped waiting for them in August. Perhaps he had never waited for them and only pretended to wait, tricking himself, lying to his conscious self in order to keep on living through the daily impulse to work. "When my younger brother returns . . . " he used to say. Now he says nothing. The time for deception is gone; the lucid man must face those pieces of his ruined life that remain.

I remember well Hélène B. who was deported with her father and mother. They came from an old family that had lived in France for centuries. During the Occupation, I saw her in the Latin Quarter near the Sorbonne on her bicycle, with her books, wearing the yellow star on her jacket, which almost ennobled this magnificent creature. She was so gifted—she had been working on a thesis that people already talked about—as musical as music itself and admirably generous. After a year of strenuous effort and heroic courage, helping those around her to live in the hell that was Birkenau, she died one morning in Bergen-Belsen. She was exhausted, no longer able to get up, clubbed to death by the woman who directed the camp. "She suffered more than Christ," writes her sister.

We must stop drawing up these lists that would fill volumes just with names of friends, relatives, and acquaintances. But I often think of S., a fragile creature who was imprisoned for two years for supporting de Gaulle. She came back to her two small children and waited for her husband who had been arrested during her absence. "Now that you are here, papa will come back," said the little four-year-old girl. Papa never came back and his young wife wrote me: "I just want to let you know that I no longer have any hope of finding my E. on this earth. But I think that if there are any blessed ones in heaven, E. is among them. Happy are those who are pure in heart for they will see God."

I cannot get used to the idea that I will never see him again, my kin, my brother, that I will never again hear his laugh, that I will never again see him so tall, so young, nor catch his occasional air of absent-mindedness, his deep, searing look, or his wonderful brilliant smile. I cannot get used to hearing nothing about him, to perhaps never knowing anything—where he died, or how, or on what day, or in what horrible way, if he ever wrote poetry in the slave camp, he who wrote such beautiful poetry, nor what he dreamed about, nor what his visions were in the final days of his suffering before he died at the age of thirty-two. For nothing. I think that his wife and children will often call out to him during the night, because people who love each other call to each other beyond life and death, and stretch out their arms of flesh and their arms of shadow to find each other at the moment when sleep begins to resemble death. They hold each other tightly in a mystical embrace that will never be subject to the vagaries of life.

Thousands of human beings are looking for each other and calling out to each other in the night in this desolate Europe. Thousands have waited for each other in spite of the growing certainty, the mystery and horror of their destiny. Perhaps, deep inside, we still believe that they will open the door and come in. And yet thousands are dead, after thousands of torments. We still hear the moaning of these hearts in pain, of those who died without graves, without funerals, and without cadavers, of this blood that flowed and demands justice.

The crime has been committed, the massacre is total; only a handful returned from this country of slaves, and all the rest perished. Six million Jews in Europe, a million eight-hundred-thousand Jewish children, thousands of Resistance fighters from every nation. . . . Now we know everything or almost everything of the scope and the horror and the variety of the German crimes. The camps hold no more secrets for us, and if every new tale still makes us tremble, it is not because we are surprised, but because we can bear no more. Our task will soon end. Then should we devote ourselves only to tears? Do we owe nothing more than a little help and love to the survivors, and only silence and oblivion to so many dead?

"Avenge yourself like a man," Ross said to Macduff, with his primitive and lordly conception of honor, and Macduff himself cut off Macbeth's head. But whose head will be thrown out to us? We need a hydra with a thousand heads, twenty-thousand, thirty-thousand; we would never be able to cut off so many heads. Will the survivors of these herds of slaves, continually beaten—these martyrs who, with supreme disgrace, were driven to fight over a piece of bread—will they have the strength and the energy, remnants of a love of life, to avenge themselves or demand justice, like citizens of a civilized world?

"What are you complaining about?" you might ask. The monsters of Bergen-Belsen are being judged and they will hang.

And indeed a trial is taking place that follows the rules perfectly. And English policemen help Irma Greese* out of her truck, coming to the help of this girl who beat the dying, people unable to keep walking, with steel rods and made lampshades out of the skin of the dead. The reporters tell us that she is

---

*A young female guard in Bergen-Belsen known for her brutality. Tried by the British, she was executed at then end of the war.

wearing a light blue blouse and silk stockings, and that Josef Kramer,* the dog handler, said that the weather was good. That's enough to satisfy quite a few people. But I must admit that no matter how much this trial reveals about the unbelievable collective and administrative sadism that found its ultimate expression in Germany in the twentieth century, the trial and punishment of the "Beasts of Belsen," as the *Daily Mail* calls them, is not nearly enough for me. We are told that German civilians are indignant and insult these monsters. What great courage, really. It is about time they stand on this mountain of cadavers to shake their fists at these prisoners in chains.

Aren't these Germans responsible for everything that happened, with their autumn gardens full of roses, their daughters so charming, they who love birds so much? Didn't they permit this? For thirteen years, didn't they allow this poisoned air to grow and flourish, leading to injustice, blindness, barbarism. Isn't it rather natural for there to be innumerable twenty-two-year-old Irma Greeses in this land drenched in fanaticism and idolatry? Every citizen is responsible for his country and its government, just as we French are responsible for our negligence and our defeat in 1940 and many of the things that followed. In the same way, each German is responsible for this government whose sad song from the Buchenwald camp is already thirteen years old. It is easy to be indignant when we hear the crimes of these brutes: "These people are monsters." Then we come home, have a quiet dinner, and sleep with a clear conscience! If there were so many monsters, it is because there was something strangely conducive to the birth and development of these monsters, something complex and latent in us all that we helped to nurture. . . . Nazism unveiled a strange thirst in Germans for destroying their world in order to create in its place, in their collective delirium, their near-madness, a world of death brought back to life from some obscure medievalism, dripping with sadism, blood, and darkness.

Alas, in France, too, there were sad and troublesome events in which many people, and not the most humble, took part. And here too, it seems to me, that some consciences are too quickly appeased. When they hear the survivors' tales and the horrors of what occurred in the camps and what the Gestapo did, many cover their faces and sigh to break your heart: "How could one even imagine such horrors? All these monsters must be shot without pity."

And how many committed collaborators, heads of families, of important firms, are sincerely indignant when they hear of the terrible deeds of the

---

*Kommandant of the camp and known as the "Beast of Bergen-Belsen". He was tried and executed in 1945.

Jacqueline Mesnil-Amar

SOL,* the militiamen, the French and Corsican denunciators, and the Gestapo? But perhaps there were other ways of handing over victims to the savage beasts. This social class too often forgets that its loyalty to the Germans as of 1940 created a profound confusion in the country and poisoned the air we breathed. After all, there are people who do not need 8,000 francs a month to become salaried assassins and to dirty their hands with the blood of others, who do not need to receive 4,700 francs and two packs of cigarettes to turn in five children, or to put their wife in bed with some high Gestapo official, or to receive 20,000 francs per head for every captured Resistance network leader. No, not everyone must fall so low.

There are people who can come to terms with these gentlemen for the small sum of 800 million francs a year. On condition, of course, that they be provided with lots of tires, trucks, and airplanes, they do not need to be paid to propose to the Germans *before the fact* that all Jewish bank accounts be blocked, or that communists be interned. They do all this while protected by their blue military uniform jackets, in all honor and dignity. Fish rots from the head down. Yes, if there were horrible militiamen (some of whom were after all only sixteen years old), torturers, gang members in Corsica, Marseilles, or Paris; if there were so many journalists guilty at so many different levels (you do not only kill with bullets, words also kill sometimes); if there were articles in the *Pilori*, the *Gerbe*, or *Je suis Partout*** (these were also calls to kill, to massacre); if there were so many propagandists, "impartial" reporters such as the one in *Paris-Midi*, for example, who wrote about Drancy and the way of life of the well-known lawyers arrested in 1941 ("Showers at six o'clock! And we know how little Israel likes to bathe! And after that, physical labor for the good of the group; it will be the first time that Jews will do something for the good of the group"); if there were radio broadcasts, posters, or books that expressed not so much an "opinion," as we call it now (but, with the Germans on our soil, was it not simply one of the lowest and most venal forms of hate?); if there were some miserable men (but those after all at least had the courage to sign their work, to complete their mission, to take risks), it was because there was, alas, a whole class of French society, powerful and organized, an "elite" that had accepted, arranged, and exalted the defeat, the obedience to the victor, collaboration, and the reign of injustice. . .

Those were black years, 1940, 1941, 1942. Must we already forget that terrible complicity, this smug, sly cowardice, that horrible scrambling for

---

*Service d'Ordre Légionnaire, a fascist militia, which was anti-Semitic and anti-Resistance.
**names of collaborationist journals.

position—even among those who did not need it—that feverish need to please, to bow, even that occasional secret jubilation of these hypocritical citizens of the kingdom of Tartuffe?

What a punishment it was then for some of us, when we understood that the concentric circles of the danger zones were coming closer and closer to us, and that our "friends" would no longer help us.

Yes, really, I think about it. If there are people who sleep well at night, it must be because they do not believe in ghosts, and that the ashes of the dead do not speak. I think of those who agreed to turn in to the Germans the unhappy foreigners of the Free Zone. I think of the official of the Interior Ministry who answered—when someone from a philanthropic organization demanded that the inhabitants of the Gurs and Rivesaltes camps be given the right to live, those miserable inmates who were dying of hunger and thirst in our beautiful France and who were the first to be abandoned: "I don't see why that's necessary." Dear sir, you who are so elegant, so well-dressed, with your beautiful tie, behind your desk, and daily genuflecting before every new religion, where are you now and do you sleep at night? I think of those who agreed in the Armistice treaty to hand over all the political enemies of the Reich, Jewish or not: Breitscheid, the socialist leader; Theodor Wolf, the famous editor-in-chief of the *Berliner Tageblatt;* and numerous Austrian personalities. I think of those, probably the same ones, who in August 1942, turned in to the Germans the 9,000 foreign Jews of the Southern Zone. And I think of all the arrests in August 1942 in the Free Zone, those of September, October, in Cannes, Nice, Toulouse, Marseilles, Limoges, Lyons, carried out by the French, alas, in massive deployments of police, to pick up a few miserable old people, unfortunate women with their children, and veterans of two wars, sent in cattle cars via Drancy to be deported. We now know what kind of voyage these innocents were sent on by the ministers, what kind of treatment they were subjected to, what their final destination would be, all because they were poor, because they were born outside France, because they were Jews—all this as a prelude to abandoning the French Jews to these "sadistic monsters."

That is probably why some magistrates—who could well have recused themselves and refused by withdrawing into a noble silence, as some did—agreed to perform some strange tasks, for example, presiding over the Commission on Denaturalization from September 1940 on, and who are now, four years later, able to testify in Pétain's trial that they performed their duties in a perfectly satisfactory manner. Here's a man who must have a clear conscience, a good appetite, and he must sleep well; he reviewed only three percent of the files of the denaturalized. That is only about 27,000 people—all those furriers, tailors, grocers, they only needed to remain quiet in back of the ovens. He could have denaturalized many others. Among the 27,000 rendered stateless by him—and thus offered up, naked and defenseless, to the fire of the SS, to the jaws of their dogs and the snapping of their whips, to the vivisection laboratories, the communal graves, and the garbage sheds—it was only by mistake that a few of the dead had been soldiers in 1939–1940, several of them severely wounded, and that many were the old parents of soldiers that the French Republic had accepted as citizens only because their sons were of an age to fight. . . . One can see there is reason to be satisfied; it could have been much worse. And afterward when the war was lost, it was because of these people, isn't that right? Marshal Pétain and M. Joseph Barthélémy, Minister of Justice, annulled the decree that had denaturalized one of the dead of 1939–1940 whom I knew well. But the decree remained in force for the parents of the dead man who of course, had been gassed a long time before in Silesia.

Of course, the president of the Commission on Denaturalization could have done worse, he could have agreed to everything the Germans asked and signed a massive number of denaturalization decrees. But he could also have done better, he could have refused to perform this task. There are some crimes that one leaves to criminals. There were some judges who knew how to say no and who threw their resignation in their superiors' faces.

Yes, they sleep well at night, all these zealous bureaucrats who, after all, only obeyed. Often, alas, they were among the most highly placed in the hierarchy, these prefects, these trembling lords of our provinces. And I think that the defenders and friends of that prefect of Lyons, they too, sleep well at night, forgetting that this important bureaucrat whom they defend, dishonored his mandate, demanding in person that some hundred Jewish children hidden by Father Chaillet be turned over to him.

Indeed, indeed, they sleep well at night, without a doubt, the friends of Xavier Vallat who "wasn't all that bad," of Darquier, of du Paty de Clam,[*] their cousins, nephews, and underlings in the offices of Jewish Affairs, these tireless defenders of the law, these licensed looters, these distinguished purveyors of trainloads of slaves. . . . They also sleep well, those bureaucrats from the Interior Ministry, who took away US visas from the children who had already reached Marseilles and had passports and visas to leave France, half-saved already, and who were careful to deliver them alive. . . . Let them sleep, let them

---

[*]Vallat was head of the General Commissariat for Jewish Affairs in the Vichy government from 1941–42. Louis Darquier de Pellepoix succeeded Vallat and helped to coordinate the deportation of Jews to Auschwitz. Charles Mercier du Paty de Clam succeeded Darquier in 1944.

sleep a peaceful and rejuvenating sleep. These vigilant police chiefs of the Permilleux section, who so courageously urged their men to search every corner of the apartments and to bring back little trembling children, to examine with a magnifying glass the false papers of the illegal men and women in the roundups, and carry off those who looked sick to the Commissariats and to Drancy for the trip to Auschwitz.

And I think also of these words that have been spoken so often, all these words one would also like to forget forever, but which reverberate in our ears every time we hear someone sigh: "Poor so-and-so,' after all, what did he do?" or "This purging, let's get it over with, let them punish only those who ratted on people and let the others out of prison. Let's talk no more of it!" Indeed, they are right, it is true, let us end it. Let us speak no more of it. But let those other elegant and well-pitched voices also keep quiet and go away, those voices that told us such peculiar things, the voice of that private secretary who told us about the decree that rendered stateless an entire family whose sons had fought for France, and thereby turned them into camp fodder, the contrite voice of the young man, who answered in a resigned tone of voice "What can I do? There are too many of them!" Too many to live. . . . Chase away, too, these terrible words pronounced by the woman from Secours National[*] in her hard, dry voice, when a Sister of the Poor came begging for four kilos of potatoes and noodles to feed children hidden in a convent, "Don't you think those little Jews are too demanding?"

You, bourgeois of France, my friends, my compatriots (and among you are also many devoted, courageous, and admirable friends), why did so many of you turn your back on us in order to verbally or tacitly subscribe, without a word, without a gesture, to a drama that would turn into a carnage? And what did you think you were defending in the end, what good more precious than justice did you think you were saving in abandoning us? Because you did not know, it is true, you could not guess, isn't that right, the ovens and the rest. You thought those were stories, a little brainwashing, some excesses, almost tall stories. Because you lacked that intuition that does not always go with political intuition, the intuition of the heart.

Indeed, we are in the shifting domain of impossible responsibilities, in which everyone has a part, where no sanction can intervene but where only one thing is needed: that the crisis of conscience that put a part of France to sleep stop immediately and that eyes, blind for so long, finally see their errors clearly.

Because one must say that it was not only the direct delivery to the enemy of herds of innocents, there was also the tacit *refusal* to save human lives.

---

[*]State-run welfare organization

Jacqueline Mesnil-Amar

Surnames that delivered so many people to their executioners, which members of the State Council could easily have changed. In spite of hundreds of interventions and supplications, visas were denied, except to millionaires. Passports and "aryanizations" that would have allowed so many spouses to avoid deportation and death were denied. A continual and zealous verification of papers didn't let us sleep. Obligatory and regular stamping of documents, expulsions from certain towns, and forced residences (such admirable traps), and "decrees" signed with such eminent names which targeted our honor, our possessions, and our lives as citizens, condemned to ruin thousands of intellectuals and artists, before condemning them to death because they did not have the means to hide.

A *silence* emanated from high places and hung over our drama in all of France. The social organizations, at whose doors we banged so often in vain, were silent. Even the Red Cross was prudently silent, the Red Cross whose volunteers were so pretty in their uniforms and so brave at the wheel of their trucks or in the camps of prisoners, and who seemed so serene while we were so panicked and anxious. Behind this charitable silence, we could sense a clubby optimism among the delegates of the Red Cross about the fate of the deported. They seemed never to have noticed during their discreet inspections the fires of the crematoria or the odor of charred bones, the perfume of Germany. These people who inundated France as of January 1945 to investigate the fate of "these poor German prisoners" had a strange optimism. There was a worldwide conspiracy of silence about this drama, unknown until then, that not a cry or a clamor interrupted. A few servants of the state, high dignitaries and presidents worthy of their position who had some sense of human solidarity could have hidden and perhaps disguised these miserable people, even under the eyes of the occupiers. They could have tried to tear them away from the enemy, surely at the price of danger, but then they might have raised the conscience and the honor of all men. All these people who were not saved keep me from sleeping at night.

— **Translated by Eva Martin Sartori**

Simone Weil
(1909–1943)

The inclusion of Simone Weil in this anthology may surprise some readers because of the many antagonistic views that are held about her. Yet, as an emblematic "self-exiled" Jew,[1] Weil begs us examine the difficult question of assimilation as experienced by some French Jews. For this reason she has a place in this volume that aims at covering as broad a spectrum of views and their expressions as possible.

Simone Weil was born in Paris into a freethinking bourgeois Jewish family. Her father was of Alsatian Jewish ancestry and her mother, a Russian Jew, was raised in Belgium. Her parents spoke German at home whenever they did not wish to be understood by their children. The children quickly learned the language, nevertheless. Neither Simone nor her brother received any instruction in the Jewish faith or traditions, but "education and cultivation of intellect" were given a primacy "typical of a Jewish home."[2] A brilliant student, she attended Alain's philosophy classes at Lycée Henri IV before going on to the prestigious Ecole Normale Supérieure (1928–1931) where her militant left-wing positions earned her the nickname of "red virgin."

Between 1931 and 1934, she taught philosophy, Greek, and art history in secondary schools, all the while devoting her energy to political and trade unionist action, which ended with her dismissal from a school in Le Puy and reassignment to another school. In 1934, she took a leave of absence and worked briefly as a factory worker, a decision that she supported with the luminous, theoretical essay "Réflexions sur les causes de l'oppression et la liberté" [Reflections on the Causes of Oppression and Freedom], and an experience that she recorded in *Journal d'usine* [Journal on Work in a Factory]. In June 1936, she enlisted as a volunteer in the Spanish Civil War, but an injury forced her to return to France.

After the German occupation of France, she followed her parents to Marseilles, where she met Père Perrin and Gustave Thibon, two important Catholic witnesses of the spiritual and mystical quest she had embarked upon for some time. Though she came close to finding in the figure of Christ an answer to her search, Weil was never baptized. She was too profoundly attached to individualism and too distrustful of religious and political institutions—typified in her various essays about ancient Israel and ancient Rome–to become a member of one. In 1942, Weil accompanied her parents to safety in the United States, which she left for England, hoping for an assignment in the French Resistance. Instead, she died of exhaustion in England, where she is buried.

Simone Weil

With the exception of articles in trade union journals and newspapers, all of Simone Weil's works were assembled and published posthumously.

The following selections include some of Weil's fragmentary notes on Old Testament Israel and a letter written in November 1940 to Jérôme Carcopino, Secretary of State for Public Education—a letter that was probably never sent.

Weil's views on the nature and role of ancient Israel are provocative, at times shocking, and certainly disputable, but they illustrate Weil's bold exercise of intellectual independence in rereading history. They must be examined in the light of her mystical search for a God that cannot be appropriated by human "organizations" and used for worldly pursuit of power.

The letter is a no less surprising document. In August 1940, Weil had applied to the Vichy Ministry of Education for a new teaching assignment in Algeria, shortly before anti-Jewish legislation was passed, denying Jews from holding positions as civil servants (*Statut des Juifs,* October 3, 1940). On the one hand, it is a masterful philosophical demonstration—and let us not forget that Weil was a philosopher—of the impossibility of defining Jewishness. The use of preposterous, falsely candid, or falsely rational arguments and of a sarcastic tone clearly aim at subverting the validity of the Statut as a document for action. The letter also exhibits a disturbing dismissal of contemporary realities, which she could not easily ignore. She had after all visited Germany in 1932 and had been exposed to the xenophobic anti-Semitism of the trade unions.

Simone Weil embodies, perhaps in its most extreme form, the deeply conflicted condition of many French Jews, torn between their loyalty to a French intellectual heritage and to the French state, and their solidarity with a community which, in 1940 included immigrants from various European and non-European countries whose allegiance was to very different traditions.

— **Madeleine Cottenet-Hage**

Notes

1. Thomas R. Nevin, *Simone Weil: Portait of a Self-Exiled Jew*, p. 2.
2. *Ibid.*

Selected Works

La Pesanteur et la grâce. Paris: Plon, 1947.
Attente de Dieu, 2nd ed. Paris: La Colombe, 1950.
La Condition ouvrière. Paris: Gallimard, 1950.
La Source grecque. Paris: Gallimard, 1953.
Oppression et liberté. Paris: Gallimard, 1955.

Translations Into English

Gravity and Grace. Trans. Emma Craufurd. London: Routledge and Kegan Paul, 1952.
Waiting for God. Trans. Emma Craufurd. London: Routledge and Kegan Paul, 1951.
Oppression and Liberty. Trans. Arthur F. Wills and John Petrie. London: Routledge and Kegan Paul, 1958.
The Simone Weil Reader. Trans. George Andrew Panichas. New York: McKay, 1977.
The Need for Roots: Prelude to a Declaration of Duties Towards Mankind. Trans. Arthur Wills. London: Routledge, 2002.

Secondary Works

J. P. Little. "Simone Weil" in *French Women Writers,* Dorothy W. Zimmerman and Eva M. Sartori, eds. Westport, CT: Greenwood Press, 1991.
Betty L. McLane-Iles. *Uprooting and Integration in the Writings of Simone Weil.* New York: Peter Lang, 1987.
Thomas R. Nevin. *Simone Weil: Portrait of a Self-Exiled Jew.* Chapel Hill: University of North Carolina Press, 1991.
Simone Pétrement. *Simone Weil: A Life.* Trans. Raymond Rosenthal. New York: Pantheon Books, 1977.

What is a Jew?

Monsieur le Ministre,

In January 1938, I took sick leave, which I renewed in July, 1938, for one year, and again for another year in 1939. When my leave expired last July, I asked for a teaching post, preferably in Algeria. My request was not answered. I very much want to know why.

It occurs to me that the new Statute on Jews, which I have read in the press, is perhaps connected with your failure to reply. So I want to know to whom this Statute applies, so that I may be enlightened as to my own standing. I do not know the definition of the word, "Jew"; that subject was not included in my education. The Statute, it is true, defines a Jew as: "a person who has three or more Jewish grandparents." But this simply carries the difficulty two generations farther back.

Does this word designate a religion? I have never been in a synagogue, and have never witnessed a Jewish religious ceremony. As for my grandparents—I remember that my paternal grandmother used to go to the synagogue, and I think I have heard that my paternal grandfather did so likewise. On the other hand, I know definitely that both my maternal grandparents were freethinkers. Thus if it is a matter of religion, it would appear that I have only two Jewish grandparents, and so am not a Jew according to the Statute.

But perhaps the word designates a race? In that case, I have no reason to believe that I have any link, maternal or paternal, to the people who inhabited Palestine two thousand years ago. When one reads in Josephus how thoroughly Titus exterminated this race it seems unlikely that they left many descendants. . . . My father's family, as far as our memory went, lived in Alsace; no family tradition, as far as I know, said anything about coming here from any other place. My mother's family comes from Slavic lands, and, so far as I know, was composed only of Slavs. But perhaps the Statute must be applied to my grandparents themselves, perhaps we must investigate whether each of them has less that three Jewish grandparents? I think it may be quite difficult to get reliable information on this point.

Finally, the concept of heredity may be applied to a race, but it is difficult to apply to a religion. I myself, who professes [sic] non-religion and never have, have certainly inherited nothing from the Jewish

From: *Politics* 6, 11 (Winter 1969) 79–81.

religion. Since I practically learned to read from Racine, Pascal, and other French writers of the 17th century, since my spirit was thus impregnated at an age when I had not even heard talk of "Jews," I would say that if there is a religious tradition which I regard as my patrimony, it is the Catholic tradition.

In short: mine is the Christian, French, Greek tradition. The Hebraic tradition is alien to me, and no Statute can make it otherwise. If, nevertheless, the law insists that I consider the term, "Jew," whose meaning I don't know, as applying to me, I am inclined to submit, as I would to any other law. But I should like to be officially enlightened on this point, since I myself have no criterion by which I may resolve the question.

If the Statute does not apply to me, then I should like to enjoy those rights which I am given by the contract implied in my title of "professor" ("agrégée").

Israel

Christianity has become totalitarian, bent on conquest and extermination, because it has not developed the notions of God's absence and non-action here on earth. It has held on to Jehovah as much as to Christ; it has conceived of Providence in the Old Testament way. Only Israel could have resisted Rome because they were alike, and at its birth Christianity was tainted by Rome before it had become the official religion of the Empire. The damage done by Rome has never been really repaired.

God made purely temporal promises to Moses and to Joshua at a time when Egypt was aiming toward the soul's eternal salvation. Having refused the Egyptian revelation, the Hebrews received the God they deserved: a collective carnal God who, until the exile, spoke to the soul of no one (unless perhaps in the Psalms?). . . . Among the characters in the biblical stories, only Abel, Enoch, Noah, Melchizedek, Job, and Daniel are pure. It is not surprising that from a people made up of fugitive slaves—who had conquered a heavenly land that had been developed by the labor of civilizations to which they had not contributed and which they massacred and destroyed—not much good could come. It is a cruel joke to speak of a "teaching God" when one speaks of this people.

It is not surprising that there is so much evil in a civilization—ours, that is—fundamentally tainted even in its very inspiration by this terrible lie. The malediction of Israel weighs on Christianity. The atrocities, the Inquisition, the extermination of heretics and infidels, all this was due to Israel. Capitalism was Israel (and still is to some degree). Totalitarianism is Israel, notably among its worst enemies.

There can be no *personal* contact between man and God, except through the Mediator. Without the Mediator, God's presence can be felt by man only collectively, nationally. Israel has simultaneously chosen the national God and rejected the Mediator. Perhaps it has at certain times leaned toward true monotheism, but it always fell back, and could not avoid falling back, to the tribal God.

He who is in touch with the supernatural is in essence a king, for in the social world he embodies in an infinitely small form an order that transcends the social.

From: *La Pesanteur et la grâce* (Paris: Plon, 1948), pp. 189–193.

Israel

But he occupies an altogether lowly place in the social hierarchy.

As for the mighty in the social order, only he who has harnessed the energy of the beast can attain power. But he cannot have access to the supernatural.

Moses, Joshua, they represent the degree of the supernatural attained by those who have harnessed a great deal of social energy.

Israel represents an attempt at a supernatural social life. One could say that it has achieved as much as is possible in this domain. It is useless to try again. The result shows the kind of divine revelation of which the beast is capable.

Isaiah is the first to bring pure light.

Israel resisted Rome because its God, though incorporeal, was a temporal ruler at the same level as the Emperor, and Christianity was born thanks to that. Israel's religion was not high enough to be fragile and, as a result of its sturdiness, it could protect the growth of that which was the highest.

For the Passion to take place, it was necessary that Israel be unaware of the idea of the Incarnation. This is true of Rome also. (They were perhaps the only two peoples to be unaware of it.) But it was nevertheless necessary that Israel be connected to God as much as was possible, while lacking spirituality and the supernatural. A totally collective religion. This lack of awareness, this darkness, made it the chosen people. Thus may we understand Joshua's words: "I hardened their heart so that they would not understand my words."

That is the reason Israel is soiled by sin in every way. Because there is nothing pure without participation in the incarnation of divinity and in order to make manifest the lack of such participation.

Isn't this great sin that of Jacob's struggle with the angel: "The Eternal . . . will judge Jacob according to his deeds. From birth, he replaced his brother, and when he became a man he triumphed over God. He fought against an angel and vanquished him, and the angel cried and asked for mercy. . . ."

Isn't it tragic not to be vanquished, when one fights against God?

Israel. Everything is soiled and terrible, as if on purpose, from Abraham on, including him (with the exception of a few prophets). As if to show absolutely clearly: Take care! There is the evil!

A people chosen to be blind, chosen to be the executioner of Christ.

The Jews, that handful of rootless people, has caused the rootlessness of the entire globe. Their role has been to make Christianity rootless in relation to its own past. During the Renaissance, the attempt at rerooting failed because it was anti-Christian in orientation. The Enlightenment, 1789, secularism, and so on, have infinitely increased the rootlessness with the lie of progress. And rootless Europe has made the rest of the world rootless through colonial conquests. Capitalism, totalitarianism are part of this progression toward rootlessness; there is no question that anti-Semites spread the Jewish influence. But before they uprooted with poison, Syria in the east and Rome in the west had already uprooted by the sword.

Primitive Christianity manufactured the poisonous notion of progress through the idea of divine pedagogy that instructed men to receive Christ's message. Such an idea reinforced the hope of the universal conversion of all the nations and of the end of the world as close at hand. But since neither occurred after seventeen centuries, this notion of progress was extended beyond the moment of the Christian Revelation. From then on, it had to turn against Christianity.

The other poisons mixed in with the truth of Christianity have a Jewish origin. This one is specifically Christian.

The metaphor of the divine pedagogy dissolves that of individual destiny, which alone counts toward collective destiny.

Christianity wanted to find harmony in history. That is the seed of Hegel and Marx. The notion of history as controlled continuity is Christian.

It seems to me few ideas are more completely false. To look for harmony in becoming the opposite of eternity. A bad union of opposites.

Humanism and that which followed are not a return to antiquity, but rather a development of Christianity's interior poisons.

It is supernatural love that is free. When one tries to force it, one only substitutes a natural love. But, conversely, freedom without supernatural love, that of 1789, is utterly empty, a mere abstraction that can never become real.

— **Translated by Eva Martin Sartori and Madeleine Cottenet-Hage**

Anna Langfus
(1920–1966)

Anna Langfus was born in Lublin, Poland, into a well-to-do Jewish family that was annihilated during the Holocaust. At age seventeen, she spent a year studying in Belgium, married, and returned to Poland where she joined the underground Resistance against the Nazis. She was caught, sent to the political prison of Plock, and remained there until liberation. In 1946, she immigrated to France, remarried, and began writing fiction and plays, all the while attempting to develop cultural activities in Sarcelles, the Paris suburb where she lived. She died unexpectedly in 1966, while working on her fourth novel.

Langfus's three novels deal exclusively with the experience of war, destruction, and loss after the Holocaust, weaving autobiographical material with fiction. *Le sel et le soufre [The Whole Land Brimstone]* which received the Prix Charles Veillon, retraces the war years in Poland, the destruction of the Lublin ghetto, the annihilation of the protagonists, a comfortable middle-class family, and the fight for survival of the central character, who has been renamed Maria in the course of one of several reinventions of her identity to ensure that she will pass as a Christian. The fear that grabs hold of the Jewish community, its early denials of impending doom, the German atrocities, as well as the shameful participation of Jewish officials in the deportation of their own community are narrated through the eyes of Maria. She herself fights off fear by fleeing into her own forms of denial: sleep, dreams, illness, and reckless roamings along the city streets. In one of many unreal and haunting scenes, she leaves a party where she has drunk more than her share of champagne and hires a coachman to drive ever faster through the city. Langfus's horse becomes the infernal steed of mythology, an emissary of death as she imagines that the men asleep in their beds behind the windows are all murderers. "Each of them has a corpse under his bed—a neat little corpse with the same face as himself. . . . [He] has killed [the man he was yesterday], strangled him—glug, glug—then stowed the corpse under so as not to see him."[1]

Maria rapidly moves from being an overprotected, irresponsible young woman to a decisive agent, as she arranges for her family's escape from the ghetto, though her father refuses to leave, arguing that his looks would soon betray them. The second half of the novel tells of the harrowing events that follow their escape: the couple's imprisonment and torture, the death of her husband, the descent into despair.

Throughout, Maria is remarkably wary of pathos and avoids manicheian representations of a world gone insane. In one memorable scene, Vic, a German doctor, saves the couple by arranging for them to stay in the very eye of the storm: a German military base, where he ensures their protection. Hardened by her experience and her suffering, with a lucidity that helps her cope with her anguish and her anger, Maria witnesses and records the evils of widespread anti-Semitic hatred, often disguised behind the lure of money to be earned by exploiting the victims; the infinite cruelty of humans revealed beneath the veneer of civilization; the dissolution of morality and human dignity under the effect of fear. Not even her own behavior escapes her lucid probing.

Les bagages de sable, [The Lost Shore] for which Langfus received the prestigious Prix Goncourt in 1962, can be read as a sequel to the 1960 novel, as Maria, who has come to Paris from Poland, attempts to "resurface." But whereas the previous Maria was able to find in herself the power to resist and rebel, the fighting spirit and the will to live have left this new protagonist. She is physically, as it were, haunted by the ghosts of the lost loved ones, and moves between reality and a state of numbness that breeds indifference to the outer world. An old man falls in love with her. She allows the relationship to evolve. A brief encounter with a group of young children in the south of France momentarily draws her out, while the suicide of one of its members, an unloved young girl, forces her to face her own "cowardice" in not going all the way to the end, and choosing between death and life. But life circumstances decide for her: the old man falls ill, his wife runs to his bedside and asks Maria to move out. We abandon the protagonist in a no-man's land, poised at dawn between hope and despair.

Saute, Barbara [Jump, Barbara], is also set in France and deals with a similar scenario. The inability of a survivor to let go of the past and turn to the business of living is told through the story of Michel, a Pole who fled from Germany with a child he abducted because she reminded him of his daughter. He has named the girl Barbara in her memory. In a conclusion that restates the impossibility of building a new life, Michel returns Barbara to Germany and dies after shooting a German—an act of revenge that Maria failed to accomplish in the previous novel.

Langfus's characters experience the present or "time after" the Holocaust as a series of disconnected fragments that cannot, indeed must not, be allowed to reconnect, lest time flow forward and the past recede from memory. Theirs is the guilt that some survivors have experienced: the guilt of not having died like the others. *"Les bagages de sable"* (the baggage of sand), a title borrowed from the surrealist poet André Breton, might evoke, among other images, the paralyzing weight of sand, a metonymy for time past and time passing, at the end of which human beings meet the silence and absence of memory: death. That very experience of numbness of the soul, of the loss of desire, and the desire for loss shape both Langfus's characters and her fiction in that the act of writing seems not to have empowered her to escape from the reenactment of the scenario of death branded into her memory. In the end, the witness sinks with the burden of her testimony.

In the first of the following excerpts, Maria dines with Jewish relatives in France who had escaped deportation. In a ferociously satirical scene, she describes the abyss that separates the penniless survivor from the well-off hypocritical relatives who had lived through the war in France unscathed. In the second passage, Maria meets a man whom she believes might be her soulmate: a Polish Jew who, like her, fought in the Polish Resistance and, like her too, has lost his family. Once again Maria understands that suffering erects barriers, rather than establishes connections. Furthermore, the existence of a community of Jews united in remembering and denouncing the Holocaust is a delusion. In Langfus's world, human beings are despairingly alone.

—Madeleine Cottenet-Hage

Notes

1. *The Whole Land Brimstone*, p. 21.

Selected Works

Le sel et le soufre. Gallimard, 1960.
Les bagages de sable. Gallimard, 1962.
Saute, Barbara. Gallimard, 1965.

Translations Into English

The Whole Land Brimstone. Trans. Peter Wiles. London: Collins, 1961.
The Lost Shore. Trans. Peter Wiles. New York: Pantheon Books, 1963.

Secondary Works

Interview with Maurice Marc. *Les Lettres Françaises* (23–29 August 1962).
Interview. *Nouvelle Critique* (June 1965).

Anna Langfus

Madeleine Cottenet-Hage. "Anna Langfus et les risques de la mémoire." *Les Lettres Romanes*. Special issue: "La Littérature des camps: la quête d'une parole juste entre silence et bavardage" (1995): 25–39.

E. A. Fine. "Le Témoin comme romancier: Anna Langfus et le problème de la distance." *Pardès* 17 (1993).

Clara Lévy. "La Guerre dans les textes littéraires d'Anna Langfus: La Mise à distance de l'expérience" in *Esprit Créateur* 40, 2 (2000): 52–60.

Judith Clark Schaneman. "Writing to Survive: The Novels of Anna Langfus" in *Women in French Studies* 9 (2001): 92–105.

The Lost Shore

So it was three days since I had left my room, and now, in the early evening, I heard someone knocking at my door. A series of crisp, resolute raps. I sat up in bed. Again came the knocking: three taps this time, impatient, closer together. My feet lowered themselves to the floor, with a dignified lack of haste. By now the raps had intensified to a regular pounding. Such a degree of arrogant persistence nettled me, and I shouted:

"Wait a minute, will you!"

Time to take the few steps that separated me from the door, and my head was in a whirl. The handle kept slipping from my clammy grasp. Finally I succeeded in turning it. My exquisite cousin stood before me. Already her eye had taken in the poky little room, the rumpled bed, and my displeasure.

"So this is where you live."

She screwed up her mouth in distaste. I shut the door and waved her into a chair. Then I climbed back into bed.

"They're expecting you at home," she said. "Will you come?"

"Not this evening," I said. "I'm too tired."

"But this evening is the very time you must come. My parents insist on it, and I do too."

"What is so special about this evening?"

She came closer, leaned over me and said: "Get dressed. Get dressed quickly. We're in for a good laugh."

"Thanks all the same," I said, and lay full-length on the bed again, "but I can have a perfectly good laugh all by myself."

"My parents have the best of intentions towards you: you mustn't let them down." She chuckled, showing all her pretty little white teeth. "Poor relations have to be obedient."

"Get out of here," I said. "I want to sleep."

At this she sat down beside me and coaxingly took my hand.

"You know perfectly well this absurd rigmarole is none of my doing." My dress was lying on the back of a chair. She snatched it up. "Do get dressed. I promised I would take you back. There's a lovely surprise in store for you."

"I'll come tomorrow," I said.

"Tomorrow there will be no surprise. You simply must come and look. Believe me, it's worth making the effort."

From: *The Lost Shore*. Peter Wiles, trans. (New York: Pantheon Books, 1963) pp. 30–37, 158–169.

She chuckled again. Then she noticed the blanket on my bed—worn, stained and of an indefinable hue. She leaped up and rubbed her hands over her skirt several times, as though to obliterate all trace of the blanket's touch. In her usual, unconcerned voice she said: "I'm waiting."

I cared nothing for what might be hidden behind her mask, but this physical resemblance between us troubled me. There had been a time when I had exhibited the same vivacity of movement, the same quivering impatience.

"Well?" she said, and she drummed her fingers on the table. I smiled.

"Don't fret—I'll come. But I'm very much afraid you will have gone to all this trouble for nothing. I am not feeling at my best today."

Carefully, unhurriedly, I got dressed. Standing by the table, she followed my every movement. When I was ready, I smiled—and my smile was only a poor imitation of hers.

"Let us be on our way then, dear poor cousin's cousin."

I closed the door with studied slowness. I loved to see impatience light up glints of malice in her eyes. We walked along without saying a word. She had succeeded in her mission, and now she seemed to be losing interest in it. For my part, I was rediscovering the street, with its lights and its people, as though I had just come back from the ends of the earth.

We were there. My overwound little aunt was dancing before me on her high tapering heels. My uncle was stretching out his arms towards me. My cousin was waking up and observing the scene with interest.

"Darling, we are going to introduce you to our great, our best friend."

And with my aunt's arm round my shoulders, I stepped into the drawing room. We drew up in front of an armchair, from the depths of which a man of about fifty was gazing at us. A large sunburnt hand was being extended towards me, so far from the body that it seemed all at once to have broken away from it. I was scared to touch it, I was scared of its remaining in mine—a queer, cumbersome object.

"Come now, darling," said my aunt, "fancy a big girl like you being so shy!"

To get it over with, I touched this hand and it closed on my fingers. Simultaneously, the man rose. He was tall, sturdily built and well dressed. His darting eyes appeared to be observing several different things at the same time. Beneath the small moustache, the mouth was unsmiling. Then, I found myself sitting in another armchair, beside his, with a cup of coffee in my hand. Somewhere in the shadows, I could sense the smile on my cousin's face. The man sat quietly drinking his coffee; his active eyes were surveying me. As for my aunt, she was telling him the story of my life.

"Poor child," she said, "she needs lots of warmth, lots of feeling. Who could understand her better than you, dear friend?"

The man nodded, but as though in response to his own thoughts, rather than to her words. He set his cup down on a small table. I was still holding mine. He took it from me without a word. Then he said:

"I am alone, just as you are."

I said nothing. I had nothing to say. He did not interest me. He was too far away.

"Alone," he repeated. And he waited. My aunt's high heels were beating out a rhythm somewhere.

"When two lonely people like us are thrown together . . ."

I turned abruptly towards him and looked at him. He left the sentence unresolved. Finally he said:

"Forgive me. I do not express myself well, but I say what I think"

The words that I had been preparing to fling at him suddenly struck me as childish and pointless. I continued to sit silent. He continued to talk.

"You need someone to look after you. People always need someone to look after them. I am much older than you—I was a father once."

His crisp, precise voice faltered, weakened. I looked at him: his eyes were dry. He handed me a photograph. A thirteen- or fourteen-year-old girl was smiling at me. Thick plaits framed a round face blooming with health.

"She was deported. With her mother."

He held his hand out in my direction and I gently set the smiling girl down in his palm. He slid her back into his wallet, carefully. And at the very moment when something had been about to blossom within me and go out to this man who so displeased me, he laid his hand on my knee and said proudly: "She was top of the class in French." He inclined his head towards mine. "I am as familiar with suffering as you are. Nobody can understand you better than me."

The fingers on my leg became animated, and the gesture might have been that of a merchant assessing the quality of a piece of material. The child must have been still smiling against the man's breast. The large sunburnt hand slapped hard against the leather of the chair. I left all the doors open behind me. The staircase was a chasm at which I hurled myself. In the street, it was with relief that I re-encountered the anonymity and indifference of the passers-by. I slackened my pace. There was no longer any cause to run away. These were merely ghosts brushing by; one was free to look at them, to accord them whatever semblance of life suited one's momentary whim, to credit them with whatever idea took one's fancy, to bestow on them the very advantages that one lacked, or to overwhelm them with the weight of one's sufferings. One was free to find them pitiful, generous, cowardly, noble or mean-spirited, depending on one's mood and on the kind of theatrical entertainment to which one had decided to treat oneself. Innumerable ghosts: it was simply a question of choosing whatever was appropriate to one at a given moment, an inexhaustible supply of leading parts to be enacted just once before vanishing into the blue again. Today, every one of them bore his little paper corpse concealed in his wallet. From time to time they would extract it, to show it to someone or to give it a little fresh air. Why not? It was quite harmless.

Nothing more to fear from that quarter. From now on it would always wear the same expression, the same look, the same smile. For the corpse was invariably a smiling one. A secure, stable, predictable property, one of those things on which one could confidently rely, one of those things which lent an orderly pattern to life, which gave it its bearings and a sense of security, as it were, a sense of comfort. A live human being was incapable of offering anything of equal value. Precious little corpse, captured forever in its eternal, its untarnishable youthfulness, for naturally it had died young, petrified in the love which it had borne one and which a single glance brought back in all its pristine freshness; well-trained, indefectible corpse, always at one's service, even facilitating one's dealings with other people, since one had only to extract it gingerly from its leather tomb for strangers to regard one with interest and with a respect which they might not accord one's own corpse, even if it was staring them in the face, so great is the prestige of the dead who have loved one. One learned to cultivate this prestige, one strengthened it year by year with the aid of a few judicious details, of a few retouches which would have been beyond the capabilities of the photographer. Life was difficult and one had to turn everything to account. I wondered whether I myself would one day achieve this perfection. Why should I be any less gifted? Any less skilful? Why shouldn't I, as well, scale these peaks on the art of reconstruction? Why indeed? It was a question of being patient. Perhaps the stairs that I was climbing would likewise change, the steps become less steep, the banister rail less long. All this was highly possible. One simply had to wait. Wait.

Darkness had accumulated above me. I struggled, I tried to push it away, I threw off the blanket. I found myself lying on my belly, and I let the shadows bury me.

The man was still smiling and resting his hand flat on my knee. Suddenly the wall slid away. Outside, it was night. I leaned out a few inches so as to discover the source of this light which was eating, here and there, into the heavy, opaque darkness. Down below, a small square courtyard was lit by a single bulb hanging from an invisible wire. The young girl with her plaits and her pinafore was standing there, very erect, with her head held high. In front of her stood a German, examining the loading-clip of his revolver. Then he said:

"Right now, I'm going to kill you."

And the girl made herself taller and jutted out her chin.

"You cannot kill me," she said, "I was top of the class in French."

But the German pointed the gun at her.

"If you don't believe me," she said sternly, "ask my father."

And her finger was pointing at us. The man sitting before me got up, red-faced with anger, strode towards the gaping darkness and, standing so close to it that I saw one of his legs hanging in empty space, shouted:

"You can kill her, but it will make no difference. She was always top of her class in French."

A few belated tourists, enthusiastically seeking out the after-dark atmosphere of the village, watched me go running down the street. As soon as I reached the outskirts, I affected the gait of a girl taking a summer evening stroll. That speck of brightness which I could make out some little distance away was he. I slowed down still further, to allow myself time to recover my breath.

We shook hands and swapped a few stock phrases of the kind exchanged by all those who have nothing to say to one another. Then he pointed to a motorcycle with glittering new chromium work, set against the kerb a few yards from where we were standing.

"Shall we be on our way?"

I seated myself behind him, on the pillion. Amid the deafening backfire of the engine, I heard him shout:

"Hold on tight!"

My hands closed on his waist. And as we gathered speed and the wind grew bulkier, I huddled ever closer against the back that was screening me. The road twisted and turned through darkness shattered by the fierce light of headlamps. Sheets of particularly dense blackness would sag down on us, and I would tighten my hold. We had become a dual being careering towards the past at full tilt, eating up the kilometres of time . . . I felt like shouting to him: "For goodness' sake don't drive so fast! We shall get there, whatever happens. It is the only place we can possibly get to."

We slowed down as we approached the town. Were we there already? How was one to tell? At night, all towns look alike. He closed the throttle and, with his foot, guided the motorcycle over to the kerb.

"This is the place," he said.

We went down a few steps, into a colourful half-light where faces and eyes and hands drifted in a haze of voices . . . I knocked against a sharp corner. I hurt myself. It was an expanse composed of overlapping fragments, devoid of coherence, scoured by furtive gleams which occasioned sudden moments of glare and fleeting spells of darkness—a three-dimensional stained-glass window which I had penetrated I knew not how, and which was at this very moment solidifying about me. Yet the man was drawing away from me. I saw him moving unrestrainedly through this mysterious geometry, as though familiar with its logic. I tried to follow him, and a table flung itself down between us. I warily edged my way round it, and inexplicably found myself still in the same position. The man had vanished. A laugh shrilled through the drone of voices, and the sense of being ridiculous, the conviction that my embarrassment was the object of malevolent scrutiny, impelled me to dart into the sinuous cleft which had just opened before me. I walked two or three paces, then stumbled. A grinning face rose towards mine, and I hurriedly apologised. Something was being said to me, but I could not make out what. I was surrounded by a ring of staring eyes. Someone standing a few yards away was signalling to me. Just as I was about to look away, I realised that it was he.

"We are lucky to get a table at this hour," he said, when I succeeded in joining him.

The small stools on which we sat down were very uncomfortable, and it took me some time to hit upon a posture that was not unduly painful. My first agreeable impression of the place came from the feel of the chilled glass which was set before me. On the small stage, three men in blue jackets were jerking about. No sooner had I noticed them than a dance tune emerged from the dinning background. I followed the man on to the cramped floor, and we insinuated ourselves among the dozen or so couples who were swaying gently to the unimpassioned strains of the music. We were dancing on the spot. From time to time, an eddying movement would make us knock into one another, and the man would politely say sorry. I saw the couples around us standing cheek to cheek, with a far-away look in their eyes, determinedly celebrating the indeterminate rite of some somnambulist god, undulating, gliding slowly along, or coming to rest with a tremulous uncertainty, anticipating the currents which were going to sweep them along, and which did indeed sweep them along, just a yard or two at a time, without even a momentary chink appearing in this strange isolation in which they had armoured themselves. When we were once again perched on our narrow stools, a certain embarrassment settled between us, as though we had just abetted one another in some forbidden act. Hoping to derive a modicum of relief from the coolness of its touch, I wrapped my fingers round the glass and then, since this proved entirely ineffective, carried it to my lips, drank a mouthful of alcoholic liquor, and set it down at the same moment that the man sitting opposite me set down his own glass, which he had just drained.

"If this place doesn't appeal to you," he said, "we can go somewhere else."

"Where else?" I asked.

"To another night club."

"We are perfectly all right where we are," I said. "Do you come often?"

His expression seemed to condemn my question.

"Now and then," he said.

Shyly, I touched the hand that he was resting on the table. It lay quite still.

"Did you really feel like coming here this evening?"

"Things are just the same here as they are anywhere else," he said.

"We could simply have gone for a walk," I said.

"I was afraid you might be bored," he answered.

I knew quite well this was untrue. He had been afraid of being alone with me. Just as I had been afraid of being alone with him.

"Do you suppose all this can make the slightest difference?" I said, letting my eye wander over the tables, the dance floor, the band.

"We are on holiday," he said gently.

I said: "Yes, of course we are," and added:

"Who did you lose?"

"My parents, my wife, my daughter." Then he said:

"Come on."

We returned to the dance floor. The rhythm, faster this time, had disunited the dancers, plucked them apart, and—each one of them the prisoner of his or her small private frenzy—they were striving to join one another again.

"How old was she?" I asked, almost as soon as we were back at our table.

"Who?"

"Your daughter."

"Four. It was just after her fourth birthday."

"And where was this?"

"In Warsaw."

"And you were where at the time . . . ?"

He looked me straight in the eye and laughed unpleasantly.

"Me? I was in the forests. Serving with the Resistance."

"In what year?"

"Nineteen-forty-three."

"I was there too," I said. "With the guerillas of the National Army."

"With those skunks?" I nodded. "They used to fire at us whenever we ran into each other."

"I know," I said.

"What a funny thing," he said, "you may have fired at me."

"That is very unlikely," I said, "I never fired a shot."

"Why did you join them?"

"I fell in with them quite by chance. Besides, I had someone to save. Wouldn't you have done the same?"

He did not answer. So then I smiled at him. "Of course you would have done it. That and a good many other things to which one wouldn't care to give a name."

"Possibly," he said.

"Unquestionably," I said. "So according to you, we were all skunks."

"No doubt about it. I seem to remember I was quite a decent human being, before."

"And . . . ?"

"I've changed. Haven't you?"

I had an urge to say absolutely anything that might hurt him. I was furious with him for bringing me here, for dancing, smoking, drinking, being so beautifully mannered, so reserved. All day long I had been thinking about him. I had been prepared to go to any lengths in order to see him again. Perhaps I had been hoping to find in him a destroyed human being who would need me; perhaps I had been lured by the thought of the scars which I had attributed to him and which he would have laid bare to me, of those old wounds which were to have been so raw and tangible within my grasp, proof against time. Yes, doubtless I had been craving for the bleak and contemptible satisfaction of commiserating with others, of playing the comforter.

"Shall we dance?"

A magnificent blonde was swaying her hips close to us. I stared at her.

"What a beautiful girl," I said.

It was his turn to look at her. "Yes, indeed," he said, and his voice was expressionless.

"Was your wife a blonde or a brunette?"

"A brunette."

Why didn't he hit me? I kept my eyes lowered as we returned to our table. I dared not look at him now.

"Drink up," he said.

I emptied my glass, and he ordered another round.

"This place is perfectly all right really," I said.

"Where were you at the time of the Liberation?" he asked me, as though suddenly realising that this was the only possible subject for conversation between us.

"In prison," I said.

"I was in the ghetto."

"You couldn't have been!" My second glass was almost empty, and my head was spinning round. I was walking along streets that no longer existed; my feet were sinking into the ashes. "There was nobody left."

"I expressed myself badly," he said. "I meant under the ghetto. A hiding-place, beneath the ground. I was down there for six months."

He thought I was drunk and was telling me anything that came into his head.

"You were not in the ghetto," I said sternly.

"I went back to the ghetto," he said, "afterwards."

"After what?"

"After the death of my wife and child."

Tears came easily to me now.

"Monsieur," I said, "please forgive me."

He patted my hand gently.

"There is nothing to forgive," he said, "nothing to forgive."

"Were they denounced?"

"Not exactly. My wife had the yellow card, the prostitution card. The best papers she could possibly have had. Even when there was a round-up, she had nothing to fear. All she had to do was go along to the hospital every Monday for a medical inspection. That was a bad moment for her, but afterwards she could live in peace for the rest of the week. My wife was always good at getting out of tight corners."

His glass was empty again.

"Waiter!" he called.

"One day a hoard of gold was found in the house she was living in. They were all shot. The child as well. There was no reason for me to stay in the forest any longer, and I went back to the ghetto."

He went back there to die, I thought, and he hid underground for six months to save his life. I wanted to throw my arms round him, to pat him on the back and say: "You and I are the perfect pair, we cannot help but get along well together. I, too, wanted to die, and here I am, keeping company with an elderly gentleman, building up my health." He noticed my smile.

"Another drink?"

I said yes. He was growing very friendly. Now that I had a few drinks inside me, I had ceased to be dangerous. Perhaps I would even be fun.

"What do you think of all these people," I asked stupidly.

"They are like we were, before."

Anna Langfus

I stopped smiling. It was all very well his sidestepping my questions and putting on his best, politely attentive mask: he would follow me the way a dog follows his master. I would sweep away the world that surrounded him and see him as he had been during the "other life." And I would at long last be able to speak, myself. I would lead him back to all these familiar things, without having to fear either astonishment or suspicion or disgust. From time to time, he would nod his head, as he had in the shop, and say: "Yes, that's right . . ." We might even marry. We would spend a wonderful wedding night running through our horror film together. And we would hang round one another all the time, keeping a close eye on one another, each ready to crush the other's slightest chance of escaping, each on the alert and ready to spring, ferociously. Then we would have to assume a real destiny. Both of us would be where we belonged.

And it was he who now, of his own free will, was coming towards me, he had summoned his daughter and she sat down between us, at this table, in the lovely blue dress which she had been wearing the last time he had seen her. An absurd little bun was perched on top other head. "My name is Wanda Malewska," she said, and with her left hand she made the sign of the cross. "No, not like that," said her father, "you must do it with your right hand." Obediently, the child crossed herself again, using her right hand this time. It was all a game. We were playing secrets. My third glass was empty, yet I could not remember drinking it. I sent for Jan, and now it was his turn to seat himself at our table. The little girl smiled at him. The man's eyes were blurred with tears, and the three of us were gazing at him fondly.

"Forgive me," he said. "Would you care to dance this waltz?"

Among the trails of light and shade which enveloped us as we spun round, I thought I glimpsed them again: the little girl had clambered on to Jan's knee and they were waving at us.

The man had slipped his arm round my shoulders. My head was heavy, and I rested it on his chest. I was growing giddier and giddier. Foolishly, I tried to recapture my empty glass, which was stealing away from me with alarming velocity.

"Philanderer," said a voice.

I looked up. Two globes of golden skin, half-imprisoned in pale green material, were being inclined towards the man. The arm which had been holding me up withdrew, and I toppled forward. When I recovered my balance, I saw the two of them standing face to face.

"Hallo, Gisèle," said the man.

"Philanderer," repeated the girl. She laughed.

"Allow me to introduce a friend of mine." he said to her.

The girl stood eyeing me. I dimly had the impression of having retained on my face a smile which no longer had any reason for being there.

"She is completely drunk," the girl said contemptuously. "Well done—please accept my congratulations."

The man had lost his calm gracefulness of manner.

He took a half-step to the left, a half-step to the right, a step towards me, a step towards the girl who, sure of herself, said:

"Let's have a dance, though, shall we?"

One step towards me, one step towards her, one step midway between us, marking time.

"You *will* excuse me," he said very quickly.

I propped my elbows on the table and sank my head into my hands. I was alone. I could see them, a few feet away, dancing at a standstill, celebrating the rite with rare perfection. The man had set his hands flat on the woman's hips, very low, almost on her buttocks. They stood there swaying, with stony expressions on their faces, swaying and waiting. There was a small amount of drink left in his glass; I gulped it down. The cigarettes were on the table. A man wandered over and bowed to me. I blew smoke into his face.

"Go and jump in the lake," I said.

He straightened up. He was about to turn nasty.

"Let her alone," said another man, "she's plastered."

The first man hesitated, tight-lipped with anger, then he shrugged and walked away. Making an effort, I got up. I clutched the edge of the table. So far, so good; but the hardest part was yet to come. I advanced one step at a time. I stopped at almost every table and occasionally clung to a shoulder, heedless of the jokes and laughter to which the gestures gave rise. A few steps to climb, then I was outside in the darkness. Soon I was walking along with far greater assurance. Someone was running along the street behind me. A hand closed on my arm. I broke free.

"I can walk perfectly well without your help," I said.

"I beg you to excuse me. It was a neighbour."

"Don't be ridiculous."

"Hold on tight," he said, after I in turn had settled on the motorcycle.

"Don't worry–even if I was drunk before, I am not drunk now. Besides, I didn't black out, not even for a moment. You would have liked to think I was drunk, wouldn't you?"

"You were," he said.

I kept my eyes closed, all the way back. The wind had freshened, and it was an icy hand that clung to mine when we took our leave of one another.

"Shall we see one another again?" he asked.

"Perhaps," I said.

"When?"

"I don't know. I am not alone."

I could not see him, but I pictured him nodding his head in that confirmatory way of his.

"We might manage to fit something in," he said calmly.

I snatched my hand out of his. I ran just as fast as I could. No one followed me, and it was without hurrying that I started up the slope leading to the village.

Viviane Forrester
(1929–)

Viviane Forrester, French novelist, essayist, and critic, begins her wartime autobiography *Ce Soir, après la guerre* [Tonight, After the War] with a simple existential declaration that under her pen must be read as a *cri de guerre*: *J'étais au monde* [I was in the world. I was alive.] J'étais au monde. It smelled good. Everything was pulsating. . . . I had more electricity running through me than the wind or the waves."[1] There is the electric charge of existence. Part organic delight, part shadow of a threatening predicate, this apparent truism— I was in the world—is the source of the major themes of her fiction and essay writing. For indeed, how should one fill in that verb of connection between "I" and "the world"?

Three primary threads characterize Forrester's thirty years of writing about the relationship of subject to world, or story to history: the relationship between personal and Jewish identity; the relationship of "I" as a body to other bodies, especially that of the mother; and the horrors of a world which would alternately strike the verb of connection from the sentence, sending the "I" off into madness, mask the connection through dissimulation, or cut the "I" out of the equation entirely. Frustrated being is read in a range of broken story lines, in varied degrees of fragmented syntax, in the multilingual text of *Vestiges*, in the hymn and lament to humanity in *Mains*, in the falsified plot of *Le Jeu des Poignards*. Wrenching images recur—bodies undone, empty gazes, smells, rot, camps, mud, secrets, hiding, leave-taking. Her writing is exquisitely sensual and unflinchingly horrific. It is also, thankfully, full of humor.

The question of how Jewishness might be a defining concept—a marker of "four letters"[2]—is explicit throughout, ranging from frequent references to concentration camps and European horrors, to specific questions of personal identity. "Does being Jewish here have a meaning? Can one be Jewish in this season?"[3] "Is she Jewish?. . . . Does she bear this detail, this veil, this invisible signal, this flag, this rupture, this tie?"[4] Are one's parts Jewish?—"my so-called Jewish hands, which were hands, two enigmas among so many others."[5] "Are my dreams Jewish?" muses the narrator of *Le Grand festin*. For the adolescent protagonist of *Ce Soir*, history moves over in the equation to the side of the I — what happens in the world is happening directly to her. Hitler "was saying bad things about me." "He couldn't stand it that I was Jewish; I didn't give it a thought."[6] Her Jewish identity is given her by others before it has any independent meaning for her, and as soon as she is given it, she must hide it to save it. Eventually, she will have to hide outright.

The relationship to family is likewise fraught with ambiguity and anguish, especially where the mother's body is concerned. One is born of a line, into a class, into a race, but born more specifically of flesh. "Oh mother, in what land do we land outside of you?"[7] Characters are haunted by images of their mothers' bodies, bodies loving men, rotting, squashing oily garden pests, wandering in search of lost lovers, making milk. Fathers are embodied originators as well, as the daughter/lover reading her father's re-plotted life story in *Le Jeu des poignards* is agonizingly aware.

And always, the world is there, "preventing us from living"[8] the word *horreur* coming back time and again in her work to mark its presence. Beneath the unveiling of the horror of history runs a yearning for communion with natural surroundings and, indeed, an escape from history. "I want to forget the source. Notice the details."[9] In Forrester, the organic élan must struggle in a perpetual *Résistance* against all that would quell its vitality.

Two recent texts resisting globalization as a force of economic injustice have made Forrester a controversial star in France *(Une Etrange dictature; Economic Horror)*. Born into the privilege of a Parisian banking family (she speaks in *Ce Soir* of her parents "collecting" privileges), she knew early on that she would be a writer and teacher, a refugee from her father's moneyed world. Her autobiography is as much the story of a dual vocation, literary voice and voice for the economically invisible—*au monde* but excluded—as it is of life in an assimilated Jewish family under the occupation.

The adolescent narrator of *Ce soir, après la guerre* comes of age politically, professionally, privately, and as a Jew in a world of both gentle and cruel irony. Her Aunt Elsa prays to the saints and makes a pilgrimage to Lourdes on Yom Kippur, fasting; her father holds her to upper-class riding techniques as they follow their guides through treacherous ravines escaping into Spain; her parents have secrets in their pasts; her beloved grandmother has coldly abandoned her sons to their poverty far away. She first sees the face of her deepest love only after he is shot dead. History hunts her down as she has barely begun her own life story. The writer is kind to her people, noting these anomalies with neither ridicule nor exaggerated indulgence. In this translated segment, the narrator chastises her young self for her facile militant stance, yet offers a literary solution to the girl's filial quandary by painting with a loving though piercing eye a wealthy father the girl professes to hate. All the while, she examines what lies beneath surfaces and silences.

"I was in literature," Viviane Forrester seems to have asserted in echo to her existential *cri*. She is indeed very much in her own literature: *Ce Soir* is a perfect prelude to the novels and essays to which her life and identity have provided so many of the images, voices, and tensions. Books entered her body at the moment in which she is forced out into the "occupied" world; in writing she occupies the world. Books have become her verb of connection, her way of being, and her being Jewish, in the world, in this season.

— **Lauretta Clough**

Notes

1. *Ce Soir, après la guerre*, p. 9.
2. "Juif", in *Le Grand festin*, p. 9.
3. *Ibid.*
4. *Ibid.* p. 11.
5. *Mains*, p. 19.
6. *Ce Soir*, p. 29.
7. *Vestiges*, p. 113.
8. *Grand festin*, p. 173.
9. *Ibid.*, p. 15.

Selected Works

Ainsi des exilés. Paris: Gallimard, 1970.
Le Grand festin. Paris: Denoël, 1971.
Virginia Woolf. Paris: Equinoxe, 1975.
Vestiges. Paris: Le Seuil, 1978.
Les Violences du calme. Paris: Le Seuil, 1980.
Van Gogh, ou, l'enterrement dans les blés. Paris: Le Seuil, 1983.
Le Jeu des poignards. Paris: Gallimard, 1985.
Mains. Paris: Séguier, 1988.
L'Horreur économique. Paris: Fayard, 1996.
Ce Soir, après la guerre. Paris: Fayard, 1997.
Au Louvre avec Viviane Forrester: La vierge à l'enfant avec Sainte Anne, Léonard de Vinci, 1492–1519. Paris: Louvre, 2000.
Le Crime occidental. Paris: Fayard, 2004.

Viviane Forrester

Translation Into English

Economic Horror. Blackwell, 2000.

Secondary Works

Grahame White. "Fictive Footprints" in *Language and Style: An International Journal* 15, 4 (1982): 283–288.

Tonight, After the War

The day of the *baccalauréat* was upon me. Essay topic: "The Nineteenth Century French Novel." I had read so many, dreamed so many. I had plumbed their mysteries with my mother, but I didn't know a single quote. A sudden flash: a manor house near Dieppe, my Uncle Jacques' library. Miles of old leather-bound books, Voltaire's correspondence. What grader, even the most learned, was going to be able to confirm a quote picked out of thousands of pages? I fudged Voltaire, had him expressing prescient formulae miraculously adapted to Balzac, Stendhal, and Flaubert.

I treated the math question, which I didn't understand in the least, as an easy problem. My proof must have surprised them in its strange sophistication, but it was irrefutable, as was my solution to the problem to which the aforementioned proof bore no apparent relation.

The verdict was announced by phone from Nice. I made the call without much hope. The list was short, passing grades were few, and then I heard my family name. But what about the first name? I called back, it was definitely me. I must have heard wrong; I called a third time. The secretary had a fit, yelled my name into the receiver, spelled it, and expressed her most fervent hope—never to hear my voice again.

My mother's fit was even more violent. An iniquitous decision! An affront. Both vice and laziness, that bad other mother, had been rewarded. I had failed to work hard every single day of the year and yet I had passed. What arrogance! I was corrupting my sister. My future would pivot on this egregious error and I would suffer for it for the rest of my life. She envisioned me lying in the gutter, waiting for the guillotine's fall, or worse yet, getting no dinner party invitations.

Like everything else, the exam slipped away from me. Even with a pass, I had no right to it. Everything I touched came to nothing.

My father and Ninette,[*] her mouth still open in an "O" of premature joy, were looking at my mother dumbfounded. "And what if she had failed?"

"I would have comforted her," said my mother regretfully, nonetheless sheepishly taking from her wrist the only jewelry she wore. It was her fetish, a slender ocelot band with a miniature clasp like in a notions shop, set with tiny diamonds. She was giving it to me. The warmest, closest, most familiar object to me, it was from "before."

---

[*] the protagonist's younger sister

From: *Ce Soir, après la guerre* (Paris: Fayard, 1997), pp. 109–122.

And then. . . . "Things are starting," my father warned one morning, his face ghostly pale. "There were raids not long ago. In Nice. Your mother and sister aren't here. We'll have to tell them." He gave me an embarrassed look, a plea for forgiveness, as if he had gotten me into a real mess. I wanted to hug him and ask him to hold me, protect me. But his eyes grew cold again, reclaiming their unencumbered, golf course gaze. He was sure of himself once again, and he said in a voice growing firmer, "We might not have anything to worry about." They were only arresting foreign Jews, or Jews naturalized since 1927, "the ones with an accent who give us a bad name."

I wished I had never been born. I wished I was Polish or Hungarian, in Nice, with only Yiddish on my tongue. My father was worse than Hitler. Not a doubt left in my mind, none, forever. Since my father was as despicable as the others, it meant he was in no way different. Being Jewish didn't make you different the way the posters, the papers, and the radio were saying. Neither good nor evil. I had always thought so and now I knew for sure. I had proof that nothing could be judged that way. Nothing and no one. Ever. I can still picture my father's bedroom, the balcony and the ocean beyond, and me leaning on the desk, torn between the horror of despising my despairing father, of having lost even that buffer between myself and horror and the delight in discovering yet a further reason to condemn him. For a minute, I thrilled at the thought of telling M. Laile[*] about this abject episode, but I knew I wouldn't say anything.

Not even to my father either, for that matter. My childhood was over, crossed out. I was no longer guilty for having hated (or believing I hated) my father and I was dismayed at being proven right.

I said nothing. He was looking at me with such compassion, such uncertainty. He murmured, "I don't know what to do anymore." And then, regretting that he had shown his emotions and worried me further, he said, "I won't make any mistakes. I'll save all three of you."

But I was thinking of the Jews in Nice, the ones with the accent.

There were children in Nice who had been left alone, not because anyone had intended to spare them officially, but because their parents had managed to hide them with neighbors. A committee divided them up among families like ours. A little girl came to stay at our house. She was practically a baby. I decided to make her my reason for living. Loving and dependent, she spoke only to me. I adored her. I took her out on the water every day in our boat and taught her songs, forever ruining both her ear and her voice in the process. I asked if I could keep her instead of the ocelot bracelet as a prize for passing the *baccalauréat*. It was a crazy time; everything seemed absent, equal, and

---

[*]former tutor

improbable—flesh, soul, and bracelets. They agreed. And that's how I got her "for life."

A few days later, her mother came for her. She had managed to get away. I knew I was supposed to be happy. It was dreadful. I spent a long time with the woman. I wanted to know everything about her but she no longer had any feeling. We would have had to revive her, she was somewhere far away, inexpressive, feeling neither fear nor hope. Her husband hadn't made it. She took the little girl by the hand as the child clung to me. The mother didn't look at her child, didn't look at anything. It was she who said "good luck," to me. She had an accent.

I watched them go.

Toward what?

M. Laile still looked like Rimbaud. He spoke less and had started playing awful records like "Night on Bald Mountain." Pale, inspired, and solemn, he conducted the orchestra, or rather the record player with such self-absorbed energy that I too felt it. Sitting silhouetted on the windowsill with his hair all tousled, he'd hold forth on the century's infamies and rightly so. He'd give an overview of colonialism and Fascism and graze the surface of Nazi horror. But when he came to the crimes of banks, in general, and of my father, in particular, there was no stopping him.

After the war, I saw him quite by chance in his hi-fi shop near Cannes. He looked like M. Liard, friendly and plump, as bald as the famous Bald Mountain, which he had pretended to conduct, his curls buffeted by the wind. He told me about his investments and his vacation house, and about his faith in real estate. "Stone is the only thing I believe in." He remembered my father's profession. What would my father advise? How did he manage his own money? How about mine? He couldn't believe at first when I told him my father hardly had any money left, and that I didn't have any at all. Then when he finally did believe it, he told me he admired me for having "dared to admit it."

But I'd stayed with the perspective he'd taught me. I saw myself back in 1943 when I was ferocious, pitiless, and critical, eager to espy my father's least weakness, ever ready to pounce and to judge, jubilantly. A man in dire straits, who barely let on. A man truly in anguish. A man who—had he not been Jewish—would probably have been one of our persecutors. My father, who had perhaps a visceral, traditional, mute, unconscious knowledge of cruelty, which he had not passed down to us. My father, with the still recent memory of the refugee business from which he would have liked to distance both himself and us, but which was unfolding with limitless fury.

The war had been over for a long time and I was looking at M. Laile's bare scalp surrounded by hi-fi equipment, remembering with disgust how, conquered by both his hair and his enthusiasm, I had once thought we were together on a mission for the good of the world's common people. I suddenly felt alone, with values judged to be of little use (even less today), while my father's principles, with which M. Laile now allied himself, had triumphed.

We were interrupted by customers, the sound of the cash register. With even less pleasure, I remembered the neo-sentimental turn our conversations had taken. My father, who bore the brunt of their ideological consequences, was at the point of cutting me off. No allowance, no haircuts, no books, no occasional pastries. And what ever was I going to do about getting him a present for his birthday in August?

M. Dargère came up with the solution. Berlitz was having trouble finding a math teacher for their summer classes. He would recommend me. I was completely ignorant of even the most basic principles, the very ones I would need to be teaching, but so what? He was, after all, my math teacher. He could teach me what I needed to know as we went along. I was to refuse the salary offered and take advantage of the low market supply to raise the stakes—my colleagues would benefit as well. I also had to lie about my age and use a false name.

With my nana's old glasses poised on my nose, my hair pulled back, and my haughty manner, I was able to extract conditions that made the director wonder how he had managed to hire such a troublesome teacher. I left his office with a dramatic flourish, teetering blindly behind lenses that blurred everything and flew straight back to Rochelongue.

I found my father waiting on the bench in deep conversation with Mme. Liard. I triumphantly announced my new social status: I was a teacher. I was earning a living. Mme. Liard went off to get a bottle of something ghastly to celebrate with. My father didn't get angry, dammit, he looked at me with a smile on his face. "Math," he murmured dreamily. He had had a passion for it. Besides, I was becoming a bit more like that imaginary son of his who would become an Inspecteur des Finances.

On the morning of my first day on the job, Luc Tausson rode his bike with me to the school. Crazed with nervousness, I didn't hear a word he was saying. It got to the point where he screamed: "Will you marry me?" at the top of his lungs. People were looking at us. "Make up your mind," someone prompted. Marry him? He had no sense of priorities. I was destined to educate the masses, the ones going to Berlitz, at least. I screamed back, "no," so that he would let me continue the recapitulation, alas brief, of my meager scientific acquirements. Why was he being so tactlessly insistent? I could only come up with one immediate reason for my refusal: "You're so religious, and the church where you serve mass reminds me of a bathroom." I deemed it sufficient. It wasn't. Church reminded Luc of the same thing. My next move was to raise the issue of pedagogical urgency. Which must have seemed less urgent when I stopped to tell my new professional and romantic achievements to a friend of my cousin who'd been snubbing me from her twenty-four-year-old perch. Luc, living proof of my accession to maturity, was waiting off to the side. "Poor kid," she murmured, not without directing a self-interested look at the unhappy candidate, who might have made a better choice. "You're not supposed to talk about things like that. I'm going to tell your family about your poor judgment," she promised, before continuing on to her weighty seaside celibacy.

But I had wings and I got the overjoyed director to give me a blackboard and some seat cushions. There was talk of a raise.

Alas. It took barely a few seconds for my first two pupils, both boys older than I, to do four equations wrong and the remainder of the hour for them to deny it. The debate was over my head; I learned about the interminable passage of time. The next student was a nine-year-old who seemed like a gift from heaven. He didn't understand a single thing in the fourth grade curriculum. Neither did I. It bound us together.

These students were real; they weren't figments of my imagination. I was getting to know people who wanted to learn and even more, to pass the previously failed tests with a second attempt in the fall. Our sessions were being paid for by their parents. For the first time, I was responsible and I knew it. Thanks to Mr. Dargère, I became a satisfactory teacher and, on the twenty-eighth of August, I gave my father a copy Clemenceau's *Memoirs,* which was very hard to come by at the time.

One of my pupils was the butcher's son, and he used his vacation to deliver clandestine steaks to Rochelongue, among other places. Although the meat was less clandestine than I myself was to become, I was forever on the lookout. The secret exit planned in case of danger became my obsession; if he should ever see me and talk about me as his teacher to my cook—why, I imagined Francine laughing until she cried. I would have done anything to have a vegetarian family!

My real family had other things on their minds: identification checks at every corner and, increasingly, raids. Threats from all sides, and what happened when it happened? Where were the deported people going? We never found out. Where were they going? Where might we go? Their destination remained a secret, but we did have a gnawing sense of exactly what we didn't want to know—the unthinkable. Proof of this was the relief we felt when we convinced ourselves that the answer was labor camps near the hardest hit German towns like Hamburg or Dortmund. Labor camps would still be human: a human violation.

A man named Donati, an Italian, came often to meet with my father, who would appear even more worried after his departure.

My mother threw herself into her favorite game, chess, with the unshakeable Luc Tausson, who would lose from morning until night. It was diplomatic of him, as well as utterly super-human, given the way my mother played. She took advantage of these visits to discourage him, holding forth on my faults with convincing delight, describing to my suitor the burden that would befall him should I accept his proposal of marriage. My whims would be his ruin. I'd spend all my time reading, draped languidly over the furniture, while he, dead tired, would be doing the dishes, in our disaster of a house. His life would be reduced to a series of affronts. I was a fickle anarchist who destroyed everything and respected nothing. She'd report these excessive statements to me, moved by her own devotion. "Unbelievable," she'd sigh, "that such a perfect, virtuous, upstanding, sincere boy, a chess aficionado no less, should have this crush on you. Now, if he'd known you in Paris, well . . ." and this would spark in us dreams of this faraway, inaccessible place, of the days when we had been so close, and "home."

M. Donati's visits grew more frequent. Fewer and fewer Italian soldiers patrolled the streets.

M. Dargère asked me if I'd step in for one of his friends. I was to go see families who had had a son sent to the STO, Vichy's mandatory work program that sent young men off to work in Germany. I was to say I had been sent by the government, carrying in my hand a sum of money supposedly owed to the families. I was to pay attention to the way they reacted, taking special note of the names and ages of the other children. M. Dargère's friends would then contact the ones who would be likely candidates for the STO and get them in the Maquis.

At that time, everyone was suspicious of everyone. People were getting arrested for the slightest thing, a word, a move. The eyes of the French militia were everywhere. Getting information was no easy matter.

I discovered slums hidden behind the fancy facades of the rue d'Antibes, but mostly I discovered people. People who would grovel at the mention of Vichy or Pétain, hastening to show me the picture of the Maréchal reigning from the mantle. I was supposed to exude ease with them saying, "Here you are, among friends!" I would smile and feel like hitting them. We were likeminded good people of France. These people were happy to provide me with details, but sometimes I hoped they were trying to deceive me.

Then there were the poverty-stricken, to whom I was offering false hope.

There was the man who, at the word "Vichy," called Pétain a pile of manure, Vichy a garbage can, me a bitch, and threw me out. He was a fisherman from Suquet. He was risking a lot. I so wished I could tell him the truth.

Then there was the former porter of a fancy hotel, terribly old, poor, and alone, ensconced in a dark bedroom. He began to cry silently; his grandson, my pretext, was dead, and his son was far away. I went to see him often; I'd steal food for him. The days in Cannes were numbered. I didn't know it. I didn't know anything. No one did.

M. Donati left Rochelongue, came back, trying very obviously to convince my father, who kept it all to himself.

The beaches were there. The weather was still nice. Women were no longer allowed to lie down with their feet pointing toward the boardwalk, so as not to shock the German families vacationing on the Riviera. This crude statute made me loathe even to go near the sand.

They had stamped the word "Jew" on our identification cards at the French police station with forced smiles, as if to say sorry. It was June 9.

One day when I was in our living room, three men came in. The police. They produced their badges and asked to see my father. I was just about to give the warning signal that would tell him to leave by the back way, when he came in. He saw the men, saw their badges, but didn't see me. I must have been as ashen as he. He didn't flinch. The chief stepped toward my father and held out his hand. My father put his hands behind his back.

He was no longer the man who had spoken those shameful words. Now he was the hero who had taken action, instinctively, thinking himself alone and on the brink of the worst.

The worst? In fact (but he didn't know this either), this particular Vichy squad was concerned about . . . the cow we had boarded out in the country! "How much butter did she produce? How much milk?" they feverishly inquired. When they had gone my father and I burst out laughing. And then we stared at each other for a long time, sensing that it might be our last chance.

I never tired of staring at my sister Ninette, so blond, so pretty, so ethereal and happy. The Germans too had fixed their eyes and set their sights on her as well.

My mother was still telling stories of the front in World War I, the dances, her past conquests, but she didn't mention the German philosopher she'd met in Grindelwald anymore. Every once in a while we would hear about another man, possibly the only one she had ever really loved. Everything in this story was left unsaid, blanks, distress. Someone from outside her immediate circle, much like the philosopher, much older. He was an antiques dealer. She had seen him once since her wedding. Near Paris, on a golf course. He had seemed so old. They had teased my father, and this stranger with the mysterious role had sunk to the grass, forlornly sitting down in the middle of the green. "Your father was gleeful," she recalled, tickled at the thought of his jealousy. But of whom? Why? The Mediterranean stretched on, silent and still, and my mother said no more. We enjoyed the absence of the Liards, however brief. We breathed the sticky air. Everything was temporary.

§   §   §

My father was on the list of Jews they were going to arrest. "Right at the top," he would point out. The opposite would have distressed him.

I still continued to go to Antoine's beauty salon, where there were still white lacquered stalls, soft aprons, smiling manicurists, pretty trays with fake coffee served among flowers from his garden, where hair would be drying under domes. Once again, one might have thought nothing was happening.

"There's something happening," announced a stylist from the doorway. "Come see, ladies." His voice sounded funny. A few of us went over to join him. It was a beautiful day. The buildings were gleaming in the sunlight. Down the street, we could see a black Citroën parked in front of a house and an old man being led out by three men in trenchcoats and fedoras. They pushed him into the car. I had seen his slender, fragile silhouette, his wrinkled, colorless, expressionless face, his blank stare. The car started up. So I had seen one. Quick, quiet, simple. An arrest. Probably the French militia, imitating the Gestapo. The street was empty and, as ever, there were palm trees, the scent of mimosa. The stylists and manicurists said nothing. "A Jew," said a woman walking by. From a customer: "I knew him. He used to be an antiques dealer." She spoke of him in the past and mentioned his name.

I went home. Everything seemed different. Was that what life was? My mother was reading on the verandah. I told her the story, hardly believing or comprehending what I was saying.

My mother repeated the name, looked at me, looked away. She was trembling, but not out of fear. She was very pale, she would have been anyway. "In front of you?" She avoided my gaze. "You saw," she murmured. "You." And I wondered why I had been present at the end of a story I didn't know. My mother looked back again as if to absorb the scene through me. She said simply, "I knew him." I had already understood. We didn't mention it again. Ever.

— **Translated by Lauretta Clough**

Liliane Atlan
(1932–)

Liliane Atlan's writing offers evidence to the fact that a writer who has not directly experienced the Nazi concentration camps can nevertheless write honestly and convincingly about the tragic fate of European Jews during World War II. The influence of the Holocaust on Atlan and on her written and spoken texts has been immeasurable. Her sense of Jewish identity, like that of other postwar French intellectuals of Jewish origin, was profoundly affected by the experience of the Nazi occupation and the Vichy regime. In Atlan's view, the crucial question that has dominated her life and literary production is "how to integrate into our consciousness, without dying in the attempt, the radical experience of Auschwitz."[1]

Born in Montpellier into a Jewish family from Salonika, Liliane Atlan (née Cohen) lived an ordinary middle-class childhood for seven years. Between the ages of seven and fourteen, however, during the years 1939 to 1945, she was in hiding with her younger sister in the south of France and in the Auvergne. The Cohen girls and their parents survived the Shoah, but her mother's family was deported and died in the extermination camps. Atlan believes that her theatrical creativity and her lifetime preoccupation with the Holocaust germinated during that period.

When the war ended, Atlan's father became active in Jewish relief efforts; her family gave shelter to refugees from the concentration camps. Her parents eventually adopted a young man, an incommunicative survivor who gradually told his painful stories to a receptive listener, the fourteen-year-old Liliane. During those early postwar years, this vulnerable and sensitive Jewish girl became seriously ill with anorexia. Eventually, she recovered and attended the Sorbonne where she studied literature and philosophy. She lived for a year at the Ecole Gilbert Bloch in Orsay, a religious school that gathered European Jewish youth in an attempt to heal their emotional wounds through spirituality. There the future playwright and poet spent many sleepless nights with her companions studying the sacred texts of the Torah, the Talmud, the Zohar, the midrashic commentaries and other repositories of Jewish knowledge and belief.

These living echoes of the Holocaust—the testimonies from her stepbrother and other survivors, her intensive immersion in traditional and mystical Jewish texts, as well as her subsequent investigations of historical archives—form the major sources of Jewish identity embodied in Atlan's literary productions. She is best known for her plays which have been performed in France, Belgium, Austria, the United States, Japan, and Israel. Atlan has also

Liliane Atlan

published numerous volumes of poetry and narrative, as well as radio and video scripts. Her eight-hour long work *Un Opéra pour Térézin*, was performed by actors and musicians in Montpellier during a single night in July 1989 and simultaneously transmitted in a national radio broadcast. In 1997, an abridged version was performed in Naples in French, Italian, and English.

Atlan's literary works make use of Jewish cultural and religious elements in intertextual resonances of secular and sacred Jewish writing and contain traces of Hebrew, Ladino, and Yiddish, in, as she puts it, "my everyday language . . . a language of the Jewish subconscious."[2] Through imitation of scriptural commentary and traditional Jewish parody, a lexicon rich in mystical imagery, incantatory rhythms and liturgical syntactical patterns, her plays, poetry, and spoken texts evoke the Judaic sources she studied during the postwar period and afterwards. Yet, in spite of the pervasive presence of signs connoting and denoting (her) Jewish identity, Atlan's writing, like that of other postwar French Jewish writers, struggles against a crushing sense of loss.

Monsieur Fugue ou le Mal de terre, the first of Atlan's plays, has been the most widely performed and translated of her dramatic works. The most representational of her texts, it is based on the principal of a school in the Warsaw ghetto who voluntarily accompanied a group of Jewish children to the gas chamber and told them stories until the end. In the play, one of the soldiers, Mister Fugue, chooses to befriend the children and rides in the back of the truck that carries them to Rotburg, the Valley of Bones, where they will all be killed.

The work incorporates a number of characteristics of Atlan's later, more postmodernist theatrical experiments. Eschewing realism, the ghetto remains unnamed, as does the country in which the event takes place. While confined in the annihilating space of the truck, the children, with the help of Mister Fugue, resist the forces of destruction by telling stories, by fantasizing an entire life course through language and theatrical gestures. The children chant irreverent ritualistic refrains, identifying themselves with the soulless golem, and parody sacred prayers. They use abrasive, vulgar slang in one moment and in the next recite lofty, poetic passages that evoke mystical images of humans transformed into giant birds, sea, mountains, and limitless spaces. The imaginary life the children enact in the back of the truck conflates the past, present, and future, and thus deconstructs the play's apparent linear temporality.

— **Judith Morganroth Schneider**

Notes

1. Liliane Atlan, letter to Judith Morganroth Schneider, December 4, 1989.
2. Lilane Atlan, *Theatre Pieces: An Anthology*. Trans. Marguerite Feitlowitz (Greenwood, FL : Penkevill, 1985), 23–35.

Selected Works

Plays

Monsieur Fugue ou le Mal de terre. Paris: Seuil, 1967.
Les messies, ou le Mal de terre. Paris: Seuil, 1969.
Les musiciens, les émigrants. Paris: P. J. Oswald, 1976.
Leçons de bonheur. Paris: Crater, 1987.
Un Opéra pour Térézin. Paris: L'avant-scène, 1997.
Je m'appelle Non: une piece de théâtre pour personne adulte et des adolescents. Paris: L'Ecole des Loisirs, 1998.

Poetry

Lapsus. Paris: Seuil, 1971.
L'Amour élémentaire: poème, monologue. Toulouse: L'Ether Vague, 1985.
Bonheur, mais sur quel ton le dire. Paris: Editions l'Harmattan, 1996.
Peuples d'argile, forêts d'étoiles. Paris: Editions l'Harmattan, 2000.

Prose

Le rêve des animaux rongeurs. Toulouse: L'Ether Vague, 1985.
Les passants. Paris: Payot, 1988.
Quelques pages arrachées au grande livre des rêves. Paris: Editions l'Harmattan, 1998.
Petites bibles pour mauvais temps. Paris: Editions l'Harmattan, 2001.

Liliane Atlan

Translations Into English

"Story." Trans. Judith Morganroth Schneider. *Centerpoint* 3 (1978): 93–94.

Mister Fugue or Earth Sick, The Messiahs, The Carriage of Flames and Voices. In *Theatre Pieces: An Anthology.* Edited and translated by Marguerite Feitlowitz. Greenwood, FL: Penkevill, 1985.

The Passerby. New York: Holt, 1993.

Interviews

Bettina L. Knapp. "Collective Creation from Paris to Jerusalem: An Interview with Liliane Atlan." *Theater* (Fall–Winter 1981).

"Interview with Liliane Atlan." In *Interviews with Contemporary Women Playwrights,* compiled by Kathleen Betsco and Rachel Koenig. New York: Beech Street Books, 1987.

Secondary Works

Bettina L. Knapp. "Cosmic Theatre: *The Little Chariot of Flames and Voices.*" *Modern Drama* 17 (1974): 225–234.

_____. Introduction. In *Theatre Pieces: An Anthology,* by Liliane Atlan. Greenwood, FL: Penkevill, 1985.

_____. *Liliane Atlan.* Amsterdam: Rodopi, 1988.

_____. "Mal-être. L'Oeuvre scénique et poétique de Liliane Atlan." *Les Nouveaux Cahiers* (Summer 1995).

Yehuda Moraly. "Liliane Atlan's *Un Opéra pour Térézin.*" In *Staging the Holocaust: The Shoah in Drama and Performance,* Claude Schumacher, ed. (Cambridge: Cambridge University Press, 1998), 169–183.

Judith Morganroth Schneider. "Liliane Atlan: Jewish Difference in Postmodern French Writing." *Symposium* 43 (Winter 1989–1990): 274–283.

Mister Fugue

The mouth of a sewer. The ruins of a ghetto. Barbed wire. Flames. The Commandant, Christopher, Grol, Grobbe *and* Frobbe *contemplate the fire. A beat.*

The Commandant: For eight days, this ghetto's burned. The rats that lived here are dead. Those fleeing toward the forest, we captured and sent to Rotburg. Those who stayed in the sewer, we hosed, for fifty-six hours you've guarded every exit, all of them drowned. The affair is done. We can leave.

They separate. Christopher *detains* Grol.

Christopher: Loosen this cover. Not too much. So it looks natural.

Grol, *dazed, obeys.*

Christopher: Lie down. Play dead. If any of those rats are left, you're going to see what they'll do to you.

Grol plays dead, his eyes open. He doesn't move, is preoccupied, distressed. Christopher *slips into his pocket bread and cigarettes, then moves off. Sound of a truck pulling away.*

The cover is lifted. The cadaverous, emaciated faces of Yossele *and* Raissa *become visible. They climb out without a word. They creep about; both, but especially* Raissa, *are like nightbirds. Then* Iona *(holding to his chest a death-doll with a skeletal gaze, enormous head and skinny limbs, a doll that resembles them) and* Abracha *emerge from the sewer. They're wild-eyed and in rags.* Yossele *and* Raissa *have seen the bread, snatch it without a word. Silently,* Abracha *and* Iona *rob* Grol, *take his boots, see the bread and jump* Yossele *and* Raissa. *They devour it on the ground, all the while on the look-out.*

Yossele: *(in a broken voice)* Shit, there's fire everywhere.

Raissa: *(even more broken-voiced)* We go back down?

Abracha: *(the most emaciated of all, in a thin, reedy voice)* You crazy, or what?

Yossele: We're gonna tear down the wires. Quick.

They do, except for Iona, *who hangs back, muttering.*

Raissa: There hands somewhere in all this blood?

From: *Theater Pieces: An Anthology.* Trans. Margaret Feitlowitz. (Greenwood, FL: Penkevill, 1985), pp. 23–36.

Yossele: Damn well better be.

Abracha: Iona, where do you think you are?

Raissa: *(spitting)* He's praying.

Abracha: To a shit god.

Yossele: Pray tearing down these wires, at least that would help.

> *Iona helps them, holding the doll and never ceasing to pray. THEY don't see Christopher watching them from behind. Grol sits and watches them; neither can he see Christopher.*

Abracha: Pray and I'll break your face, you hear me?

> *Furiously, THEY tear down the barbed wire, wounding themselves. Iona is crying like a child who has been chased for a long time. HE keeps trying to stop, but cannot.*

Grol: Stop, for God's sakes, it won't get you anywhere.

> *Iona mutters even more as HE tries to escape, Abracha cringes, Yossele and Raissa are like hyenas, ready to pounce.*

Grol: *(he suddenly gets up)* Come, children. I'll drive you to the forest. (*The Children don't move.*) I'm a soldier, it's true . . . I set fire to this ghetto, it's true . . . I played dead in order to catch you, that's true, too, but for God's sake, come quickly!

> *The Children huddle together, keeping their distance from Grol. Christopher appears, laughing.*

Christopher: Just as I thought. Like bugs, they always come out.

> *Beat. He whistles.*
> Frobbe!

> *We see the mouth of the truck. The Children, huddled close, move back, still keeping their distance from Grol. The Commandant returns.*

The Commandant: So there were some left.

Christopher: Four, Commandant, the last of them.

The Commandant: You've got a flair for this, Christopher. Have them join the others in the Rotburg valley.

> *The truck moves forward, driven by Frobbe and Grobbe. It is a huge, wire cage, full of straw, the kind of half-van, half-bus used to transport animals. Though it's a machine, there is something both human and bestial about its mouth. There's an elevated, windowed cab, from the inside of which one can observe the interior of the truck proper.*

THE COMMANDANT: And so, children, you're going to join your parents. Hop in. There's meat in this truck, you're going to eat. *(THEY don't obey.)* Get in. *(Beat)* Get in. *(HE hits them with his stick)* Ladies first, be gallant, good sirs. *(HE hits them again with his stick)* Get in. Get in.

    GROL: *a flash. HE wants to climb in behind the children, without saying a word.*

THE COMMANDANT: Don't bother, Grol, such a light load!

CHRISTOPHER: If Sergeant Grol had had his way, Commandant, these rats would have gotten away.

THE COMMANDANT: You've never been to the Rotburg valley, Grol? To the Valley of Bones? *(GROL doesn't answer)* I should have you shot on the spot? *(GROL doesn't answer)* Then take your place next to the driver, Sergeant Grol. You'll be less chilly there. *(GROL still doesn't answer)* Special treatment, you know what that is? *(Beat)* Sergeant Grol, do you persist?

GROL: I'm no longer Sergeant Grol.

    HE pushes THE COMMANDANT aside and gets into the truck.

THE COMMANDANT: *(to CHRISTOPHER)* Consider him as one of the inferior race.

    THE COMMANDANT moves away.

CHRISTOPHER: How long, Frobbe, for this last trip?

FROBBE: Should be about an hour, Lieutenant, but with this fog . . .

CHRISTOPHER: *(shaking off his fatigue)* Let's go.

THE TRUCK IN THE FOG

    The truck starts. The noises of the fire soften, are replaced by those of the motor.

GROBBE: It's the first time, Lieutenant, we're making a trip for just four.

CHRISTOPHER: Five.

GROBBE: It's not many, Lieutenant, four or five.

CHRISTOPHER: But they're the most important. The last ones.

GROBBE: The fog's getting worse, Lieutenant, we're not finished yet.

CHRISTOPHER: We got 'em, we'll finish.

    In the back of the truck, THE CHILDREN huddle together in a block, facing GROL.

ABRACHA: So, it's sure, they're going to kill us?

GROL: Yes. *(Beat)* Me too.

YOSSELE: We'd rather be alone.

GROL: I know.

YOSSELE: So why don't you leave?

GROL: People say I'm a little crazy, I don't know.

YOSSELE: Leave, go up front.

    GROL doesn't move. Beat.

IONA: *(as though possessed by the doll)* May TAMAR sit down?

RAISSA: Yes, she may. Here, you may.

ABRACHA: *(to TAMAR)* And you may even make noise. Here, play with this.

    HE gives her one of GROL'S boots.

IONA: *(trembling)* She doesn't want to play.

RAISSA: She's caught her death again.

IONA: *(frightened)* No. I don't want that. Not that.

RAISSA: *(tough, to TAMAR)* Don't bother to make a fuss, there're no more sewers, no more hiding, and it isn't cold.

    IONA-TAMAR starts to cry

YOSSELE: *(to TAMAR)* Don't be dumb, I can't go running after doctors here.

RAISSA: She still caught her death.

YOSSELE: What did she say?

IONA: I don't know. She just vomited blood.

ABRACHA: It's nothing. It's 'cause she's scared of the flames.

IONA: That's not it, she hasn't seen them. I didn't want her to see that.

GROL: *(to IONA)* Don't tremble like that, I beg you, you're making me sick.

YOSSELE: Shit. He's sick.

    Barking laughter from the kids. Beat.

IONA: *(to TAMAR, like a lullaby)* Don't tremble, don't tremble, it's not really cold. Here, the cart won't take you away.

    Anguished, the children lean over TAMAR. RAISSA hums something, a lullabye without words. Slowly, GROL gets up, covers the doll with his overcoat, then returns to his place. Beat. Then suddenly:

RAISSA: *(giving him back his overcoat)* We don't want it.

Iona: We do, too.

Yossele: *(taking back the coat)* We didn't get her out of there so she'd . . .

Raissa: Bah! All she does is groan.

Grol: I know lots of stories.

Yossele: She doesn't believe stories anymore.

Grol: *(to the doll)* Once upon a time, there was a truck. Its name was Earth. It rolled toward the trenches. It's been a long time since the drivers stopped trying to stop it.

Iona-Tamar keeps crying, as hard as before

Yossele: She doesn't like that one.

Grol: Once upon a time, there were some children. They hid in the sewers. They had turned the hoses on them. They would climb out and the soldiers would capture, then kill them.

Yossele-Tamar: That's not a story.

Grol: *(still to the doll)* It's something you can believe.

Beat.

Raissa-Tamar: Something else.

Grol: *(to Raissa)* Once upon a time, there was a soldier. He would have wanted to lead them to the forest, but the children hadn't followed, he could have lied to them, but he didn't, the proof, he got in the back of the truck, they'll kill him in the Rotburg valley.

Yossele: That doesn't interest us.

Beat.

Grol: *(to the doll)* They've often thrown lots of people into lots of trucks, some in back, others in front. Some were killed, others killed them.

Yossele: And then?

Grol: *(to the doll)* I was among those who killed. I was so afraid of being killed myself.

Raissa: Shit. We're going to end up comforting him.

Barking laughter from the children.

Grol: *(to himself)* The soldier climbed into the truck, to his place. They didn't try to escape, you can't get away from the earth. But there are the stories, they told them to each other.

Yossele: *(sad, without aggression)* The real stories, you don't know.

GROL: *(putting on his boots)* Before the war, I didn't work, I didn't like anything, like the others, they told me I was stupid, from time to time I'd go away, so the children in my village called me Mister Fugue, I liked that name because it's true, I didn't much like all that earth, so I'd go away.

YOSSELE: Where?

GROL: To the city. I'd stare at the streets, I loved their lights. But the people made me sad! When I had money, I'd give it away to see them laugh. But they didn't laugh, ever, war broke out. I set fire to houses, I wounded people, I was happy, there were no longer any doors. And then we waited, fifty-six hours, I counted them, near the sewer for you to come out and we set this trap for you. So I saw you when you were still down there, as you are now (looking at TAMAR) especially her, she hurt like no one ever has, she'll hurt forever, it's as though we'd been family in I don't know which world, I recognized you, everything hurt and in my head I started everything all over again-from the earth's beginning, without soldiers, without people in pain.

Beat.

YOSSELE: You must be a little nuts, Mister Fugue, we'll take your shirt.

GROL smiles sweetly and awkwardly, morbidly, painfully good. HE tends to YOSSELE with awkward gestures. From now on, They'll call him Fugue, or Mister Fugue.

YOSSELE: Start with her, that's Raissa, my fiancée. We're not old, but since we're going to die, Iona will marry us. That's him, he knows all the prayers. He said the one for the dead while we took their clothes. That way, we weren't doing them any harm.

MISTER FUGUE: *(tending to RAISSA)* For me, Iona didn't say prayers.

YOSSELE: Who knew you were crazy. That's Tamar. She spent two years in a closet, won't sit or stand without asking permission. They hid her at a neighbor's house, that's why. And then the neighbors died. That's Abracha, he went searching for Tamar and her doll, and we took them with us. Abracha can worm his way into anyplace. He ran guns, papers, everything. That's how we kept from dying. Tamar, she couldn't. They covered her with old newspapers, they came with the cart, but Iona snatched her doll, and Tamar was on the shuttle again with us. And then, there was no one anymore to take what we were running, we left this sewer because we were too hungry.

Mister Fugue

MISTER FUGUE: That's right, there's meat . . . Christopher, the meat. We promised it to them.

Anguished, religious silence from the children.

CHRISTOPHER: Grobbe, feed the dogs.

GROBBE throws them a little meat through the bars. The children madly tear into it, devouring it, except for IONA.

IONA: Blessed Art Thou, Lord of the Worlds, thank you for this meat.

HE eats, the doll in his arms.

ABRACHA: *(mouth full)* Shit on prayers.

MISTER FUGUE: Right, and shit on the whole world. But not so fast, don't eat so fast.

THEY'VE finished their meat and are waiting for more. CHRISTOPHER pretends to throw them more, keeps it, then suddenly makes his throw. THE CHILDREN do as they did before. Beat.

YOSSELE: *(anguished)* Why aren't you eating?

MISTER FUGUE: I'm not hungry.

ABRACHA: It's no good. The meat's no good.

HE is taken with a fit of trembling.

YOSSELE: *(mouth full)* Sometimes, it's all night he shakes like that, then it's over.

Beat.

RAISSA: *(drying her mouth with her fingers)* How long until this valley?

MISTER FUGUE: The whole Earth.

RAISSA: He's crazy, this old geezer.

YOSSELE: Completely.

ABRACHA: *(still trembling)* If he had just a small ration of bread, he'd look like my grandfather, also a nut who prayed, was praying but they shoved him to the left and when they fired at him . . . and when they fired . . .

MISTER FUGUE: And when they fired at him?

ABRACHA: He died, what do you think?

Barking laughter from the children.

CHRISTOPHER: And here's dessert, some chocolate, ready?

IONA: My God, chocolate!

Raissa: *(almost smiling)* Of course, chocolate!

> Christopher, *without a word, throws the chocolate out of the truck. The Children press their faces to the wire grating.* Christopher *laughs.*

Mister Fugue: Stop this truck, stop it.

> Christopher *laughs harder.*

Mister Fugue: Stop it, or I'll . . .

> Fugue *lunges at* Christopher, *throwing himself against the bars.*

Yossele: Don't yell, Mister Fugue, with them, it doesn't do any good . . . we just ate.

Iona: But not the chocolate. *(He forgets about* Tamar*)*

Abracha: Blessed Art Thou, Lord of the Worlds, that you did not want us to eat chocolate . . . The prayer machine broken, Iona?

Iona: You're the one who broke it.

Abracha: It broke when my grandfather went to the left and instead of praying . . . or before, I don't know anymore. Or when they split my sister's kidneys with a hatchet, it gushed over everything, he's red all over, our merciful God, and I piss on him.

Mister Fugue: Abracha, you worry us. It was men who did all that, not God. Hey, I'm going to tell you the story of the crazy captain. He steered his boat into the cliffs, which wrecked it, then he said, "Goddamn those cliffs."

Abracha: I don't know what they are, cliffs.

Yossele: Me neither. We've never seen any.

Mister Fugue: Cliffs, well, they're hard to explain. They're hard things, the sea crashed into them. The sea never dies, neither do the cliffs. They get worn down a little, that's all. And in the morning, and at night, sea birds gather there. They have large feathers, warm and white, they come from far away, from a land that fell long ago, they have hoarse, broken voices, they tell love stories forgotten for millenia, they themselves don't understand them, then they take off, again alone.

Yossele: What good does that do?

Mister Fugue: None. It's marvellous, that's all.

Raissa: *(hurt)* You are really very stupid, Mister Fugue, you believe in things that are marvellous.

Mister Fugue

Mister Fugue: Of course!

Raissa: In this truck?

Mister Fugue: Where else?

Abracha: Love, they do it on the stairs, in front of everyone, before they die. I know, I stood guard.

Yossele: Or on the cobblestones, in the streets, as long as there are streets. We've done it too, but it's not funny.

Raissa: Tell them, tell your fairy tales.

Abracha: My brother, he wasn't married long, I often stood guard. But when they came, he didn't hesitate, he gave over his wife.

Barking laughter from all the kids except Iona; he's occupied again with Tamar.

Raissa: So, what about those love stories of your big white birds?

They laugh, even more savagely. Beat.

Mister Fugue: The great white birds come from another world where trucks don't exist, where children don't stand guard. They descend to earth at high tide, they cry with their strange, broken voices words of love from another world. They look at one another, and they recognize each other. Then they take to the air again, and disappear, for millenia.

Raissa: It's stupid, your story.

Yossele: Tell us about the sea instead. Boats.

Mister Fugue: The sea, she is a great lady, she, too, is slightly stupid. She seems to be sleeping, then strength takes hold of her, making her whirl, throwing her over black holes, boats pass, happy, tranquil, but strength leaves her, so now the sea, sick, eats the gathering blackness. She forgets everything, closes in on herself . . .

Yossele: That's not the sea.

Mister Fugue: Maybe, I never saw her.

Yossele: Me neither. But I know the sea, that's how you escape, and one day you see chimneys smoking, far away, that's the promised land guarded by soldiers, and guarded so well you can never get in. That's what the sea is, she smells of gunpowder and cannons, 'cause of the soldiers who have fired on her.

Iona: Even on God.

Yossele: Now God, he went crazy, he knocked around in the sea like a fish, in the air like a bird, nothing but barbed wire, he doesn't dare anymore to sit or stand, he steals passes, but he doesn't leave, he doesn't dare anymore to do anything. He's sick, our good God.

ABRACHA: There were some like that in the ghetto, and to finish with it, they slept in the snow, near the soldiers who were firing at them.

RAISSA: You remember the dancer—who—recited—psalms?

Barking laughter.

RAISSA: *(Miming)* The soldiers were hitting him and he was dancing, like this, he was old and thin, so thin you heard his bones creak. He closed his eyes, leaned his head like at shul when you pray, you know, like this, and he rocked, he jumped, and the soldiers were hitting him like madmen, they were red, they'd been drinking (ABRACHA *and* YOSSELE *mime the soldiers*) the more he hopped, the more they hit him. He recited psalms, the ones for the Day of Atonement Ani Kéli mále bouchá, I am a vase full of shit, and he drooled, I swear it, he drooled.

ABRACHA: And after that, he barked. Like this. *(HE barks)* They killed him anyway.

Laughter.

RAISSA: Your big white birds, they're not so funny.

ABRACHA: Even when he was barking, he didn't stop reciting psalms.

YOSSELE: "from the Red Sea to the charnel house / my tribe carried the star . . . / full of shit . . ."

Laughter.

ABRACHA: My grandfather, when they fired at him, he did it in his pants.

Laughter.

RAISSA: You don't know life, so you, you talk about birds, but birds, I'm gonna tell you, birds . . .

Crazed laughter.

YOSSELE: They came right into the street to eat our dead.

RAISSA: That's why we covered them with newspapers.

Laughter, in crescendo. Beat.

RAISSA: *(not laughing anymore)* Birds, that's how they were, Mister Fugue.

MISTER FUGUE: I didn't know. I was only a soldier.

RAISSA: So tell us about that.

MISTER FUGUE: I'm ashamed.

Yossele: He's ashamed!

Raissa: Ah shit.

> *Beat.*

Iona-Tamar: What's shame?

Mister Fugue: It's a black doll that eats your heart.

> *The truck stops suddenly.*

Yossele: Shit.

Abracha: Rotburg.

> *They press their faces to the wire grating.*

Christopher: *(who was dozing)* What is it, Frobbe?

Frobbe: I can't see, Lieutenant . . .

Yossele: Can't see anything.

Frobbe: It looks like a wounded animal, I'll go see.

Iona: Does it hurt to die?

Mister Fugue: Of course not.

Raissa: You're lying.

Mister Fugue: Just a little, Raissa.

Frobbe: It's a deer, Lieutenant. Run over.

Grobbe: Probably by the last convoy.

Christopher: The bastards.

Yossele: He's right, it doesn't hurt. What hurts is not having been grownups.

> *They keep standing, one against the other.*

Christopher: Let's go now.

Frobbe: There, Lieutenant,

Grobbe: Christ, it's cold.

Christopher: *(passing the canteen after taking a drink)* Drink some of this, it'll warm you up.

> *The truck starts up again. Its noise. This will not fade as the children dream again, will not disappear until they are totally absorbed in their game.*

Abracha: We're going again.

Yossele: The next time it stops, it'll be for good.

Sarah Kofman
(1934–1994)

Sarah Kofman was born in Paris on September 14, 1934. During the war, she suffered the trauma of her father's deportation (he died in Auschwitz) and the disruption of her family (her brothers and sisters were dispersed to the countryside for their protection). Sarah refused to be separated from her mother and they remained in Paris, hidden in the apartment of a non-Jewish friend, "Mémé," until the end of the war. After studying at the Sorbonne, Kofman wrote extensively on philosophical and psychoanalytic subjects. Her contributions to these fields were, however, not fully recognized until 1991 when, after twenty years of teaching at the University of Paris I, she became a professor and was awarded the title of Chevalier des Arts. Kofman committed suicide in Paris on October 15, 1994.

Freud and Nietzsche are the anchors of Kofman's multidisciplinary and polyvocal work. Freud provides her with an invaluable instrument for reading philosophical and literary texts. She analyzes and demystifies his approach in a number of her works. Kofman also wrote a great deal on Nietzsche.

Kelly Oliver has commented on her identification with the philosopher:

> Kofman seems to have identified with Nietzsche, perhaps with his suffering, perhaps with his dual genealogy. She wrote at least four volumes on his work. She committed suicide on the 150th anniversary of his birth. Like Nietzsche, she was sick most of her life, suffering from digestive problems from the time of her early childhood, and she lost her father when she was young. Might Kofman identify with what she calls Nietzsche's "fantastic genealogy"? Or perhaps her identification with Nietzsche and her philosophical fathers is her own fantastic genealogy, her own family romance, through which she attempts to give birth to herself.[1]

In "A Rhapsodic Supplement," the conclusion of the two volumes of *Explosion* (1992, 1993) devoted to Nietzsche's *Ecce Homo* and to his "madness," Kofman writes most revealingly of the symbiotic relationship, both fertilized and fertilizing, that binds her to Nietzsche; the strategic opposition Freud/Nietzsche that enables her to neutralize their authority as absolute *maîtres à penser* [intellectual masters]; the funerary ceremonial character that can be attributed to the explosion of *Ecce Homo;* her rejection, like Nietzsche's, of the ascetic ideal and of the will to nothingness; madness as final idleness. She also offers a rich and illuminating semantic commentary of *contre* [against], with the tension generated by readings of proximity, exchange, and comparison.

Autobiography was a third interest derived, she believed, through *routes obligées* [obligatory channels] from the earlier two. Works devoted to autobiography include *Autobiogriffures: Du Chat Murr d'Hoffman* [Autobiographical Sketches: On Hoffman's Tomcat Murr], leading through *Paroles suffoquées* (1987; *Smothered Words*) to Kofman's own lived experiences in *Rue Ordener, rue Labat* and the problem of anti-Semitism in *Le mépris des Juifs: Nietzsche, les Juifs, l'antisémitisme* in which she shows that Nietzsche was not an anti-Semite. Other works by Kofman deal with ideology, Auguste Comte, Kant, Rousseau, Derrida, Kierkegaard, Marx, Sartre, Hoffmann, Molière, Shakespeare, Blanchot, and Antelme. She had also published numerous interviews, which still await analysis and interpretation.

Kofman's point of departure is her position as a woman. She delves into the genesis of philosophical and psychoanalytical systems: the subjective factors that led to their development, Freud's theory as matricide, and the mutation of the hateful mother into the Dionysian mode of Nietzsche. She subtly analyzes the implicit metaphors unquestioned by philosophy and brilliantly examines the "analytic and philosophical novels" (those which Freud rewrote based on seminal texts by Empedocles, Hebbel, Jensen and Hoffman; those of Plato, Hegel, Kierkegaard and Nietzsche that, at their core, "have deeply to do" with Socrates). She kept a lively dialogue with Derrida, aspects of whose *Le Spectre de Marx* she anticipates in her book *Camera obscura*.[2] With Derrida, Jean-Luc Nancy, and Philippe Lacoue-Labarthe, she edited the series, *Philosophie en Effet*. In her writing, Kofman was consistently open to a plurality of perspectives, anti-dogmatic, deliberate in her use of quotations and fragmentation, and "rhapsodic" as she often said quoting Kant.

The following selection is an excerpt from *Rue Ordener, rue Labat,* her only literary text. The book seems to set Kofman's lucid and tacit implosion against the Nietzchean madness of *Explosion*. As pointed as *Explosion* is expansive, this autobiographical text soberly recounts the atrocity of the war which, to an extent unacknowledged by Kofman, constituted the secret core of her writing. In this episode, the child, resenting her mother whose determination to defend her Jewish way of life is, she believes, responsible for their misery and daily humiliation, she replaces her with "Mémé", a non-Jewish woman. Mémé does not need to hide and therefore ensures her simpler, happier existence. An evocation of Leonardo da Vinci's *Madonna and Child with St. Anne* and of Hitchcock's film *The Lady Vanishes* deepens, rather than elucidates, the mystery of the maternal "doubling" that appears to be connected with the later doubling of her father via a couple of philosophical fathers. A child with two mothers, she feels vaguely guilty at her preferences and her desertions, aspiring to a life of freedom and nevertheless relieved when her mother takes her back. Kofman in this text ventures far from the peaceful reading of the life and works of philosophers, tilting to the void of a lived text that was finally to be impenetrable, unlivable, and whose writing she could not long survive.

— **Sanda Golopentia**
Translated by Eva Martin Sartori

Notes

1. Kelly Oliver. "Sarah Kofman's Queasy Stomach and the Riddle of the Paternal Law." In *Enigmas: Essays on Sarah Kofman,* Penelope Deutscher and Kelly Oliver, eds. (Ithaca, NY: Cornell University Press, 1999), p. 183.
2. See Pierre Lamarche. "Schemata of Ideology: Camera Obscura and Specters of Marx." In *Enigmas: Essays on Sarah Kofman,* Penelope Deutscher and Kelly Oliver, eds., (Ithaca, NY: Cornell University Press, 1999), pp. 110–111.

Selected Works

L'enfance de l'art: Une interprétation de l'esthétique freudienne. Paris: Payot, 1970.
Nietzsche et la scène philosophique. Paris: U.G.É., 1979; Galilée, 1986.
L'énigme de la femme: La femme dans les textes de Freud. Paris: Galilée, 1980, 1983; Librairie générale française, 1994.
Le respect des femmes (Kant et Rousseau). Paris: Galilée, 1982.
Paroles suffoquées. Paris: Galilée, 1987.
Explosion I: De l'Ecce Homo de Nietzsche; II: Les enfants de Nietzsche. Paris: Galilée, 1992; 1993. ("La philosophie en effet").
Le mépris des Juifs: Nietzsche, les Juifs, l'antisémitisme. Paris: Galilée, 1994.
Rue Ordener, rue Labat. Paris: Galilée, 1994.
L'imposture de la beauté et autres textes. Paris: Galilée, 1995. ("La philosophie en effet").

Translations Into English

The Childhood of Art: An Interpretation of Freud's Aesthetics. Trans. Winifred Woodhull. New York: Columbia University Press, 1988.

Sarah Kofman

Camera Obscura: Of Ideology. Trans. Will Straw. London: Athlone Press, 1998.
The Enigma of Woman: Woman in Freud's Writings. Trans. Catherine Porter. Ithaca, NY: Cornell University Press, 1985.
Smothered Words. Trans. Madeleine Dobie. Chicago: Northwestern University Press, 1998.
Rue Ordener, Rue Labat. Trans. Ann Smock. Lincoln: University of Nebraska Press, 1996.

Secondary Works

Les Cahiers du Grif (nouvelle série), 3 (1997), numéro spécial "Sarah Kofman."
Penelope Deutscher and Kelly Oliver eds. *Enigmas: Essays on Sarah Kofman*. Ithaca, NY: Cornell University Press, 1999.

Rue Ordener, rue Labat

XVI

One Sunday evening we'd lingered longer than usual at L'Haÿ, our arms full of irises. We had just time to catch the last bus back to the Porte d' Italie, but we missed the last Métro.

We had to get home by foot. When we arrived at the Gobelins Métro station, I was completely exhausted, and we still had to get all the way to Marcadet-Poissonniers.

Mémé decided we'd stay overnight in a hotel. I was relieved and at the same time, without knowing why, extremely worried.

We slept in the same bed. Mémé got undressed behind a big mahogany screen, and I, curious, watched from the bed to catch sight of her when she emerged. Back on the Rue Labat, to the amazement and irritation of my mother, she routinely walked around the apartment in pajamas, her chest uncovered, and I was fascinated by her bare breasts.

I have no memory of that night in the hotel, save of that undressing scene behind the mahogany screen,

The next day we took the first Métro. My mother was waiting, sick with worry, certain we'd been arrested and obviously unable to inquire at the police station.

I had completely forgotten her. I was quite simply happy.

XVII

My mother suffered in silence: no news from my father, no means of visiting my brothers and sisters; no power to prevent Mémé from transforming me, detaching me from herself and from Judaism. I had, it seemed, buried the entire past: I started loving rare steak cooked in butter and parsley. I didn't think at all any more about my father, and I couldn't pronounce a single word in Yiddish despite the fact that I could still understand the language of my childhood perfectly. Now I even dreaded the end of the war!

One day, all the bells of Paris started to ring at once. The next day we went on foot all the way to the Champs-Elysées to see the parade. There was white bread again in the bakeries. No need anymore to sift bran flour or to buy things on the black market. Some women from the apartment building had their heads shaved, and it was quite a surprise to see a tenant who had

From: *Rue Ordener, Rue Labat*, Trans. Ann Smock (Lincoln: University of Nebraska Press, 1996), 55–66.

been collaborating only the day before sporting an armband of the Free French!

It was the liberation of Paris.

And of my mother. She was finally going to be able to leave the apartment, live again, get all her children back, perhaps see her husband again! She was finally free, but penniless and homeless. She would have had to sue to recover our apartment, which, after being sealed off, was taken over by a collaborationist doctor. And my mother had other things on her mind: first of all, to reclaim me from the woman who wanted to "steal" me on the pretext that my own mother had more than enough to handle with five other children and wasn't looking after my best interests—which were, according to Mémé, not to be raised by my own mother but rather to be brought up by Mémé herself.

My mother felt nothing any more but hate and contempt for the woman who'd saved our lives. Better to go live in a hotel than stay with her a second longer!

It tore me in two. Overnight I had to take leave of the woman I now loved more than my own mother. I had to share my mother's bed in a miserable hotel room on the Rue des Saules, where we warmed up our store-bought meals on a hotplate that burned butane gas. I refused to eat and spent my time crying until my mother consented to let me go back and see Mémé: "One hour a day," she decreed—just to get me accustomed to the separation—"but no more than that!" If I stayed away a minute too long, she would beat me with a strap. Strangely enough, she had thought to bring that strap with her the day we escaped through the window that gave onto the veranda. . . .

I was soon covered with bruises and began to detest my mother. Life at the hotel with her became intolerable. We went to stay for a while with one of her Jewish friends who lived very far from the Rue Labat. My mother was afraid to let me take the Métro alone, and she rescinded my right to see Mémé.

But I eluded her watchful eye and decided to go and to stay with Mémé, who wanted nothing more than to keep me! However, the law required that I return to my mother, and my mother knew it. So she brought a suit against Mémé. The hearing took place before an improvised Free French tribunal in the play yard of a school. Mémé was accused of having tried to "take advantage" of me and of having mistreated my mother. I didn't understand the expression "take advantage," but I was convinced that my mother was lying. I was outraged to see her falsely accuse the woman to whom we owed our lives and whom I loved so much! I in my turn accused my mother, showing the court my thighs covered with bruises, and I succeeded in making everyone feel sorry for me. The Jewish friend who had taken us in and who had heard the worst imaginable stories about what had happened on the Rue Labat was herself scandalized and promptly switched sides. She confirmed that my mother beat me with a strap.

The Free French tribunal decided to entrust me to Mémé.

A few moments later, Mémé and I are in a phone booth, in a little café on the Rue Marcadet. She is holding me by the hand and smiling, and she is calling her friend Paul, "We won. I'm keeping my little girl!"

Without understanding why, I feel a very strange uneasiness: neither triumphant nor completely happy nor altogether secure.

As I left the café my stomach was in a knot. I was afraid. I peered around me in the street as if I had just committed a crime—as if once again I were "wanted."

I was, in fact. On the fifth floor of the apartment building on the Rue Labat, my mother was waiting on the landing, accompanied by two men. They tore me violently from Mémé and carried me in their arms all the way down to the street. My mother hit me and shouted at me in Yiddish, "I am your mother! I am your mother! I don't care what the court decided, you belong to me!"

I struggled, cried, sobbed. Deep down, I was relieved.

XVIII

For the cover of my first book, *The Childhood of Art,* I chose a Leonardo da Vinci, the famous London cartoon of the *Madonna and Child with St. Anne.* Two women, the Virgin and Saint Anne, each with the same "blissful smile," bend side by side over the infant, Jesus, who is playing with Saint John the Baptist.

Freud: "The picture contains the synthesis of the history of Leonardo's childhood: its details are to be explained by reference to the most personal expressions in Leonardo's life. In his father's house he found not only his kind stepmother, Donna Albiera, but also his grandmother, his father's mother, Mona Lucia, who—so we will assume—was no less tender to him than grandmothers usually are. These circumstances might well suggest to him a picture representing childhood watched over by mother and grandmother. . . . Leonardo's childhood was remarkable in precisely the same way as this picture. He had had two mothers: first his true mother, Caterina, from whom he was torn away when he was between three and five, and then a young and tender stepmother, his father's wife, Donna Albiera. By his combining this fact about his childhood with the one mentioned above (the presence of his mother and grandmother) and by his condensing them into a composite unity, the design of his 'St. Anne' took shape for him. The maternal figure that is further away from the boy—the grandmother—corresponds to the earlier and true mother, Caterina, in its appearance and in its special relation to the boy. The artist seems to have used the blissful smile of St. Anne to disavow and to cloak the envy which the unfortunate woman felt when she was forced to give up her son to her better-born rival, as she had once given up his father as well. . . . When Leonardo was received into his grandfather's house before he had reached the age of five, his young stepmother, Albiera, must certainly have taken his mother's place where his feelings were concerned."

XIX

Hitchcock's film *The Lady Vanishes* is one of my favorites. I have seen it several times, and each time I am seized with the same visceral anguish when the nice little old lady, Miss Froy, seated in the train opposite the sleeping heroine (a young Englishwoman named Iris), vanishes. It is even worse when she is replaced by another woman who passes herself off as the first. And my agony is excruciating when Iris, having left her seat to look throughout the train for the lady who has vanished, returns to her compartment half-convinced by the pseudodoctor from Prague that the blow to the head she received before getting on the train has caused her to have hallucinations (according to the doctor, Miss Froy—the good little old lady—has never been on the train at all, and seated opposite Iris has always been this other woman who, in fact, has been put there in Miss Froy's place by the conspirators). The part that is always unbearable for me is to perceive, all of a sudden, instead of the good maternal face of the old lady (and everything in the film suggests that she represents the good mother: she calls the mountains at the little ski resort baby's bonnets; she always has extra food with her; when there is no longer enough to eat at the inn, she manages to get cheese for the other guests—especially the English ones; on the train she invites Iris to share her "special" tea in the restaurant car; she's concerned about Iris, advises her to sleep; she poses as a governess, a children's music teacher) the face of her replacement (who is wearing the clothes of the good lady, who is really a secret agent for the Intelligence Service and who is at this point in another compartment, bound and gagged by spies). It is a horribly hard, shifty face, and just as one is expecting to see the good lady's sweet, smiling one, there it is instead—menacing and false.

The bad breast in place of the good, the one utterly separate from the other, the one changing into the other.

Hélène Cixous
(1937–)

Widely regarded as one of the most influential French feminist theorists of the late twentieth century, Hélène Cixous has produced a body of work whose impact cuts across the disciplines of philosophy, psychoanalysis, linguistics, and literary studies. She has written numerous novels, essays, and plays whose intellectual and political project involves nothing less than finding new ways of thinking. Like other French feminist deconstructionists of her generation, she questions not only the social and gender hierarchy, but also the very conceptual premises underlying western culture itself. That is, she disputes the fundamental beliefs that there is only one mode of thought, the logical; that every word or thing has a single, transparent meaning; and that the human subject is a fixed, coherent entity who can grasp all that is knowable.

Instead, Cixous argues that intellectual authority and human mastery are myths that have come to dominate by excluding any values and practices that questioned them. Ways of thinking that lie outside the norm have been viewed as different, as unassimilable, as "other" and have therefore been rejected. But Cixous takes her critique of western philosophy further by sexualizing it: She draws on both Simone de Beauvoir's tenet that woman is "other" in relation to man *(The Second Sex)* and the French psychoanalytic notion that what the psyche represses is "the feminine." Thus, "real" women (social and historical beings) and the abstract "feminine" (the irrational, ambiguous, and unknown) have been the victims of this destructive power dynamic that supports the dominant or "masculine" order, a system Cixous calls "the Law of the Father." In place of this violent relation between self and other, masculine and feminine, men and women, Cixous calls for a new one that affirms life rather than death. It is within this overarching problem of "otherness" that Cixous's connection to Jewish and female identity must be situated.

Cixous was born in Algeria to parents representing two different Jewish diasporas: her mother's German family displaced by conflicts in Europe, and her father's family descended from North African survivors of the Spanish expulsion. These multiple Jewish affiliations were further complicated by the fluctuating position of Algerian Jews with respect to French nationality. Granted automatic French citizenship, like all Algerians, by virtue of the 1870 Crémieux Decree, the Jews were stripped of it in 1940 by the Vichy government. It was not until the Cixous family immigrated to France in 1955 that their French nationality was reinstated.

In addition to these historical dispersions that undermined her sense of Jewish belonging, French colonial rule of Algeria and the war for independence also tangled Cixous's identities. Most Muslim Algerians saw the highly assimilated Jews as allied with the colonizer. Anti-Semitic incidents, which had generally been the work of European settlers, were increasingly associated with North African nationalist movements. Cixous was therefore both oppressor and oppressed; she was at once French, Algerian, and neither. Given these shifts in the Jews' status, Cixous rejects the notion of a fixed, predetermined Jewish identity. She also, until recently, attributed no particular importance to her own Jewishness. In this sense, Cixous has viewed being Jewish as a philosophical, rather than a religious or ethnic question. Just as she sees "woman" as the "other" who has been repressed, both conceptually and materially, in the masculine order, so too "Jew" as idea and as reality has been subjected to violence.

Yet, despite her earlier inattention to her own biography, Cixous acknowledged, even back in the 1970s, the traces left on her "Jewish unconscious" by the anti-Semitism she experienced as a child.[1] The anxiety and guilt aroused by her childhood encounter with hatred have continued to haunt her characters, whose inner struggles reflect the alienation women and Jews have experienced. Moreover, she points to the importance given to books and words in Jewish tradition as having shaped her allegiance to writing, the only "native country" she now recognizes.[2]

The two texts below span Cixous's career. The poetic essay *"Sorties"* ("Exits," in *Newly Born Woman,* 1986), appeared in 1975, the heyday of new French feminists and their radical critique of "the Law of the Father" and all patriarchal systems. *Bare Feet,* a short work of fiction, is more apparently autobiographical, part of a recent trend among French Jewish intellectuals to explore identity labels. The two works represent Cixous's overall shift from theoretical, atemporal analysis to personal narratives more anchored in historical events. Neither explicitly treats Jewish themes, but both condemn the encroachment of power on Jews' and women's bodies and minds, and both push for freedom from physical and conceptual constraints. Further, in a spin on Jewish nomadism, both texts insist on the "journey" of Jewish or female protagonists who confront their fears and desires as their stories unfold. Finally, through wordplay, both question the dominant language that has silenced Jews and women in the past.

The invented word "Jewoman" (in the *"Sorties"* excerpt, "The Dawn of Phallocentrism") melds the two incomplete labels, "Jew" and "woman," suggesting the damage done historically to both groups; it also evokes Cixous's refusal of stable identity categories. Using the Jewish hero in Kafka's parable "Before the Law" to illustrate the exclusion all "others" have experienced,

Cixous shows how he is further alienated by his ignorance of his own ability to act. By internalizing the lie that he is "nothing"—as the paternal "Law" deems him—he makes this fiction real and ultimately dies. For Cixous—a non-believer—God, too, is a paternal fiction whose power rests on the suppression of female authority. She exhorts Jews and women to expose these illusions, in order to free themselves from their devastating effects.

Bare Feet uses allegory to evoke the contradictions of Cixous's childhood as a Jew in Algeria. Her fractured world—Jews/Muslims; natives/French; city/country; women/men—is further unsettled by the story's fragmented time and space. In the first part, a little girl wanders up a sacred mountain near Oran and connects with the dead, symbol of her origins. Deciphering ancient signs, she, along with the adult author, unites with her roots: the mother, the Bible, the land. But, in keeping with Cixous's refusal of narrative closure, the girl's quest is incomplete, undermined by both war and colonialism. Set in 1941, it presents a drama of persecution in which a middle-class Jewish girl and a poor Arab shoeshine boy act out a dynamic of hate and desire. The girl's pain and confusion are interwoven with the adult author's understanding of the violent cultural script being performed. This early wound—"blood on my soul for eternity"—rends the girl's sense of self. As the first passage suggests, she reconstitutes her Jewishness by forging familial ties of suffering and survival.

In almost all her works, Cixous both announces and subverts her Jewishness and her femaleness. At once rooted and unrooted, she embraces this freedom as a way to reconceive human differences and to reinvent relationships through her writing. Ironically, Cixous's profoundly ethical commitment to life-giving connections resonates with the Jewish heritage she believed she had left behind when she moved from Algeria to France and embraced revolutionary feminist thought.[3]

— **Elissa Gelfand**

Notes

1. "Avee Hélène Cixous: Etre femme-juive." *Nouveaux Cahiers* 46 (1976): 94.
2. *Hélène Cixous; Rootprints: Memory and Life Writing*. Trans. Eric Prenowitz (New York: Routledge, 1997), 204.
3. *Ibid.*

Hélène Cixous

Selected Works

Tombe. Paris: Seuil, 1973.
La Jeune née (with Catherine Clément). Paris: Union Générale d'Editions, 1975.
Photos de Racines (with Mireille Calle-Gruber). Paris: Éditions des femmes, 1994.
La Fiancée juive, De la tentation. Paris: Éditions des femmes, 1995.
"Pieds nus." In *Une enfance algérienne*. Leïla Sebbar, ed. Paris: Gallimard, 1997: pp. 53–63.

Translations Into English

The Newly Born Woman (with Catherine Clément). Trans. Betsy Wing. Minneapolis: University of Minnesota Press, 1986.
Inside. Trans. Carol Barko. New York: Schocken Books, 1986.
The Book of Promethea. Trans. Betsy Wing. Lincoln: University of Nebraska Press, 1991.
The Hélène Cixous Reader. Susan Sellers, ed. New York: Routledge, 1994.
The Terrible but Unfinished Story of Norodom Sihanouk, King of Cambodia. Trans. Julie Flower MacCannell, Judith Pike, and Lollie Groth. Lincoln: University of Nebraska Press, 1994.
Three Steps on the Ladder of Writing. Trans. Sarah Cornell and Susan Sellers. New York: Columbia University Press, 1993.
Hélène Cixous, Rootprints: Memory and Life Writing. Susan Sellers, ed. Trans. Eric Prenowitz. London, New York: Routledge, 1997.

Secondary Works

"Avec Hélène Cixous: Etre femme-juive" (with Jacqueline Sudaka). *Les Nouveaux Cahiers* 46 (1976): 92–95.
Verena Andermatt Conley. *Hélène Cixous: Writing the Feminine*. Lincoln: University of Nebraska Press, 1984.
Julia Dobson and Gill Rye, eds. *Revisiting the Scene of Writing: New Readings of Cixous*. Special Issue of *Paragraph: A Journal of Modern Critical Theory* 23:3 (November 2000).
Claudine Fisher. *La Cosmogonie d'Hélène Cixous*. Amsterdam: Rodopi, 1988.
Elaine Marks. "Juifemme." In her *Marrano as Metaphor: The Jewish Presence in French Writing*. New York: Columbia University Press, 1996: 143-153.
Morag Shiach. *Hélène Cixous: A Politics of Writing*. London: Routledge, 1991.

The Dawn of Phallocentrism

What is a father? "Fatherhood is a legal fiction," said Joyce. Paternity, which is a fiction, is fiction passing itself off as truth. Paternity is the lack of being which is called God. Men's cleverness was in passing themselves off as fathers and "repatriating" women's fruits as their own. A naming trick. Magic of absence. God is men's secret.

> Among the precepts of Mosaic religion is one that has more significance than is at first obvious. It is the prohibition against making an image of God, which means the compulsion to worship an invisible God. I surmise that in this point Moses surpassed the Aton religion in strictness. Perhaps he meant to be consistent; his God was to have neither a name nor a countenance. The prohibition was, perhaps, a fresh precaution against magic malpractices. If this prohibition was accepted, however, it was bound to exercise a profound influence. For it signified subordinating sense perception to an abstract idea; it was a triumph of spirituality over the senses; more precisely, an instinctual renunciation accompanied by its psychologically necessary consequences. (*Moses and Monotheism*[1])

Jewoman:
And in the same story, as Kafka told it,[2] the man from the country, the one-who-doesn't-know-but believes, comes before the law. A doorkeeper stands before the law. And the gullible man asks to go into the law. But even though the door opens, one doesn't go in. Maybe later. Nothing keeps the poor fellow from entering. Except everything: the doorkeeper, the way he looks, his black beard, the door, the fact of its being open; the fact that nothing keeps him from entering the law, except what the law is; except that it is what it is. And waiting.

> In the first years he curses his evil fate aloud; later, as he grows old, he only mutters to himself. He grows childish, and since in his prolonged watch he has learned to know even the fleas in the doorkeeper's fur collar, he begs the very fleas to help him and to persuade the doorkeeper to change his mind. Finally his eyes grow dim and he does not know whether the world is really darkening around him or whether his eyes are only deceiving him. But in the darkness he can

From: *The Newly Born Woman,* Betsy Wing, trans. (Minneapolis: University of Minnesota Press, 1986), pp. 100–104.

now perceive a radiance that streams immortally from the door of the Law. Now his life is drawing to a close. Before he dies, all that he has experienced during the whole time . . . condenses into one question, which he has never yet put to the doorkeeper. He beckons the doorkeeper, since he can no longer raise his stiffening body. The doorkeeper has to bend far down to hear him, for the difference in size between them has increased very much to the man's disadvantage. "What do you want to know now? asks the doorkeeper, "you are insatiable." Everyone strives to attain the Law," answers the man, "how does it come about, then, that in all these years no one has come seeking admittance but me?" The doorkeeper perceives . . . that his hearing is failing, so he bellows in his ear: "No one but you could gain admittance through this door, since this door was intended only for you. Now I am going to shut it.[3]

And no one is there now to learn what the man devoted his whole life just to begin to think, no one to reap the discovery that could come about only at the price of a whole life, at the moment of death. There is never anyone there when what has never been not-open or open closes, the door, the threshold of the law. What is the law? The law where? who? whose?

But the Real has very clearly crystallized in the relationship of forces between the petitioner "outside-the-law" and the doorkeeper, the first in a series of representatives of the L—, the cop, the first level of a power with a thousand laws. "Outside" the law? What is inside the law"? Is there an "inside" to law? A place? A country maybe? A city, a kingdom? As long as he lived, that is what he believed.

Was he ever outside in relation to the desired inside that is reserved for every man—that place, that L—, which he believed was his good, his right, his "accessible" object. *Into* which he would enter and which he was going to enjoy.

So it is the L—that will have served as "life" for him, will have assigned him his place before the L—, permanently. Immobilized, shriveled. And no one will have been there to learn from the dying man, from the dead man, what he began to think maybe at the last second: that the law isn't within, it has no place, it has no place other than the gullible man's body that comes to rot in front of the door, which has always been in the L—, and the L—has only existed to the extent that it appears before what he doesn't see it is behind, around, before, *inside him* that it is nothing without him, that its apparently absolute power is inexhaustible, because like Moses's God, it doesn't exist; it is invisible; it doesn't have a place to take place; it doesn't have anything. It "is"

Dawn of Phallocentrism

hence it is only if he makes it; it is nothing more than the tremendous power of the invisible.

Exploited by thousands of its representatives—supposed-to-represent-it, who draw their dissuasive, repressive power, their calm and absolute violence from this nothing that is out of sight.

You will not pass. You will not see me. A woman is before the door of the law. And the bearded watchman—his beard so pointed, so threatening—warns her not to go through. Not to go, not to enjoy. And by looking toward, and looking in, and feeling herself looked at without knowing where the L—'s look is coming from, she gets it to come, she believes she sees a glimmer radiating, which is the little flame that the constant flow of her gaze keeps burning in emptiness, in nothing. But from always being looked at without seeing, she pales, she shrinks, she grows old, she is diminished, sees no more, lives no more. That is called "internalizing." She is full of this nothing that she imagines and that she pines for. Sublimation? Yes, but negative, turning the power—whose source she is without knowing it—back against herself. Her powerlessness, her paralysis, her feebleness? They are the measure of her power, her desire, her resistance, her blind confidence in their L—. Suppose she "entered"? Why not have taken this step? Not even the first step? Does she fear the other doors? Or does she have forebodings? Or is it the choice between two mockeries of life inscribing themselves in the nothingness that she embodies and that rivets her in the visible, on the lowest level, in relation to her nearest interlocutor: fleas in the doorkeeper's coat, a flea herself.

Or maybe there is an L— and it is the petrifying result of not-knowing reinforced by the power that produces it.

And they told her there was a place she had better not go. And this place is guarded by men. And a law emanates from this place with her body for its locus. They told her that inside her law was black, growing darker and darker. And a doorkeeper preached prudence to her, because beyond it was even worse.

And she doesn't enter her body; she is not going to confirm the worst, it is not even properly hers. She puts it in the hands of the doorkeeper.

So, the resounding blow of this same trick echoes between Jew and woman. In the tabernacle it is metamorphosed as a box full of nothing that no one would miss. The trick of the "omnipotent." The voice saying "I-am-who-I-say-I-am." My name is "the-one-who-is-where-you-aren't." What is a father? The one taken for father. The one recognized as the true one. "Truth," the essence of fatherhood, its force as law. The "chosen" father.

And one day—as Freud sees it still inscribing itself in the Oresteia—the matriarchy is done for, the sons stop being sons of mothers and become sons of fathers. The question of filiation swings, changes tack: What is a mother? And they no longer ask themselves which is more certain, but which is stronger?

On one side there is mother, belly, milk. The bond passing through flesh, blood, and milk, through the life debt. What is owed to her? A debate begins over sperm and milk: does she provide food only, or does she also provide a germ? Who begins?

How hard it all is for Orestes who is at a turning point in time and whose action, a matricide—until now the crime of crimes—marks the end of mothers and inaugurates the sublime era! How do you estimate the value of the mother's murder? What value does blood have? What is the value of words? In the struggle between Blood and Words, the marriage pact—a commitment made with word and will—is stronger, Apollo claims, than the blood-tie. The link to mother loosens. The link to word tightens. We are still in the age of the organic. From now on legality is to come to the assistance of the father's order. A new relationship between body and justice will have to be instituted.

Notes

1. Sigmund Freud, *Moses and Monotheism*. (New York: Knopf, 1939), 152.
2. *Vor dem Gesetz [Before the Law]*, in Kafka's *Parables and Paradoxes* (Schocken, 1975), is also the key to the end of *The Trial*, in which the riddle is revealed in an "interminable" explication. The necessity for K.'s death is inscribed within it.
3. *Ibid.*, pp. 63-64.

Bare Feet

Oran always was *The City,* the Absolute and sacred City, Ortus, the site of Signs where Alea, the God of my story's ventures, had left me to be born. Minuscule and scattered, I grew in front of its gigantic buildings, my neck stretched tiny twisted toward the heights, vigilant like a kitten among elephants. Immense, impassive, Oran would move around imperceptibly, its skin so dry that I would hear its wrinkles and its descending alleys rustle.

Oran was native: one could not not be born, not be birthed, from that white-hot summer's nest. The patient and modest basin made to give birth. The Mount of Venus was to me mysteriously called Santacrousse, sent across, they said it was "the mountain"; the family used to go there on Sundays as to a Roman mass, Saturnalia-style, treading on paths other generations had tracked, the tightly packed omelets made with potatoes; surely they descended from thousand-year-old omelets, and throughout the climb the predecessors' passages were repeated and one reconnected pleasantly with the dead. It was the Moors who slept informally all along the side of the mountain, barely covered with a grassy patch and a pretty, brightly colored mosaic on their head. We would walk between them, on them, we'd sit down with them, and it was good, this hospitable company; never again did I find that peaceful congeniality later on, that sharing of the earth, that acquiescence. Later on I encountered discontented cemeteries, strictly upright, austere, merciless, rushing to be separated, hirsute like soldiers entrenched behind their stony uniforms. Never again did I find my gentle Moorish friends who were dreaming smiling beneath their delicate and fresh masks. It was good to die an Oranian like I was born. And to find ourselves together the warm familiar mixture—centuries the dead the Moors children uphill climbers rising descending all in agreement as if united in one natural alliance, all we were doing was going on.

Continuing to enjoy climb sleep clamber toward the summit about which I only knew dozens of years after having left my generous Ortus that it was called Santa-Cruz and that it lifted its name and its sword on my mother's head.

I felt the dead loved me. I sensed it in the love of trust with which I inhaled the strong scents on the way up. Powerful feelings can be smelled: love, hate, the urgency to murder; first you receive them in the face, they strike, you open a door, you go in, and the bodies in the room emit their olfactory messages. They would give me time, all the time. No, I had not fallen out of the sky. My appearance had been prepared for a very very long time.

From: *An Algerian Childhood*. Marjolijn de Jager, trans. (St. Paul, MN: Ruminator Books, 2001) pp. 51–59.

Hélène Cixous

I clambered where they had clambered, I sweated where they had sweated, I put my bare feet down on the stones that had known their feet, I stepped where earlier steps had been made, and I went back all the way back to the family of the Creation, the steps hewn into the rock to the size of my earliest ancestors, I had to take three steps for one of their strides, I was limping and skipping in the authoritarian smell of the brush and the Barbary figs. The original scent: it weighed on my head like the hand of eternity. Sweet and pungent fragrance of thyme and resins. Climbing up to the Planters on Sundays when you are three years old always meant having five thousand years around you and starting them all over again. Oran had not broken with eternity. Clambering up I would take off my sandals and put my feet in the hands of the dead, and I'd caress the imprint of their feet with the soles of my own. They had been expecting me, I had come, I was the result of that geomancy, I never had any doubts about the ancient necessity of my birth. The pine trees were witnesses.

I lived at 54 rue Philippe and that was a whole different story. A narrow street smelling of urine, which led to the harbor, it seemed, by all sorts of innuendoes. It went downhill. I liked going up. If you followed it you'd end up at the nuns' school, but I didn't know that and don't remember it. Further along it dropped into the navy district. I imagined the world of sailors and the big-bodied ships that would go off, strangers that they were. Sometimes, from the grasping sea, charming small human figures would surge up beneath a beret with red pompoms, messengers of distances. They'd surface suddenly at the top of the rue Philippe, and as they emerged from the neck they'd collide with the layer of dense sun. Like flowers on their stems you'd see some of them drop off on the Placedarmes. They'd go to my aunt's, who ran a tobacco shop at the corner of the Placedarmes and the rue du Cercle-Militaire. It was Ali Baba's place and its front bore the name: "In Two Worlds." Thus the shop, and me with it, was dedicated to a universe of two worlds. But I never clearly knew, neither explicitly nor implicitly, which two worlds those were. The world was two. All worlds were two, and there always were two to begin with. There were so many double-worlds.

(One day, I shall tell about the sailors. It was through them that I later became naturally linked with Jean Genet. Sailors were one of the species characteristic of the rue Philippe. They were French, foreign visitors, elegant nomads who would call at my aunt's to stock up on marvelously refined objects: braid with which they'd decorate their suits, and pink glazed postcards, dragées for the eye. For the sailors were engaged and sent their French fiancées pink hearts shaped like Mickey Mouse ears. The word *fiancé* united everything that was sweet and salty between the wars.)

The natives of the rue Philippe were different from the pretty pink-and-blue sailors in every aspect. Having come out of the grottoes and caverns, they slowly went up (while the sailors emerged like bubbles), not yet separated from the earth and the pavement, water carriers, laden with their goatskin containers. The sea petals would be gone with the wind. But the water carriers were the former gods with two bodies, one a man's and one a goat's, without which the City could not have lived; they gave us to drink since biblical times, and heavy tired condemned calm heralds of fresh water; they announced themselves in the dark street by their name wearily ejected in French: "Water carrier." Devoted to goodness by definition. Passersby would stop them to buy a bowl of fresh water. (One day I will also tell about water, need, thirst, the verb to *quench,* the country that was the source of sources and was not called Algeria.) Wanting a bowl of fresh water. Water flowing from the goatskin in a promising spurt. Water a promise and an achievement. Wanting water, do you remember? The taste of the tasteless, the pure taste of fresh water, the sweet tasteless taste of purity, the taste of purity's fresh water, you remember.

In the rue Philippe, a narrow bed in which human waters and urine mixed, molecular flows. Oran's body composed of Arab, Spaniard, Jew, Catholic, military, and French, was not free. No matter how I loved it. It was a political body, swollen, limbs inflamed, a monster people, mouths gasping tongues laden with gobs of saliva ready to be spit in each others faces, puffy knees, throats thick with afterthoughts, strangers to themselves, foreign, furious. Joy stayed up on the mountain. It stank below, and this hatred couldn't be ignored, this flagrance that would burst loose between all double-worlds.

The century's entire history had already been written, the date on walls, squares, in staircases was 2000, but the inhabitants didn't want to read it, they said they were in 1940.

It was in 1941 that my father was no longer a doctor or a soldier or a Frenchman or anything at all. That we were pariahs consoled me in an obscure way, like true beings, like barefoot beings on the path of the Planters among the tombs. In order to survive, my father became a pedicure. I don't know why Vichy, which had taken the care of bodies away from him, still left him the care of corns. He had his office in a clockmaker's cubicle not much larger than a clock located next to the Two Worlds. Finally we had come out right: we were no longer part of the oppressors. It seemed to me that New Time was opening before me. I knew the peace of the poor and the exultation of the outlaw. Without a homeland, without a ghastly heritage, with a chicken on the balcony, we were unbelievably happy, like savages absolved from sin.

One day a pair of white sandals appeared in the house. It was a lady from the rue des Jardins whose daughter wouldn't wear them; they were completely new. I leapt up.

There I was in the rue Philippe, my feet dazzling as if I had a laurel wreath wrapped around my forehead, as if I had gained a rooster's spurs and two crests. There I was, a queen, an emperor, there I was, poisoned. With that intoxicated step I was going to show my glory to my father chained to the neighboring clock. For, as all narratives tell us, for triumph to be triumphant it must be reflected in the light green eyes of the father; I hadn't read the narratives, but I was already caught in their jaws. I rushed from sin to sin, avid, in love, oh my feet my sandals my beauty.

That was when, and I heard it as such, the dry and ominous gavel sound of the Supreme Judge resounded in the middle of the rue Philippe. Little shoeshine boys (to put it in one word) do not send their cry up to the windows like water carriers. They wouldn't shout, they wouldn't call. They tapped. They hit the tops of their brushes against their boxes with short dry taps. The box would give a stubborn, imperative sound. Because it addressed itself to feet covered in shoes as sloppy and silly as sheep. The box would bark: here! And the shoe obeyed, nose to the ground. Come here! Lie down! Stop! Here! The order snared me. I was struck with compliance. But why? Because without wanting to I had read the whole Book written in advance on the walls, and never again would I be able to act as if I didn't know what had to happen and what would happen. And I wasn't the only one. The small boy who played the role of the shoeshine boy in this children's play, and I was not yet five and he was not yet seven years old, was already rehearsing the role he was to play when they would present the End of the Two Worlds. I knew. But I was too young to believe that a child of five could have read the whole Book and I didn't dare believe myself.

Suddenly I was a grown woman and I hurried to hide that enormous impropriety even to my own eyes. I resolutely pretended to be the little girl I had been ordered to be. Again the feeling of shame that accompanies our lies invaded me. And it is that shame that is the sign of our childhood. For children painfully force themselves to imitate "the child" they never are, and, as they cannot manage this, they pretend and devote themselves to hiding their deception.

I saw the face of the phony little shoeshine boy, and I recognized the sparkle in his eyes: it was the lust of hatred, the first shimmer of desire.

Trembling, I put my foot on the box as a fierce blow of the brush ordered me to do. I confessed. I was guilty. Before his tribunal, the acquittal I had enjoyed since Vichy was of no value whatsoever. I lived in the rue Philippe on the second floor, and I had been given sandals that were almost entirely new. I confessed.

We knew everything. I could have fled. I wasn't able to flee. Had I been innocent I would have yelled, I would have fled. I could have condemned his hatred, unmasked the man who was pretending to be a six-year-old shoeshine boy. I could not accuse him without accusing myself. Where did it come from, my clear recognition of the sparkle? I was not innocent. I knew it. But how could I accuse a six-year-old child of wanting to commit murder? I accused myself of sheltering a similar thought. It was springtime in the rue Philippe, and I should strike the child on his knees on the pavement?

Full of anxiety but not surprised, I stayed, mute, because I couldn't ask him: why do you hate me?

What I didn't know was the form the blow would take.

Then the shoeshine boy took out one of his boxes of polish, opened it, rubbed his brush on the bright red cream, and smeared my white sandal with a greasy layer of thick blood. I was convulsed with horror. I was horribly wounded. Oh, no, not that! The red awakened rebellion in me.

Finally I could stand up for myself. As if my sandals had been made of flesh. And I wasn't going to let my other hand be cut off. Yet, I wasn't able to measure the enemy's range. In a clinch would it not be easy for him to mutilate me entirely in red? I chose a ploy. I acted like a child, refined. I told him that I had to go home and get money to pay him. I extricated myself from the trap and moved away with dignity, my foot red as a scream, blood on my soul for eternity.

Elisabeth Gille
(1937–1996)

Elisabeth Gille was born on March 20, 1937, the daughter of the novelist Irène Némirovsky and the banker Michel Epstein, both Russian-Jewish immigrants to France. In 1940, when some of their relatives sensed danger and left for the United States, Gille's parents, who did not feel threatened, chose to remain in France with their two daughters. In July 1942, her mother was arrested, sent to the transit camp at Pithiviers, and from there deported to Auschwitz. Her father was arrested three months later and also deported. Neither survived. Elisabeth and her sister escaped deportation and were hidden in various religious institutions until the end of the war. It was in these institutions that Elisabeth met Odile who was to be her great friend and to whom she later dedicated *Un Paysage de cendres* [A Country of Ashes]. At the end of the war, Elisabeth was adopted by her friend's parents and brought up with Odile.

Gille's entire career was in publishing. She worked as a translator and editor. She specialized in American literature and translated Peter Taylor, Mary Gordon, Alison Lurie, and J.G. Ballard among others. She also wrote three novels. The first, *Le Mirador* [The Watchtower] is an imaginary autobiography—"dreamed memories"—her mother might have written. Two years later, Gille published *Le Crabe sur la banquette arrière* [The Crab in the Back Seat], about the cancer that soon was to take her life.

"No, said Léa." This opening phrase of *Un paysage de cendres,* signifying refusal, rebellion, and the lack of resignation, is one of Gille's principal themes. It is an echo of her mother's novel, *David Golder,* published in 1929, which also opens with a "no." But above all it introduces Léa's cry of revolt against unhappiness and death that resonates throughout the novel. Léa Levy is five years old when, in the middle of the night, she is left in a religious boarding house by the Resistance fighter who had saved her from the Nazi roundup of Bordeaux Jews in which her parents had been picked up. That night, miserable at being separated from her parents, Léa fights to hold on to her doll and the pretty clothes the nuns insist she exchange for a gray uniform. Little by little, Léa is introduced to the world that will be hers until the end of the war, but which she never accepts. Whether she takes refuge in silence or explodes in rages, she rejects the discipline imposed by the nuns. She washes herself by completely taking off her clothes, a practice frowned on by the nuns; remains motionless during gym; and continually asks embarrassing questions about God during catechism class.

In this hostile environment, only Bénédicte, who is two years older, finds favor in the eyes of the young rebel. The two forge a bond that only death will sever some years later. Neither receives packages from her parents or news of her family throughout the war. To fill the void, the girls invent an imaginary life in which they continue to believe that their parents will return. But only Bénédicte's parents, who had been in the Resistance, do return to claim their daughter. After liberation, Léa is adopted by Bénédicte's family and, without the knowledge of her adoptive parents who want to protect her from the truth, she begins to gather information on the concentration camps that had swallowed her parents.

As she grows to adulthood, Léa explores the various aspects of her identity, linked to an exploration of what it means to be Jewish. Renamed Eliane Lelong, by the sisters in the boarding school to save her life during searches Léa still knows nothing about Jews. Asked if she is Jewish, she coldly answers that she is not.

Jean-Paul Sartre's *Reflections on the Jewish Question* provides her with the rationale for rejecting her Jewish identity. According to Sartre, a Jewish identity is conferred by others. Thus, an individual can decide not to be Jewish. "I have decided that I am not," she asserts. But later she discovers the work of Vladimir Jankelevitch, a Jewish philosopher of Russian origin and as uncompromising as she. Her doubts about her identity are suddenly removed: "He [Jankelevitch] was a Jew, as she was. Maybe it made sense. Maybe Sartre's explanation, which had seemed so satisfying and so clear, was inadequate. She read his work, she listened to him, and she observed him for months, with her usual mistrust. Was it possible to accept Jewishness freely without becoming a believer or a Zionist? Could one love others without forgetting or forgiving?"

The following selection shows Léa trying to find information about the atrocities committed during the war. In 1945, in secret, but helped by Bénédicte, she begins a frantic search—by listening to the radio "illegally," collecting newspaper photographs and articles, and sneaking into military tribunals —and discovers in the ashes an all too recent past.

— **Pauline Reychman**

Selected Works

Le Mirador, mémoires rêvés. Paris: Stock, 1992, 2000.
Un Paysage de cendres. Paris: Editions du Seuil, 1996.
Le Crabe sur la banquette arrière. Paris: Mercure de France, 1994.

Translation Into English

Shadows of a Childhood: A Novel of War and Friendship. Trans. Linda Coverdale. New York: New Press, 1998.

Shadows of a Childhood

They were wrong. Léa knew all about it. Or at least all she'd been able to learn since the end of the war. In August of 1945, in Saint-Palais, she'd begun listening to the radio, even though she had been forbidden to touch it. The Gaillacs slept late when they were on vacation. The years of boarding school and the nighttime air raids had trained the girls to sleep lightly and wake up early. At six-fifteen on the dot, they both opened their eyes. After a glance at her friend, Bénédicte would roll over and stick her head underneath her pillow. Léa would get up, put on her bathrobe and slippers, and steal down the creaky stairs, one hand on the railing, the other holding up the thick blue plush folds of her robe, which had been cut, like Bénédicte's, from an old blackout curtain. At that hour, the steps were visible in the faint glimmer filtering through the fanlight, but Léa knew her way so well that she could have found it in complete darkness even with both hands tucked in her pockets.

She would push open the pebbled-glass door to the little room, strictly off-limits to children, where the big radio sat in splendor. Léa was small enough to huddle in the space between the perpetually damp wall and the armrest of the battered brown couch of worn corduroy. Turning on the radio, she would glue her ear to one of the two speakers—its circular outline faintly discernible behind a screen of what looked like yellow raffia—and adjust the volume as low as possible. She solved the problem of the luminous screen, which might have given her away, by covering it with her handkerchief after setting the dial on the Programme National, which broadcast the first news of the day at half past six.

That was how she followed the trial that ended with a death sentence handed down to the old Maréchal, who was immediately pardoned. At eight years old, she didn't understand everything, but she noticed that although much was said about dealings with the enemy, treason, and the humiliation inflicted upon France, the fate of those referred to as "racial deportees" was never mentioned. It was the same for Laval's trial, which took place shortly afterward, in October, and which she again followed secretly in Bordeaux, listening at different times, depending on whether Bénédicte's parents were around or not, and when they got up in the morning and went to bed. It was quite late on the evening of the fifteenth, after they'd gone upstairs for the night, and only after she'd waited a long time in the dark before daring to sneak down for the last newscast, that Léa was able to savor a young reporter's laconic announcement: "At twelve thirty-nine, Laval paid the final penalty."

From: *Shadows of a Childhood*. Linda Coverdale, trans. (New York: The New Press, 1998), pp. 91–102.

That night, in a frenzy of joy, she stuck a chicken feather carefully saved from the previous Sunday's dinner into her hair and danced around the shadowy living room furniture like a Sioux Indian, muttering incantations.

This man, who had been revived after his attempted suicide and sent to the firing squad wearing a tricolor sash across his white vest, had still claimed only a few days earlier that foreign Jews—like Léa's parents—had been sacrificed to save French Israelites. The latter, however, had quickly been deprived of their nationality and turned back into ordinary Jews, complete with the yellow star. Jews? Israelites? Léa didn't know what those words meant and to tell the truth, she didn't care. Right after they'd left the boarding school, she'd told Bénédicte that she didn't believe in God, because there couldn't be an almighty God mean and stupid enough to create men simply in order to exterminate them. Bénédicte had accepted this reasoning without argument. Her parents weren't church-goers. For her as well, the catechism lessons, the endless Masses in the frigid chapel, the papery host placed on the tip of one's tongue and absolutely not to be chewed on pain of instant death (but the two girls had done it a hundred times, with pounding hearts at first, then as a routine provocation)—all that belonged to a sordid and unreal past.

Bénédicte covered for these sessions with the radio as she did for everything else. In Saint-Palais, when her parents would go off to the seaside café to enjoy once again their ritual cocktail hour, inviting the girls along for a lemonade, Bénédicte would accept while Léa declined, to no one's surprise, since she kept herself so stubbornly aloof. When it was time to go home and fix dinner, Bénédicte would frisk about, running on ahead of the grown-ups, dancing backward to rejoin them, then rushing off singing at the top of her lungs so that her parents would grow used to her antics, which allowed her to dash into the house ahead of them to warn her friend. In Bordeaux, keeping a lookout was easy because the apartment was empty all afternoon. Jean-Pierre Gaillac worked late, while his wife—who had become interested in the Communist Party when she joined the Resistance—was off at political meetings, and the cleaning woman only came in the mornings. No doors were locked, so Léa had complete access to the living room and its radio, which was newer than the one in Saint-Palais. When you raised its cover, you could see a record player and a picture of a dog, his ear cocked, listening to "His Master's Voice" on a phonograph.

One Monday at four o'clock in the afternoon during Christmas vacation in 1945, she discovered a program called "Bulletin Board for Prisoners and Deportees" that was rebroadcast at night and that she preferred to listen to later, half asleep in the darkness. For fifteen long minutes, an impassive voice would read lists of names into the silence, pausing lengthily after each sentence.

With your ear right up against the loudspeaker, you could even hear regular breathing and the rustle of pages being turned. "Paul Weil is looking for his wife Emma and their children Hélène, eleven, Max, ten, Françoise, seven, Albert, two, who left Drancy in November '42 . . . Elise and Jeanne Ackerman would like to meet anyone able to give them news of their parents, who disappeared in July and October '43 . . . André is searching for his comrade Jacques, who was being treated for dysentery in the infirmary after the liberation of Buchenwald . . ." During each pause, the names fluttered painfully away, like moths that could barely move their wings, and were sucked into an endless void. Léa let herself be swallowed up by this other world that had engulfed and drowned all those living, breathing people. She listened to this silence that would linger during the pauses, then shake itself as though flinging off raindrops when strains of chamber music signaled the end of the program. If Léa had been listening since the very first broadcast, would she have one day heard the anonymous voice say in that monotone, "Léa Levy, eight years old, is looking for her parents, last seen at the camp in Mérignac in November '42"? The Gaillacs might very well have taken such a step on their own. She never bothered to ask them such a useless question.

Léa got caught only once, in Saint-Palais, in September 1947, during the trial of Xavier Vallat, the first Minister of Jewish Affairs, which she was following with keen interest at a time when Bénédicte was in bed with the flu and unable to stand guard. When the grown-ups came into the living room unexpectedly, Léa barely had time to change stations. Blushing furiously, she admitted with downcast eyes that she sometimes gave in to temptation and listened in secret to her favorite radio series, *Sarn*, which was broadcast at that hour on another program relayed by a local transmitter. Rather relieved to find her taking an interest in something, and even to find that the ten-year-old had a tiny romantic streak, her guardians forgave her.

The year before, in fact, they'd been astonished when she returned silent and unmoved from her first real movie. For Bénédicte's eleventh birthday, her mother had taken the two girls to *Gone with the Wind*, the legendary film the French had been waiting impatiently to see. Before its official premiere, some American officers had held a few screenings for special guests in a private club in the city. Having already seen it herself at a previous showing, Madame Gaillac had dropped the girls off at the club and returned for them after the show, expecting enthusiastic chatter about Vivien Leigh's flirtatiousness, Clark Gable's dashing manner, and the dress of green velvet whipped up from a set of drapes. Sure enough, Bénédicte's eyes had been red, probably from weeping over Melanie's death. Léa had not been crying, however, and she hadn't said one word. Jacqueline Gaillac assumed Léa had been distressed by the scenes of war, by all the dead and wounded, and she reproached herself for having exposed the child to images that had perhaps brought back cruel memories.

But Léa hadn't seen any of the burning of Atlanta—although it had been much more spectacular, in technicolor, than the bombing raids on Bordeaux—because before the film, for the edification of these handpicked spectators, the Americans had shown a documentary on the camps. There was the Soviet Army, discovering the gas chambers and crematory ovens of Auschwitz in January 1945. Later, at Bergen-Belsen, a young English soldier, weeping and holding a handkerchief over his nose and mouth, drove the bulldozer that shoved thousands of emaciated corpses into a pit. The wasted bodies tumbled slowly over one another in postures like grotesque couplings. Flies clustered on the staring eyes, while dirt filled the gaping mouths. In the Little Camp at Buchenwald, the dead lay in jumbled heaps on the bunk beds inside the blocks. In Mauthausen, two detainees supported a third one, a bag of bones that would have collapsed like matchsticks without its envelope of skin. When the girls got home, Léa went straight to their room without even asking to be excused from dinner. Turning to face Bénédicte, who had run up after her, she slowly clawed scratches in her cheeks with her nails. Bénédicte tried to put her arms around her. Léa stiffened, then gently freed herself, and lying flat on her stomach, she slipped under her bed, where she stayed all night long. That evening, Bénédicte came close to admitting to her parents that her protégée's problems were beyond the therapeutic skills of her eleven years, but faithful to her promise, she did not. She made excuses for Léa, claiming she had been upset by the film, and babbled bravely all through the meal about Scarlett's run-ins with her corset and her black mammy.

From that day on, Léa's silence and her obsession grew steadily worse. Bénédicte did all she could to draw Léa out, but she felt so unnerved by the haunted look in her friend's eyes that she restrained her own natural gaiety when they were together. She tried to interest Léa in something besides that endless parade of tortured shadows her friend never stopped seeking in books, movies, newspapers, and radio programs. On Sundays, the two girls often went to the flea market on the Place Mériadeck, where one could find piles of old magazines and secondhand books among the chipped basins, rickety armchairs, and tarnished silver. Bénédicte would hunt for novels to supplement her parents' library at home. She became a voracious reader as she was growing up, and in a few years went from the sentimental stories of Hector Malot and *Little Lord Fauntleroy* to Alexander Dumas and Victor Hugo, then on to the Brontë sisters, whom she worshipped. Léa read constantly, too, out of friendship, through habit, but without love. Only one character earned her respect: the dark and brooding Heathcliff of *Wuthering Heights,* who came back as an adult to wreak suitable vengeance on the second Catherine. Léa ferreted out old copies of *Point de Vue, Objectif, Action, Le Magazine de France,* which had devoted special issues to Nazi crimes. She collected their yellowed pages and hid them beneath the drawer liners of the chest in the bedroom she shared with Bénédicte. Emaciated figures lay sprawled on gray blankets. Skeletons exploded in charnel houses set on fire with flamethrowers. Half-charred bodies were heaped up on funeral pyres. Acres of human hair, mountains of teeth, all mapped out in detail, waited in frozen expectation of an unimaginable fate. One day Léa came across an eyewitness account published in 1945, probably the first one written by a survivor of a women's concentration camp, and she practically forced it on Bénédicte. Thinking that she might better be able to help her suffering friend if she herself were to experience some of the same pain, Bénédicte agreed to read the book.

The author, a young woman of about twenty with a thoroughly French name, described with unsophisticated simplicity her activities in the Resistance, her detention in Fresnes, a prison outside Paris, and the sixteen months she spent in Ravensbrück. The two readers did not reach the same conclusion.

"It's positive proof," insisted Léa, "that everything they say is true. People were butchered like animals in these camps, starved, tortured, gassed, burned in crematory ovens. She wrote this three months after she came back. She couldn't have lied. And now everyone's forgetting. They don't want to hear about it. It's 1948, the war's only been over for three years, and even the Jews aren't thinking about anything but the creation of the state of Israel. They don't care at all about their people who disappeared. And the French care even less."

"The author cares," replied Bénédicte. "And she's not the only one. Remember those boys at the Lycée Montaigne, close to our boarding school—they were barely older than I am now. I'm thirteen. One of them was fifteen. They gave their lives for the Resistance. My parents risked theirs, too."

"Not for the Jews," hissed Léa furiously. "Oh no, not for the Jews."

She answered with such rage and conviction that Bénédicte was shaken. Sometimes she wondered how their friendship managed to survive this gap between them. They had such different outlooks on life! Bénédicte's parents often talked about politics, and from their discussions—in which she was free to join—their daughter concluded that every wrong could be righted, every evil easily challenged through reason and altruism. Weren't they themselves the proof of this? In June of 1940, they had immediately understood where the good of the nation lay and had acted accordingly. If all the French had done as they had and rallied to the side of General de Gaulle instead of backing the old Maréchal, the Boches would have quickly been chased from France, and Léa would never have been orphaned. To avoid such tragedies in the future, one had simply to be vigilant and prepared to sacrifice one's life, like those lycée students in Bordeaux and elsewhere. Bénédicte wouldn't hesitate to do so, if necessary. In the meantime, one could try to forget the war, and above all, be willing to like most people one has just met instead of instantly suspecting them, as Léa did, of Nazism or anti-Semitism. Yet though life and morality seemed clear and uncomplicated to Bénédicte, she could still understand that things weren't the same for Léa, who had lost everything because of a bunch of cowards and idiots. Besides, Léa was two years younger than she was, and while they received the same good grades in school, her friend wasn't yet capable of the same sound judgment. When Bénédicte turned her blue gaze upon Léa—a gaze that had the property of beautifying everyone it beheld—she saw once again the exhausted little ghost that had returned from Paris in May of '45, and she told herself that by loving her, she would some day be able to show her how wonderful life was.

But even Bénédicte didn't know that the paper lining their clothes drawers concealed more than newspaper articles about the Nuremberg trials or detailed reports of the medical experiments of Josef Mengele in Block 10 of the Stammlager at Auschwitz. Léa kept a much more personal account of her private vendettas. In her still-childish handwriting, she recorded in a series of spiral notebook—with an implacable precision achieved through marginal alterations, erasures, additions, strips of paper glued on in an almost Proustian abundance—all the cases of collaboration tried in Bordeaux since the end of the war, with their outcomes: acquittals, guilty verdicts, prison terms, and often, as the years went by, death sentences. In 1950, for her thirteenth birthday, she asked for a four-color ballpoint pen, which didn't seem like much of a present to the Gaillacs, but which Léa welcomed with a most unusual twinkle of joy in her eye, to the great pleasure of her astonished guardians. This pen made Léa's record-keeping much easier, because the colored pencils she'd been using until then didn't work very well with calligraphy. Now she was able to retrace in red ink the capital letters and exclamation points calling attention to the entry in the 1948 notebook announcing the conferring of the Legion of Honor on the Prefect of Constantine, the former Secretary General of the Prefecture of Gironde, Maurice Papon.

For a long time she had tried to find a way to attend these "purification" trials in person, out of a desire for revenge, first of all, and also because of something she'd heard while eavesdropping on Bénédicte's parents shortly after her arrival in Saint-Palais. From their conversation she'd learned why she hadn't been arrested with her father and mother, thus escaping the fate of the two hundred and twenty-six Jewish children shipped out of Bordeaux during the Occupation, almost all of whom were exterminated in Auschwitz-Birkenau.

This scene of her rescue, forgotten along with everything else and which she'd never managed to recall, was what she hoped to relive one day by recognizing her would-be captors among the handcuffed defendants in court. Then she would truly know everything, because if seeing them provoked the anticipated effect, she would make them talk, even if she had to wait until she was old enough to torture them herself.

But how could a little girl sneak into a military tribunal? The one in Bordeaux was on the Rue de Pessac, in a former barracks on the southern outskirts of the city, far from her apartment and her lycée. She cut classes several times to reconnoiter the area. Getting there turned out to be fairly easy: all she had to do was take the number 9 or 10 streetcar at the Barrière Saint-Médard and get off about ten minutes later at the Barrière de Pessac. It took her no more than half an hour, walking included. At first she didn't dare get too close, and stayed hidden behind a tree. Then, on her fourth or fifth visit, she saw a fat woman wearing a plaid coat and a headscarf rooting around nervously in her shopping basket for her papers, to show them to the guard on duty at the gate. Three little kids were clustered around her, and on impulse, Léa ran over to join them. The mother was too preoccupied to notice a thing, and when she finally found her papers, Léa trooped through the door in her wake.

That day she realized that being only twelve, and looking two years younger, was not so much a problem as a blessing. On her next visit, to make the most of this unexpected asset, she brought along her book satchel instead of leaving it in the shed where she met Bénédicte after school. And taking full advantage of the opportunities offered by a military tribunal sitting in judgment on civilians, she usually managed to slip inside with one family, then find another one to sit next to in the courtroom.

After a few weeks, afraid of being found out, she boldly staked everything on another, riskier ploy: she sat right down on the first step of the dais where the judges' table stood. It was a Thursday, but she'd kept on her blue-and-white checked school smock. She pulled a textbook and some paper from her satchel and began to suck thoughtfully on her pen. Unlike everyone else, she did not rise at the entrance of the magistrates, one of whom, the public prosecutor, almost tripped over her.

"What do you think you're doing?" he asked Léa in surprise.

"I'm the cloakroom lady's daughter," she replied. "Mama told me to wait in here. She doesn't want me wandering around out in the street or to be bored at home alone. And I have to do my homework someplace . . ."

"Well, don't stay here on this platform," said the embarrassed official. "Why don't you go sit down in that corner over there? You can do your homework on your lap."

Shadows of a Childhood

And so, as the years went by, the scrawny schoolgirl—to whom no one paid any attention as she grew into a skinny adolescent—became a fixture of the tribunal. Since Léa was careful to attend the sessions only at irregular intervals, no one questioned her identity or noticed that the cloakroom lady had been succeeded by a second one, and a third, while her supposed daughter was still around. The prosecutor who had unwittingly promoted her deception began by winking at her during his solemn entry into the courtroom and wound up patting her on the head as he left. One evening when he returned to get a file he had forgotten, he asked her nicely if she received good grades in school and whether all the noise and hubbub of the trials didn't make it hard for her to do her homework. When she had the nerve to whine in reply that she didn't understand math at all, he had her come up onto the dais, where he sat comfortably at the long table in the empty courtroom to explain a geometry problem to her. Seeing her chance, she walked out to the courtyard with him, holding his hand, so as to be noticed by the guard at the gate, who from then on let her come and go as she pleased and passed the word on to the other guards. The solicitude of the prominent personage who had elected himself her protector and even her private tutor put an absolute end to whatever doubts might have occurred to any subordinate officials.

Actually, Léa hardly touched her homework during the court sessions. It was the spiral notebooks that filled up, with names she thought no one would ever decipher, since she wrote them in the childish alphabet perfected years before with Bénédicte. To represent the guilty verdicts, she used a code inspired by a game her classmates played in a completely different spirit and setting: hangman. Unfortunately, the tiny figure dangling from his gallows was completed less and less frequently now. There was a procession of collaborators, profiteers, and informers, but the time was past when women's heads were shaved, and men with signs saying "Traitor" hanging around their necks were tied to the closest tree by an angry crowd and shot. Lawyers were appealing for mercy from the court, pointing out the defendant's age, his straitened circumstances, his family responsibilities, and they always managed to dig up some Resistance member he'd helped out or a Jew he'd tipped off the night of the roundup. The stiffest sentences commuted, amnesty laws were in the wind, and "purification" was no longer the order of the day. Léa drew in the left foot of a hanged man one last time on June 2, 1953, and she drew it in all the more gleefully because it marked a double execution. On that day, after three years of appeals, on the very site of the camp at Mérignac, a firing squad dispatched a man who had taken part in the atrocities of August 1944 and another who had worked for the Division of Jewish Affairs. After a moment's thought, she made the bodies green, the color of hope, and enclosed them in a black box.

Régine Robin
(1939–)

Born in France, Régine Robin immigrated to Canada after a brilliant academic career in her native country. She currently teaches in the sociology department at the University of Quebec in Montreal. Her work as a sociologist, a historian, a translator from the Yiddish, a literary critic, a novelist, and a linguist has been recognized by numerous awards.

In the 1930s, Régine Robin's parents, the Ajersztejns, immigrated to France from Kaluszyn, Poland. "They decided to choose the land of the Rights of Man, of the Commune, in spite of the Dreyfus Affair, the home of Victor Hugo and Anatole France," writes Robin.[1] Robin was three years old in July 1942, when the French police conducted the roundup of Jews known as *"la grande rafle."* Mother and daughter escaped. Her father, who had joined the French army, had been captured by the Germans and spent most of the war years as a prisoner of war while she, her mother, and her brother hid in various places. The immediate family survived the war, but her mother's entire family in Poland was murdered. Robin's sense of herself as the keeper of the history of the family's persecution before and during the Holocaust and as the heir of a particular political ideology informs all of her writings.

The day her mother held her hand over the child's mouth to prevent her from talking and revealing their hiding place during a roundup of the Jews, Robin began to question her French identity. An immigrant by proxy—although born in France, she imaginatively lived both her own and her parents' experience—the child Robin lived both inside and outside two cultures, the French culture of her school and the Yiddish culture of her parents. This sense of belonging to several cultures led her to create multiple selves and multiple histories. Never entirely certain of herself as French (language, her family's structure and customs were not those of her classmates), she later imagined a Polish self, with no documented history (all the documents have been destroyed) suffering the fate of a Polish girl her age: "I am a little alive and a little dead, dead somewhere in Central Europe and miraculously still living in Paris."[2]

Both the themes she addresses in her fiction and her literary techniques express the problematic quest for identity caused by fear, wandering, exile, and madness, and portray the various ways in which imagination and memory preserve us from oblivion. Because Robin subscribes to Jules Michelet's notion that only fiction can "make the silences of history speak" and because she believes that "fiction has more latitude to move sociograms, to integrate them, to make them play and work together without freezing them into stereotypes,"³ she refuses the nostalgia of "folklorization" and instead weaves her grief into original narratives. The mutability of identity and the turmoils of history are sources of linguistic and stylistic creativity for Robin.

Robin's fiction focuses on the community of idealistic Jews caught first in the maelstrom of the Russian Revolution and then in the Shoah. It is peopled with Communists and Socialists, those who remained loyal to Stalin and those who joined the opposition, those who joined the Bund, the Jewish Socialist party, and the trade unionists who fled McCarthyism. Stylistically, it is a hybrid of historical events, memories, fantasies, and nightmares told in a poetic discourse that wavers between anger, nostalgia, and tenderness. The subject matter and techniques are also evident in her language. Since she believes French to be too analytic, too logical a language to translate the particularity and peculiarity of her experience and that of her community, she has invented a compound language made up of French and Yiddish.

The excerpt that follows from *Le Naufrage du siècle* (1995) [The Shipwreck of the Century] is a meditation on what constitutes Jewish identity when language and culture have largely disappeared. Robin evokes the myths, tales, ideologies, and spaces that animated the small Polish town of Kaluszyn and interweaves them with her own quest for those psychological and cultural traces that remain. In so doing, she invites her readers to explore their own sense of Jewish identity.

— **Stella Behar**
Translated by Ralph Tarica and Suzanne Tarica

Notes

1. Régine Robin, *Le Cheval blanc de Lénine* (Bruxelles Complexes), p.78.
2. *Ibid.*, p. 25.
3. Régine Robin, *Le Naufrage du sicle* (Paris: Berg/Montreal: XYZ), p. 64.

Selected Works

Le Cheval blanc de Lénine ou l'histoire autre. Bruxelles: Complexes, 1979.
La Québécoite. Montreal: Quebec-Amerique, 1983.

Le Deuil de l'origine: une langue en trop, une langue en moins. Paris: Presses Universitaires de Vincennes, 1993.
Le Naufrage du Siècle, and *Le Cheval blanc de Lénine.* Paris: Berg International/Montreal: XYZ, 1995.
L'Immense fatigue des pierres. Biofictions. Montreal: XYZ, 1996.
Berlin Chantiers. Paris: Stock, 2001.
Le Golem de l'écriture. De l'autofiction au Cybersoi. Montreal: XYZ, 1998.
Berlin Chantiers. Paris: Stock, 2001.
"Vous! Vous êtes quoi vous au juste? Méditations autobiographiques autour de la judéité." *Etudes françaises,* 2001; 37(3): 111–125.
"Autofiction hypertextuelle." http://www.er.uqam.ca/nobel/r24136/

Translations Into English

The Wanderer. Trans. Phyllis Aronoff. Montreal: Alter Ego Editions, 1997.
"Gratok: Language of Life and Language of Death." Trans. Phyllis Aronoff, in *Metrix* 54: 26–31.
"Toward Fiction as Oblique Discourse." Trans. Marie-Rose Logan. 1980, *Yale French Studies* 59: 230–242. (Includes a translation of pages 138–150 of *Le Cheval blanc de Lénine*).

Secondary Works

Edmond Cros. "About Interdiscursiveness." Trans. Jerome Schwartz. *Sociocriticism* 1985 (July 1):15–29.
Simon Harel. "Montréal: Une 'Parole' abandonnée: Gérard Etienne and Régine Robin; Théorie et Littérature." In Benoît Melançon and Pierre Popovic, eds. *Montréal 1642–1992: Le Grand Passage.* Montreal: XYZ, 1994.
Lucie Lequin. "L'Epreuve de l'exil et la traversée des frontières: Des voix de femmes." *Quebec Studies,* 1992 (Spring–Summer) 14:31–39.
Anthony Purdy. "Shattered Voices: The Poetics of Exile in Quebec Literature." In David Bevan, ed. *Literature and Exile.* Amsterdam: Rodopi, 1990.
Susan Rubin Suleiman. "Reflections on Memory at the Millenium." *ACLA Bulletin,* 1999: ii–v.

Yiddishkeit

I am getting lost as to the purpose of this book. I ask myself what could have brought me here to give an account of a personal journey, whereas for months and months, I amassed notes from my readings, I created files, I went back over what people have agreed to call "the crisis in the social sciences." It was as though I were caught up in this crisis so deeply that it would not allow for an objective discourse, in the sense of reconstructing an object by taking some distance from it, in the sense that the only possible outcome would be the spectacle of a debate with myself, a discourse flowing back toward the speaker. It was as though my theoretical discourse, focusing around the manner of elaboration and no longer around what was being elaborated, had changed its nature. Covering its tracks, mixing genres, shaking off the affirmations of its conceptual certainties, my discourse could only be reborn in the form of fiction, of aphorism or, more modestly, in the form of an itinerary, a stroll. What is involved here is not a memoir—a normalized, categorized, institutionalized literary genre—but a work of memory.

An identity cannot be acquired like an identification card at a police station with two photos, a questionnaire to be filled out and fingerprints—although my last trip to the police station on the Rue Vauquelin in the Fifth Arrondissement did serve as one of the signposts that led me to Yiddishland. I had lost all my papers: a robbery in the subway. I had to replace everything: various entrance cards to libraries, my social security card and identification card. It took forever. So, at the police station I filled out a complicated form: father's name, place of birth, mother's maiden name, place of birth. I applied myself; I did it in a routine manner. The woman putting the file together that would finally let me have a new identification card called out rather sharply, "There's an item missing, your naturalization card."

I was dumbfounded. "But I was born French, I don't have a naturalization card."

"You're going to have to prove that because with that kind of name. . . ."

I shook, and then, being something of a rather loud talker, blurted out a remark that could only hurt, seeing that she was an older woman: "Tell me something, when Pétain was in power, what exactly were you doing?"

Such anecdotes are extremely banal. All Jews are familiar with, have experienced, this kind of vexation—this reminder of something that doesn't simply work automatically. How can you prove that you are French by birth? How do

From: *Le Naufrage du Siècle* (Paris: Berg International/Montreal: XYZ, 1995), pp. 126–138.

Yiddishkeit

you go about doing that when your name is Ajzersztejn? Yet it was in America that I discovered Yiddishland.

Montreal today does not look like the Montreal of Duddy Kravitz, but I like to wander aimlessly on "main" street, St.-Laurent Boulevard. At Schwarz's, you can still eat the best smoked meat in Canada, on bread with caraway seeds that takes me back to Kaluszyn with each mouthful. You can still find Warshaw's department store, falling into ruin: low decrepit houses, stores of every type, veritable Ali Baba caves smelling of oriental spices, where feta cheese sits next to enormous black olives, pistachios in great cloth sacks next to hot peppers. Further down you find thrift shops: surplus items, old clothes, a bit of Orchard Street in Montreal. Still further down, delicatessens with the fat-bellied pickles of my childhood. This was the neighborhood, near St. Urbain, where the Jews once settled. Now there are only traces left. They have moved to Snowdon and Saint-Luc, on the west side, abandoning the center to the Greeks, the Italians—the new immigrants. Bit by bit, the neighborhood is even losing its working-class look. Real estate speculation has gutted it. Artists and intellectuals have recolonized these streets, lined with neat little houses with their fire-escape ladders. They have repainted the outside walls in apple-green, lemon-yellow and bright purple. Antique shops and restaurants with a retro look, a trifle snobbish, have recently opened their doors. You have to seek out Yiddishkeit somewhere else—a trace of nostalgia for the period between the World Wars in this big city neighborhood.

But I feel like a stranger to Saint-Luc, with all its synagogues. My ties to the Jewish community were complicated. They came to Canada some time ago, and almost all of them are English-speaking (I'm speaking of the Central European Jews, of course). I found them all very reactionary—all Zionists, all pro-American, all hostile to Quebec independence, incapable of seeing that there could be a national problem in this "other place" that was also their home, all quick to see Fascism and anti-Semitism everywhere, in short not well inclined to welcome an ugly duckling. But all it took was an invitation to dinner, sitting over the *kneydlach,* for a conversation to strike up in Yiddish which, without eliminating any of the contradictions, made them bearable. The women had the same voice as my mother, and certain common expressions she used to repeat all the time would tug at my heart. These women insisted on the same things my mother did. You had to eat. Everything was connected to food. Like a supreme gift, the recipe for a cheesecake, for *leykekh* and strudel would be given as the sign of a solemn transmission that was supposed to assure the continuity of culinary traditions from one generation to the next.

What effect did Jewishness have on me? No great ideas or grand principles, abstract patterns, or doctrinaire questioning of things. No: rather, small details, untranslatable language and idioms, its words, expressions, ready-made sentences, proverbs, and popular sayings that, by themselves, condense the whole flavor of the wanderings of the diaspora, establishing a complicity, a recognition, a human chain, as soon as they are spoken. Yes, language and food, pushing us into a thousand daily gestures in the rediscovered shtetl, to a thousand shopping trips, a thousand concerns, to allow for difference to take place. We're the people who eat this food. Yiddishland is a country where people speak Yiddish and eat Yiddish, a country like no other.

I am at Ronce Alley, on my way home from school. The weather feels muggy. There is a smell of orange blossom in the air. In the center of the courtyard is our fig tree, an unreal fig tree that the Algerian on the ground floor used to try so hard to water, to maintain, to cherish—the fig tree with no figs, as we used to call it. At the entrance to the courtyard was a street singer with his accordion; we called him "the scrambler." My mother would wrap a few coins in newspaper and throw them down to him with an encouraging bravo. She loved street singers. Maybe they reminded her of the fiddlers of her youth? I can see her preparing my afternoon snack and talking with me about America, that land from where magic packages came for us right after the war. There were little sour candies with stars on the wrappers, chewing gum, powdered eggs, powdered milk and colorful pajamas from an aunt my mother had rediscovered by placing a little ad in the Yiddish newspaper of New York, *Vorwarts [Forward]*. "I am Fajga Sagalik. I am alone. My whole family in Poland was massacred. If any of my family have survived in America, or anybody from Kaluszyn could help me, here is my address." A little while later she received a letter from one of her relatives and we received our first candy. I, too, searched for survivors from Kaluszyn, as soon as I arrived. I had a few addresses, I telephoned, and Yiddish allowed for all kinds of miracles from people I had never seen, whom I did not know. I said in Yiddish: "I'm the daughter of Shmil Ajzersztejn from Kaluszyn." And at the end of the phone line I heard: "Where are you?" "What are you doing?" "Do you need anything?" "Come over to the house right away!" "Do you have a good winter coat and boots?" It was, once again, like the Jewish restaurant in Prague—as if I hadn't left home.

In Toronto, first there was the shoemaker's family. He had not emigrated, either to New York or Paris. Perhaps because he was too poor, or through inertia or lack of awareness, or because despite everything he kept hoping, he had remained in Kaluszyn. He was still there when the Germans arrived in town. During the big fire of Kaluszyn, the whole Jewish population sought refuge in the biggest of the churches. The shoemaker owed his survival to the Soviet trains that one could still take—for a few days or a few hours—to escape far, far away to Siberia. He did not see the war go by. His memories of the Siberian years were of hard labor, blue and white spaces, and birch bark. As he tells me his story, I feel that he is still tied to that distant land, his eyes shine when he remembers the birch forests, frozen rivers, and blue snow. One day, they were told that the war was over, that they could go back home. The journey back with his wife and children was long. Dressed more or less in rags, they crossed a starving, ravaged USSR; one of their daughters died of typhus in Tashkent.

They finally arrived in Kaluszyn. There was nothing left; it was like a smaller version of Warsaw in 1945. No one was there. This they learned from the Russians who had just liberated Auschwitz and from survivors that they met and questioned. Most of the time, the shoemaker said, the look in their eyes was enough. There was no question of remaining; they had to leave as soon as possible. Ask no questions, act as though they knew nothing, but leave—escape this nightmare. We've already covered thousands of kilometers, we'll cover the whole earth, if need be: the wandering Jew.

The only possible place from now on was Israel. And so they had a long adventure in a displaced persons camp in Germany and from there took the boat to an Israel at war. After the birth of the State of Israel, their odyssey was not over, for the shoemaker was hardheaded. He owed his survival to the USSR and he refused to be caught up in what soon became the cold war. Anti-Arab racism weighed on him. In short, he did not feel comfortable. For a moment, he even had the idea of going back to Poland. A socialist Poland could hardly resemble the old land of bigots, chauvinists, and anti-Semites; there would be room for all. And so, he began to dream of Warsaw.

It was at that moment that one of his daughters, married to a Canadian and living in Toronto, contacted him. Once again, there was a long sea voyage, a new country, new snowfalls. Until his recent death, he would daydream about his past, busying himself during the long Canadian winter with writing his epic, the snowy nights of Ontario taking his memory back to the Siberian nights of the 1940s.

He, his wife, and I spent a whole night talking about Kaluszyn. He read me fragments of the intimate diary he had kept for many long years. He would read in a tired, monotone voice that was well suited to this incredible story. Through the dull, matter-of-fact sound of his voice I could see Kaluszyn in flames, and a tragic song came back to my memory, a song I once learned at the Yiddish club, and that my mother had often sung.

> It's burning, brothers, it's burning
> It's our city, alas, that's burning.
> Cruel winds, winds of hate

Régine Robin

> Blow and rip with unleashed fury,
> The wild flames spread out
>
> And soon all about starts burning.
> And you, you stand there watching
> With your hands still,
> And you, you stand there watching
> our city burn down . . . [1]

You can read in the Encyclopedia Judaica:

> The Germans came into Kaluszyn on September 11, 1939, and almost the entire Jewish population was assembled in the main church where they remained for three days. A few hundred Jews got out of this situation and managed to reach Soviet territory. In March 1941, 1,000 Jews managed to reach Warsaw. In 1942, 4,000 Jews could be counted in Kaluszyn. On September 25, 1942, almost the entire population was deported to Treblinka. On September 28, a ghetto, or forced labor camp, was established for the few hundred Jews who had not been deported with the others. In November 1942, another group of Jews from Minsk Mazowiecki were deported to the Kaluszyn ghetto. They were all exterminated in December 1942 when the ghetto was liquidated.

And then there is this sentence like a knife: "The Jewish community was not reestablished after the war."

I looked for other families, people who could talk to me about my relatives and Kaluszyn. I spent long winter afternoons in Montreal where the sun sets at four o'clock, remembering the life of yesteryear; the figure of my great-grandfather who had heard his own grandfather tell about Napoleon's troops entering Warsaw and many other legends my mother still remembered, such as the one told by Mendel Mann in *Les plaines de Mazovie:*

> On a shopping trip to Kuchary, his mother had pointed out a hill to him saying that Napoleon had rested here during the Russian campaign. The hill still bears his name. Halfway up there was a hollow where a tent had been set up for him. He stayed there a long time,

Yiddishkeit

for he was awaiting Shulamit, a young Jewish girl. But the petite Jewish girl from Sochocin did not come. She never came to the imperial tent. He had noticed her while going to Sunday mass in Sochocin in his golden carriage. She was at her window braiding her hair. The next day, a courier brought her a letter on a golden tray. The great Emperor was inviting her to his tent. She set out. All the Jewish girls in town escorted her as far as the bridge. Then she continued on her way alone, along the river, undoing her braids. She never got to the tent.

"Why didn't she get there?"

"She threw herself in the river. Her body was never found. She drowned here at this very spot. Since then there's been an eddy here. Today, the ninth day of the month of Av, is the anniversary of her death. Look, son, do you see the water swirling? You'll see her unbraided hair floating. This is the day when her black braids come back up to the surface. There they are, you see them?"

Michel blinked his eyes and said: "I see her braids."

Napoleon did not leave the hill immediately. He waited seventeen days in sadness, for he was not an evil Prince who wanted to hurt people; he really loved her. When he arrived in Moscow, at the head of his great army, it was too late. The weather had already turned cold and it would not be long before the great freeze. He had to pull out of Russia. On his way back, he went by Sochocin a second time. His horse swam across the Dzialdowka at the very spot where Shulamit had drowned and everyone saw her undone braids floating behind the imperial mount. The Jews of Sochocin went out to meet the French Emperor, bringing him bread and salt, and they saw how sad he was. The Emperor gave them a velvet banner embroidered with silk of many colors, which the Jews made into a curtain that can still be found in the synagogue.[2]

I have a suspicion that Bonaparte left other velvet banners embroidered with silk of many colors here and there and everywhere and, particularly, at Kaluszyn. My great-grandfather's grandfather might have received one in his own hands. Yes, we spent many hours on winter afternoons in Montreal, where the sun goes down at four o'clock, recalling this stern old Jew who did not joke about traditions, whose only dream was about a land where oranges grew by themselves—his ancestors' land waiting to be reconquered. We recalled my grandfather's candy shop on Varshave Gass [Warsaw Street] and my father's barbershop, the clandestine meeting place for the city's Communist party. The drawers were stuffed with bars of soap and political flyers. His closets held red flags ready to be unfurled at the predetermined moment, and even a revolver. Then there was my paternal grandfather who made his own contraband vodka and who died after carrying a vat of boiling vodka that was too heavy during a sudden raid, at the end of the World War I.

Then there was Aunt Helli who didn't want her eldest son to get married. She invented some dark story about devils that came to her at night threatening to strangle her if her son got married. The times were not right for deviltries, so the family promptly exorcised her demons and my uncle got married. And there was my mother's house with the blooming rosebush and the open structures decorated with branches and apples that were set up in the courtyard for the festival of Sukkot. And there were all those organizations in the shtetl, so many we couldn't keep them straight! Before becoming a Communist, my mother had been a Bundist. Her older sister Ita was a Bundist, too; her brother Laibou Itshok a Communist. Hersh Dovid and Moshe were Zionists belonging to the Poale Zion organization. Srul, as a religious man, did not belong to any group. Rachmil was a paid-up member of Agudath Israel, a religious Zionist group if I am not mistaken. Yankel perhaps was a member of Hashomer Hatzair, a leftist Zionist group. All this in a single family. Dinner conversations must have been quite lively.

Through all these organizations, the libraries, the charitable and athletic associations, this rich network of civil society, the shtetl opened out onto the world, humming to the tune of international politics with its two strategic poles, the land of Israel and the Soviets, sometimes thought of as incompatible, sometimes reconciled in a tenacious dream. And there was this "Lumpen" unique to the shtetl, which in Kaluszyn was called the "commando knockabouts." These were gangs of delinquents, of dreamers, of the perpetually unemployed and marginalized, looking simultaneously like de Sica's "bicycle thief" and Charlie Chaplin's "kid."

We spent hours recalling that very special humor that Freud used so liberally in his *Witz*. Jewish humor, says Albert Memmi:

> expresses at the same time the cruelty of the Jewish condition and the vanity and never completed effort to tame that cruelty. Jewish humor is an attempt to correct Jewish fate, a compromise, a safety valve . . . Jewish humor—a confession of uneasiness, an attempt to lighten the burden of being Jewish, a plea for the defense addressed to others and to themselves, an ostentatious show against the world's hostility—is an attempt to make negativity livable.[3]

Yiddishkeit

They were inexhaustible when it came to fires. In Chelm, in the middle of the night, there's this fire. The whole town is outside, lamenting or forming a human chain. The rabbi runs over. He stops the symphony of lamentations. "Praised be the Eternal, our God! Don't you see that this fire is a blessing? It would have been so dark that we would never have been able to put out the fire."

They were inexhaustible when it came to death. There was once an old man who lived in the woods. He felt very lonely and very tired. He gathered wood, as much as he could, piece by piece. One winter day, he went out to gather a bundle. He stretched a cord out on the ground and covered it with branches. Then he tied up the bundle and tried to hoist it over his shoulders. But he had no strength left to lift it. So he cried out: "God, I can't go on. Send me death." He lifted up his eyes and saw the angel of death approaching: "You called me?"

"Yes," answered the old man, "I'd like you to help me carry my bundle." Suddenly, I became afraid. All this past was falling like a weight on top of my head. This whole cemetery scattered to the four corners of the world, all these voices from beyond the grave, this voyage to the end of the night which was my own. I became afraid of FOLKLORIZATION. How simple it would be to freeze what had once been life in the shtetl into a certain number of types. There's the rabbi who knows everything, wiser and more knowledgeable than everyone else; the *yenta,* that busybody sitting on her doorstep or at the market place who poisons all human relations with a few indiscreet remarks; the matchmaker who hopes to make a small commission by finding a fiancé for such and such, a not-so-young woman; the young man from Warsaw, an emancipated Jew who rarely returns to the shtetl, speaking only Polish and making fun of Yiddish; the militant Zionist on the right; the militant Zionist in the center; the Zionist on the left; the Communist, the Trotskyite, the anarchist; the Bundist; the pious Jew; the Jewish mother wielding her strangling love; the simple-minded; the merchant; the usurer, and the fiddler—a whole world that soon risks turning into caricature, ethnic type, and stereotype. Imagine the people of the shtetl as mechanical figures on a big merry-go-round, automatons moving with jerky motions in rhythm to old droning tunes. We could even add to this big merry-go-round the stage sets of Expressionist films: low houses, little public squares, curved lines, and broken lines all askew. They would all be in their respective places, in their respective roles. It would be a reassuring sight, defying the centuries. The merry-go-round goes round and round, each figure turns about itself, busy at something, following a set path. And suddenly the mechanical action comes to a stop, each of the figures remains frozen in a clumsy position, not anticipated by the initial mechanism.

The shtetl has become something like that—a merry-go-round ground to a halt. Yes, I am afraid of folklorization. Is Yiddishland the land of the dead? Will there only be room for folklore, a certain exoticism, a taste of something archaic, dilapidated, picturesque? People would come to feel sorry for the shtetls. People would study them, the way others look into the sorcerers of Rouergue (are there really sorcerers in Rouergue?) or the shepherds of the Landes. I recall that terrifying statement by Michel de Certeau: "It's when a culture no longer has the means to defend itself that the ethnologist or archeologist appears."[4] So make way for archeology. There is nothing left to study over there. The last Polish Jews, those rare survivors, those who haven't died of grief these last few years, are warming their behinds in the sun of Tel Aviv.

Is the only way to escape this folklorization to transform the tragic into the fantastic as in this haunting story by Sholem Asch?

> ... After hearing Chopin's funeral march, others of the common folk come out of their holes to salute the victorious armies making their entrance. These people had not appeared on the streets of Warsaw for a long time; yet, they had lived and grown up here, domestically and intimately, for centuries and centuries. This was the Jewish population that could not be eliminated nor separated from the life of Warsaw. The Jews did not come from Nalevki, Krochmalna, Twarda, and dozens of other streets in Warsaw where the Jews lived. They came out of someplace, gliding, they walk and they glide through the air. They can be observed, and yet they cannot be seen. They are here, they fill the empty streets of Warsaw, they come to meet the armies that penetrate the city, pour out of the nearby streets, arrive from Marszalkowska, from the old market, from the Franciscans Street and from Nalevki. All of them, all of them have come out to meet the army. Here, finally, come the ordinary folk, all kinds of people. The streets are like a vast sea filled with heads and hands. Look at these heads; some are wearing monks' caps, velvet caps, little flat headpieces or derby hats; others come bareheaded, modern people, vegetarians who believe in nature. Look, look, all of Warsaw is here. Men with Hasidic caps, like those that used to be worn at the train station in Vienna, are here to get a glimpse of the rabbi from Ger on his way to a spa; little hats and hatless heads. A vision of the Bund demonstrators on the First of May. From the porters of Krochmalna and Gzibovo with ropes over their shoulders, their mouths toothless from brawls and shouts ready on their lips: "I'll tear Hitler's guts out, I'll slit his veins open," to the pious, reserved Jew. The Hasid from Sochatchovo, his mouth

twisted under his great beard. He stands there, full of mercy, swaying as though he were in front of the Rebbe's house; they are all here. Abruptly, everything disappeared as if it had only been a dream. The groups vanished, the sea of heads faded away, as if they had never existed. The whole Jewish community rose up into the air leaving the earth free. Suddenly, pouring out of a little alley, there appeared a little group of people with torn clothing, hair disheveled, and barefoot; there were mothers with maddened faces, their eyes on fire, carrying sick children, there were young and old, some of whom had rifles strapped over their shoulders, their hair unkempt and beards wild. Through their ragged clothing could be seen bleeding flesh, their bare feet were bloody, wounded by the stones on the road; other people were wrapped in rags. The children who were dragging behind their parents looked like little dolls. All of them looked around with eyes filled with fear, as though worried that they would see someone approach them. They looked like people who had been unearthed, their arms trembling before marching armies. . . these are the last Jews of Warsaw.[5]

Yes, escape from this folklore and obsession with the past, this regressive nostalgia; let mourning finish its work. The shtetl no longer exists. The womb no longer exists. To evoke this people requires the fantastic, the dreamlike, the metaphoric. Images. Images that move like those thousands of shoes at Maidanek that, in a poem by Moishe Shulstein, begin suddenly to walk. Images strong enough, however, to try to reconstruct a puzzle—myself in pieces. No, an identity cannot be acquired like an identification card.

In America, however, I thought I could escape folklorization. I felt that one could be Jewish and speak Yiddish without falling into the worship of relics; without artificially maintaining what no longer exists. I felt that it might be possible to speak Yiddish somewhere else besides the shtetl, somewhere besides commemorative events, ceremonies of remembrance, museums, inaugurations, cemeteries, steles, monuments. I felt that we had to stop playing at Proust's madeleines when listening to a certain song, a certain phrase; that Yiddishland could be something other than the land of memory; that one could belong to a nation without being tied to a territory or being part of a state. An old problem, an old debate. Unavoidable. A new space, a kind of rainbow between the old world and the new, an imaginary, interior territory where Lenin's white horse can jump again.

—**Translated by Ralph Tarica and Suzanne Tarica**

Régine Robin

Notes

1. Poem by Mordechai Gebirtig, quoted in Charles Dubzynski, "Le Miroir d'un peuple." *Anthologie de la poésie yiddish,* Paris: Gallimard, 1971, pp. 80–81.
2. Mendel Mann. *Les plaines de Moscou,* Paris: Calmann-Lévy, 1966, pp. 37–38.
3. Albert Memmi. *La libération du Juif,* Paris: Gallimard, p. 46.
4. Michel de Certeau, quoted by M. Panoff in *Ethnologie: le deuxième souffle*. Paris: Payot, 1977, 165.
5. Sholem Asch, excerpted from *Le buisson ardent*. Translated into French by Claude Paris in *Domaines yiddish,* no. 1, 1958.

Michèle Sarde
(1939–)

Michèle Sarde was born Michèle Benrey to Sephardic Jewish parents in Brittany during the exodus from Paris. Like many such families from the Ottoman Empire, the Benreys came from two distinct cultures; her mother's family traces its origins to Salonika, Greece, while her father's comes from the Balkans. During the war, the family escaped Nazi persecution first in Vichy France and then in the Alps, where her father—whose own parents were victims of the Holocaust—joined the Resistance and fought in the Battle of Vercors.

Sarde studied at the Sorbonne and taught French literature, culture, and women's studies courses at Georgetown University. She is the author of a number of important scholarly works and has collaborated on the memoirs of Jacques Rossi, a survivor of twenty-four years of imprisonment in a Soviet gulag. Sarde is a recipient of the Prix de l'Académie française, among other prestigious awards. In addition to her scholarly and pedagogical activities, she has written three novels. *Histoire d'Eurydice pendant la remontée* [The Story of Eurydice During Her Return], from which the following selection is excerpted, is her second one.

Histoire d'Eurydice contains several stories and levels of symbolism. It is, on the surface at least, the story of two lovers, Sophie Lambert and Eric Tosca, who are reunited some twenty years after their broken engagement, thanks to Tosca's relentless pursuit of his former fiancée. Sophie reluctantly allows herself to be convinced to fly to Rome with him. Once there, Eric tries to get his beloved to revisit their past as they wander the streets and historic sites of the Italian capital. But Sophie Lambert is more than just a passive object of desire and, over the course of their conversations, she reveals that the truth of the past is not at all what Eric thought.

Eric Tosca is in fact the son of Christian Hermesse, a famous tenor whose collaboration with the Nazis and the Vichy regime eventually led to his summary execution, witnessed by Eric as a child. It is Eric's mother who tries to erase the family connection, changing Eric's patronym and starting him along a path of deception that many followed in the postwar period. In a secret attempt to rehabilitate his father's name and restore its honor, however, Eric Tosca later accepts the pseudonym of Hermès, a name that he is given as a cover for his right-wing activities in support of the *Organisation Armée Secrète* (OAS) that opposed Algeria's successful bid for independence from France (1958–1962). In an ironic twist of fate, Eric, like his father, is thus destined to espouse the wrong side in a conflict where repression and occupation cause unspeakable suffering.

Michèle Sarde

Sophie Lambert's secret is similarly one of heritage. She was born Sarah Solal, a child whose Jewish family was all but destroyed in the Holocaust and who escapes only because the Lamberts adopt her and raise her from infancy as a French Catholic. Sarah, alias Sophie, is kept ignorant of her origins by her adoptive parents, until the return to France of her last surviving blood relative, Aunt Rachel, who ultimately forces the Lamberts to acknowledge the truth. As a consequence of this revelation, Sarah becomes a modern example of the "marrano" phenomenon in Jewish history, since discovering her true identity makes it impossible for her to fit in with either the Jewish community or the French Catholics, her "conversion" being suspect to both. For Sarah, looking back at her history as Sophie Lambert is a particularly painful experience of double exile, in which historic, social, and religious persecutions are revived and perpetuated by her fiancé's family history and personal politics. After discovering the true identity of Eric Tosca, it is his deception as well as her own trauma that Sarah had hoped to escape by leaving him and disappearing forever from his life.

The novel's three parts span the three days of this odyssey of recovery and are punctuated by excerpts of Lambert's doctoral research and meditations on the symbolism of Eurydice that reflect an intent to give voice to a woman's perspective on the Orphic myth. Lambert's feminist comments on the myth, appearing in sections labeled "Sophie's Notes," accompany and resonate with the story in a way reminiscent of the chorus in ancient Greek tragedy. Indeed, just as the researcher seeks to unearth Eurydice's story, so this novel can be seen as an attempt to bring to light the individual and collective trauma from a period of modern French history on which many would prefer to turn their backs. For if Eric Tosca and Sophie Lambert are a modern avatar of the mythic lovers, it is with an added twist; like Romeo and Juliet, they are vexed by family plots that predestine them to be mortal enemies.

The selection that follows is the chapter in which Sarah reflects on the cataclysm that discovering her Jewish identity represents in her life. Despite this secret she herself felt pressured to keep for many years, Sarah comes to see how the truth serves ultimately to reconnect her to her people's history. In working through her own ordeal, she is also compelled to face the "disaster" of the Holocaust that befell so many Jewish families. This is no doubt as to why Eric and Sarah's story is so compelling. In their search to understand their personal and familial traumas, they represent a whole generation condemned to look back on what they can never recover, except perhaps in the writing that is, after all, the legacy of the myth of Eurydice.

— **Miléna Santoro**

Selected Works

Le Désir fou. Paris: Stock, 1975.
Colette: Libre et entravée. Paris: Stock, 1978.
Regard sur les Françaises: Xe siècle–XXe siècle. Paris: Stock, 1983.
Vous, Marguerite Yourcenar: La Passion et ses masques. Paris: R. Laffont, 1995.
Histoire d'Eurydice pendant la remontée. Paris: Seuil, 1991.
Jacques le Français: Pour mémoire du Goulag. With Jacques Rossi. Paris: Cherche Midi, 2002.
Constance et la cinquantaine. Paris: Seuil, 2003.

Translation Into English

Colette: Free and Unfettered. Trans. Richard Miller. New York: Morrow, 1980.

Secondary Works

Patrice J. Proulx. "Of Myth and Memory. Rereading Michèle Sarde's *Histoire d'Eurydice pendant la remontée.*" *Religiologiques: Sciences Humaines et Religion.* 1997 (Spring) 15: 179–187.

Plate Liedeke, "Breaking the Silence: Michèle Sarde's *Histoire d'Eurydice pendant la remontée.*" *Women in French Studies.* 1995 (Fall) 3: 90–99.

The Disaster

At first, Sophie Lambert, alias Sarah Solal, only remembered fragments of her discussion with her adoptive mother. Later, she distinguished between what the latter had revealed, on that interminable February afternoon in 1957, and what her Aunt Rachel subsequently told her. In the beginning, she only retained that an eighteen-month-old baby, who was herself, had arrived in a basket on the Lamberts' backstairs doormat, at the very apartment on rue Gustave-Mahler where the revelation of her origins was made to her.

She does not recall having cried, shouted, or rebelled—as she will later in her nightmares, hammering with her closed fists on a door leading to an ossuary where a short woman dressed in black waits, ready to smother her with poisoned kisses. No. The teenager, clenched in the corset of her uneasiness and her upbringing, took it all in without a word and, on top of this new skin that was in fact the older one, shouldered a carapace in which the insanity of her elders suddenly and entirely imprisoned her. Her only dramatic gesture was to unhook the crucifix that hung over her bed. The next day, pious hands had restored it to its rightful place. She yielded.

In becoming what she was, a little Israelite, as they termed it, a daughter of foreigners hunted down and exterminated in the dark, she changed camps. She became one of the damned, those about whom Clotilde de Pondavenne spoke only indirectly now. For their disappearance seemed somehow suspicious and shameful, and the word Jew crossed the lips of Madame Lambert as seldom as it did those of her daughter.

Sophie Lambert was well placed to know how people like Nicole Lévy were considered, and in what way their image was diffracted, as if by a prism, into a spectrum of feelings that ranged from disgust to pity and derision, always ending up in some depreciatory difference in the minds of those in her parents' circles, even if they restrained themselves from making any comment. She knew from experience how they treated "those people," and how she herself had behaved to the "new girl."

Of course, the adoption furnished an alibi. It permitted one to live the exclusion under a facade of harmony. But in truth it provided her with only a superficial show to impress others, and that charade was no substitute for an identity.

The attitude of Madame Lambert accentuated this imbalance. She made it apparent how this choice, or rather, this absence of choice, was merely a makeshift settlement. For her, the adoption was not an act of love bestowed on

From: *Histoire d'Eurydice pendant la remontée* (Paris: Seuil, 1991), pp. 217–238.

an orphan who had been robbed of such affection, but rather a process of erasing an accursed origin in favor of a respectable, healthy, and marketable identity. The secret she unloaded on her daughter seemed so loathsome to the adoptive mother that it could not be revealed without her inheriting some of its infamy.

For a long time, she made Sarah feel how lucky though unworthy she was to have received the gift of becoming Sophie, her very own daughter, baptized and raised in the correct, the only possible, faith. And she had sought to foster in the adolescent the zeal of the newly converted, their fanaticism in destroying the faith of those in whose ranks they had formerly found themselves, for reasons of religious law or blood.

Later on, when Sophie alias Sarah tried to climb out of the hole in which the disaster had buried the dead and the survivors alike, she used to see in her dreams the fanatical face of her adoptive mother, Thérèse, resembling that of a Torquemada, bent on making her a *conversa,* a new Christian buying with betrayal the mercy of continued breath, of having escaped, of being on the right side.

Thanks to the intercession of the adoptive family, she was a survivor of the other one. "Without us," the mother said to her daughter, "you would have become one of those little skeletons of the living dead displayed in all their unspeakable horror in the films about the camps. Without us and without the merciful intervention of the Lord who saw fit to snatch you from their claws." And who also had, it went without saying, allowed Monsieur and Madame Lambert to perform the ultimate good deed that would ensure them, without question, a direct pass to the comforts of the afterlife.

At first, the idea that she, Sophie alias Sarah, had been chosen to survive while all her family had been sacrificed, disturbed her more than anything else.

"Their God"—she began to say "their God"—had elected her. Why her instead of another? Why that mark of distinction given to her when she, according to Madame Lambert, was so unworthy of it? Why had this Thing—which she began to capitalize since she was at a loss to find words in the lexicon of monstrosities that could name what had just happened—why had it happened to such an ordinary person as herself, and why not to Clotilde, or Véronique, or Marie-Rose Chenevière? Of all of them, Marie-Rose would have been better prepared than she. Marie-Rose would have known, better than she did, what to think, what to say, how to react, how to suffer.

Sophie was too upset to think, however. Exiled from herself and from others, she was no longer, as Eric Tosca had so rightly put it yesterday, either the daughter of her parents or the parishioner of her church. Like a house of cards, all the foundations on which she had built her existence and her convictions were collapsing. Such were her youth, her fragility, her selfishness, that she had not sought to know a single detail about the itinerary that had led her real parents from their fifth-floor apartment to the ovens of Auschwitz, and even less about the path that had brought them to that very dwelling on rue Gustave-Mahler where little Sarah alone had remained. In the beginning, she quite believed it did not even enter her head. She was only trying to salvage the pieces of her shattered identity. She watched herself floundering and wore herself out trying to find solid ground.

On the fourth day, Madame Lambert gravely entered her room and sat down at her bedside. She spoke deliberately. She explained that she had always meant to defer this revelation and that she would have waited until Sophie was able to handle it with more maturity. Perhaps, she said, she would never have revealed what was, after all, only a little secret of birth and of nature that one must not make into a tragedy. But the intrusion of Madame Abravanel into their lives had forced her to divulge prematurely what should have remained concealed.

Sophie asked why this hurried little woman, who was supposedly her great-aunt, had waited all that time to make her presence known. It was 1957. The former Sarah Solal had been adopted by the Lamberts fifteen years earlier, and they considered her to be their daughter. If this woman had wanted "to get her back," as Madame Lambert stated, why had she not done so earlier?

Thérèse Lambert did not know how to answer this question that she was in fact asking herself. This woman claimed that she had taken refuge in Argentina with her husband during the war years and had fallen ill there. This is how she explained the lost years. But Madame Lambert was herself convinced that in truth the woman had hardly wanted to be worried with taking care of a baby or a little girl, and that she had probably not had the means to feed a useless mouth. She had therefore waited until Sophie was grown , and properly brought up, to assert rights that the law did not give her, and to trouble a family's peace—a family that in the interim had taken in a little girl, had saved her from a life that at best would have meant living in a state-run orphanage, and had made her a Christian with painful memories that it was now best to forget and forget completely for the second time.

It was tacitly understood by Sophie and her adoptive mother that the story of Sarah had to be as deeply buried as possible in order to prevent it from resurfacing in any way. And also that they would no longer recall it with the least little question or allusion, so as to ensure the secrecy of this operation.

Sophie acquiesced. She was perhaps the more determined of the two to shroud in silence the unburied bodies that she had not joined. And, from her adoptive mother's lips, she lapped up the trite and yet charmed words, the balm that circumscribed the disaster by reducing it to mundane proportions, to concerns about a mouth to feed and a good education.

Once confined by silence, from that day forward she no longer dared ask Madame Lambert why she forced her to see the little woman that Sophie, to her shame, would rather have seen reduced to ashes with the others. On the basis of what undisclosed negotiations did she make Sophie entertain the aunt once a week with a properly maintained composure? When she rebelled, it was as if on a whim, a whim that Eric Tosca and other regular visitors to their home had witnessed, but that no one had recognized. Was Sophie not crossing that intransigent territory that Madame Lambert, in keeping with custom, called that "awkward age"?

Later, much later, she turned to her aunt when the pain that refused to subside and festered under the imposed silence, began to seep out.

This change of heart happened at the same time that Sophie Lambert and Eric Tosca fell in love. It was that day, the day that she had learned . . . when she thought she learned she was pregnant, that she had had the courage to hear, from Rachel Abravanel's lips, the story of the beginning of the disaster.

In her apartment in Cimiez, her aunt sat in an old caned chair because she preferred furniture that allowed her to sit straight, so as not to lose an inch of her small stature. And, that day, she had begun to tell the tale of death, as she would later continue to spin stories of life, in her inimitable accent and her somewhat old-fashioned vocabulary, learned in the Jewish Middle East of Sephardic Salonika, with her special way of rolling her r's and peppering her sentences with words and proverbs from her native Judeo-Spanish.

"Your father, Abraham Solal, they came to take him at dawn on September 14, 1942. The fourteenth of September! Since the raid of Vél' d'Hiv,[*] when they arrested the Poles and the stateless people, we had been living in terror. Communications were difficult. We had neither phone nor radio anymore. Curfews of eight o'clock had been imposed on Jews. The news that did get through was more and more catastrophic. One day, they took the Romanians, another day the Serbs, a third day the Czechs and the Turks. The most insane rumors flew about, sometimes confirmed, sometimes contradicted by the facts.

"The night before the fourteenth of September was a Sunday. My niece Esterina had gone out that day to sup at the home of some friends. Early, because of the curfew. During dessert, somebody said, 'I heard tell that tomorrow there will be a raid and that the Bulgarians will be taken. If you know any Bulgarians in your vicinity, they should be warned.' Esterina reflected for a

---

[*]The raid of Vél' d'hiv took place in Paris on July 16 and 17, 1942 when over 12,000 Jews were arrested by some 4,500 French police officers.

moment and then she thought of Abraham. When she looked at her watch, it was already a quarter of eight. She had just enough time to go home with her son Oscar, who was thirteen. Thamar and Abraham lived too far away, at number seven rue Gustave-Mahler. She figured that she would not have time herself to make the trip there and back before the curfew. Oscar, her only son, insisted:

'I will go, Mamma. On my bike. Quickly. I won't get caught, I promise you. We must warn Uncle Abraham, in case this is true!'

'No,' said Esterina, 'it's too dangerous. You risk being arrested yourself, with your yellow star. And in any case, these are always false alarms. Don't worry, Oscar. Nothing will happen to your uncle. Indeed, a man such as he who wears his heart on his sleeve and has a conscience as clear as a child's!'

"If nine-tenths of Jews had not reasoned like that *bousdra** Esterina," added Rachel, "they would not have gone to register themselves as Jews and to voluntarily accept their ticket to the slaughterhouse! But they all thought to themselves: 'I have nothing to worry about, I have done nothing wrong. It is the wrongdoers that are being arrested. It is the others. They would not dare.'

"They dared. At sunrise they arrived, at about six thirty, seven o'clock. Thamar and Abraham were asleep in their room with the baby who was you, my little Sarah. The twins were in the next room, Rebecca in the third. The concierge, who you know so well, accompanied them, at once curious and sympathetic. It was officers from the Vichy police force, Frenchmen in civilian clothes, Thamar told me. About thirty-five years old. Very polite: 'Monsieur Solal, Abraham, born in Burgas, November 30, 1910? Gather up a few things and please follow us, Monsieur Solal!'

"Thamar helped him put a few clothes, a toothbrush and a little money in an overnight case. He kissed you all and caressed your tiny hand with his own. You did not awaken, you were sleeping peacefully. And he said to Thamar quickly in Judeo-Spanish: 'You must leave right away with the children. Save yourself. I love you.'

"He went downstairs with the officers, and no one ever heard from him again.

"That afternoon Madame Georgette, the concierge, all upset, went up to see Thamar. She had protested to the officers, 'Why are you coming to arrest those people? They are respectable!'

"The younger of the two officers, the one with glasses and a birthmark on his right cheek, had answered her coldly, 'If you like those people, tell them to get out of here because they will all be taken along with all their belongings. And as for your Solal, you will never see him again!'

---

*In Judeo-Spanish, someone stupid or slow-witted.

The Disaster

"In the meantime, a family council had been convened at my sister Sarah's home. It was decided that Monsieur Joseph would be called upon to make us false identity papers and that the whole family would try to get across to Vichy-controlled France.

"Around September 26, ten days later, other alarming rumors reached us: others would be taken as well, new raids were in the works. It was necessary to make haste. The trip was organized quickly. We were to receive the false papers around the twenty-ninth and leave that day. Shortly before that time, my husband Raphaël declared that it was too dangerous to move around in a group. He had a business associate in South America who offered a refuge. He himself was protected by his Spanish passport. I was Greek. I could be arrested at any moment. Raphaël decided that we would leave for Argentina. And, from that point on, things began to happen all at once. We left Paris so suddenly, I did not even have time to kiss my sister good-bye."

After that, everything was confused in the aunt's mind. She did not know what had happened to Sarah Calderon and her husband Moses, to their daughter Thamar and to the latter's children, Rebecca the eldest, the twins David and Joseph, and the baby, little Sarah. No letter made it to Buenos Aires between the month of October 1942 when the Abravanels arrived and the fourteenth of July 1946, the day they received an envelope from the Red Cross. The letter regretfully announced that Monsieur and Madame Calderon of Italian citizenship and Madame Solal and her children of French citizenship, living since 1942 on via delle Botteghe Oscure in Rome, had been taken in the raid that had emptied the Jewish quarter of the capital and had probably been deported. Their fate was unknown.

It was then that Rachel had a breakdown that lasted almost ten years, during which time she struggled to retain her sanity in the hands of knowledgeable psychiatrists and well-meaning psychoanalysts. When she awoke from the long nightmare, she was able to make a simple assessment of the disaster. Of the large family who used to celebrate Passover in the house of her grandfather Mosseri in Salonika, there was nobody left. Besides the loved ones from France who had been annihilated, the cousins and relatives of Jewish Salonika in Greece had also been exterminated in Bergen-Belsen or in the gas chambers of Auschwitz-Birkenau. Rachel and her husband were among the few survivors of a community that within four years had been completely swallowed up, swept off the face of the planet.

On December 15, 1955, during the scorching summer of the southern hemisphere, Raphaël Abravanel was driving his car from the San Isidro neighborhood toward that of la Recoleta where he lived. He had a heart attack on Avenue of General San Martín the Liberator. His car swerved and smashed into the simulated stone fence of the zoo, right across from the Monumento de los Españoles.

Two days later, just before the funeral, Rachel received a brief note which began in this way:

> *Dear Allegra,*
> *In Buenos Aires on a stopover, I learned of your presence here, unfortunately through the obituary columns of* La Nacion. *I will come to the services to pay my respects for the last time to our dear Rapho. I share your pain and offer you my sincerest sympathies, even as I think of our people, so many of them, who did not have the chance to die as he did and to know a proper burial. At the same time, I would like to pass on to you a piece of information that has been bothering me for a while and that is of interest to you personally. Please give me a minute of your time after the funeral, since I must catch a plane that very evening for Israel, where we have been living for the last ten years.*
>
>
>
> *Myriam Saporta*
> *your friend and classmate*
> *at Notre-Dame of Zion*
>
>

Rachel had not seen Myriam since the happy years of their adolescence in Salonika, when she was still using her Judeo-Spanish first name, Allegra. She was reunited with an unrecognizable, wrinkled old woman who was then living in Tel-Aviv, where she managed a publishing house with her husband. Like her childhood friend, Myriam was mourning three-quarters of her family, deported from Salonika and Corfu during those terrible years. She told Rachel of a friend of her son-in-law, an Italian, who had been among the last to see Sarah, Thamar and the rest of the family when they were living on the via della Botteghe Oscure, at the edge of the Roman ghetto, in the old neighborhood of the Porticus of Octavia. This man, young and energetic at the time, had escaped the raid of 1943; he had been deported during the last months of the war from Cernobbio on Lake Como. But he had come back. One night, in Tel-Aviv, during a dinner among Salonikans, Myriam had spoken to him about the Calderon-Solal family. It was then that the man, by the name of Aaron, had alluded to a baby that Thamar Solal had been obliged to leave behind in France at the last minute, because she had been forgotten on the false papers. The baby was not with the rest of the family in Rome and had not been deported. Of that Aaron was absolutely certain.

"The baby . . . " Aunt Rachel began to tremble. "You mean little Sarah, the youngest?"

"I don't know—and Aaron doesn't either—what sex the baby was. But he was convinced that there were only three of the four Solal children in Rome. He remembered that Thamar was obsessed by the memory of the little one left behind. Twenty times she wanted to make the trip to go and fetch the baby. Twenty times she was prevented. Aaron was in Naples the day of the raid in 1943. He was able to hide. He told me that much later, when he himself was deported, he had thought about the child, about how lucky the child was to have been saved by chance . . . if it had indeed been saved. . . . ."

"But Myriam, where was the baby left? With whom? What became of it? . . . "

"That I don't know, nor does Aaron. That is the exact question I had for you. I myself learned this news by chance, as you see, and not long ago. I thought you knew and that you had perhaps taken steps to find the child. Rumor had it that you had escaped deportation and left Europe, but I had no idea where you were living. In fact, I thought you were in New York! Without Rapho's death! . . ."

The groundswell of memories swept away the recovering consciousness of Rachel Abravanel once again. She saw again the Solal's apartment on rue Gustave-Mahler in Paris, the little office where Abraham used to pace in circles after he lost the right to work, the blue-eyed twins who were always starving and that the Solals could not manage to feed with their disappearing savings and did not dare send to school anymore because of the star, and who played checkers for afternoons on end like silent little robots while their sister Rebecca mischievously hid the nuts that they had spent hours shelling and had set aside to savor with great delight before going to bed.

Rebecca had a long, black braid and gray eyes like her mother. She devotedly looked after her little sister Sarah, changing her, feeding her, rocking her with infinite patience. When she could not stand being cooped up in the house anymore, she took Sarah in her arms, holding her next to the yellow star so that it was hidden by the baby's dimpled little body, and breathed in the outside air with this animated doll who laughed uproariously when her sister's bouncing braid tickled her legs.

One evening, they returned home barely a minute before curfew. Rachel was expected at Thamar's house, where she was to spend the night. And so the worried aunt and niece stared anxiously at the minute hand, approaching the fateful fifty-ninth minute after seven o'clock.

"Mamma, Auntie... you just don't know... you just won't believe. . . . "

"Calm down, Rebecca. You are all out of breath. Is this an hour to be getting home? I told you a hundred times. . . . "

"Imagine this. There is this kraut soldier, he wanted to take Sarah into his arms. But I did not let him. He was saying to the other kraut *'schön'* and to me he said 'pretty child.' And he gave her a candy. I did not let her eat it. Look, Auntie . . . perhaps it is poisoned!"

And the graceful dark-haired child who seemed like something straight out of a nineteenth-century engraving burst into ripples of laughter, and pulled out a huge, slightly sticky, pink candy, wrapped in paper of the same color.

"Can I pop it in my mouth, do you think, Auntie? You know, like those tasters for the queen who try things first to make sure they are not dangerous?"

A little later, she added seriously, "You know, Auntie, the kraut did not see my star, because of Sarah. He only had eyes for her, anyway. But perhaps I should have shown it to him, so that he might understand that one can be lovely and still be a Jew. For starters, my daddy is blonder than they are . . . !"

For the first time in ten years, Rachel was lifted by a swell of hope, despite the sadness of this day of mourning. Of course Raphaël was lying there, in the coffin that had just been put into the ground. Death—albeit easy and natural—had come for him as well. He was the last in a long list of old men, children, and adults in the prime of life who had themselves been ripped away like branches of an ancient tree, in one lightning strike. But there was, perhaps, on the other side of the Atlantic, in that old, ravaged Europe where she had sworn she would never set foot again, a surviving child that the cruelty of History had forgotten. Was it a mistake made by an absurd order of things that had been driven by blind powers, or was it a calculated act of Providence? Rachel, who had put little Allegra's religious fervor on the back burner, went back to trusting once again, in a stubborn resurgence of faith.

For the first time since she had received the letter from the Red Cross, she slept right through the night, that night that was also the first of her widowhood. And she imagined herself a child again, in Salonika, embarking with her whole family and her doll for a boating excursion. Suddenly, the wind rose, a terrible wind, like the one that blew on the day of the great fire of 1917. Buffeted by the storm, the boat capsized. Daddy, Mamma, and all the others sank under the waves, but Allegra managed to swim and keep her head above water. In an instant, she saw her doll, an anachronistic plastic bather with golden eyes and a bisque ceramic face. She swam with all her might towards the bather, but the doll moved away ever faster, pushed by the current towards land. Allegra continued to advance against the waves and the current, and finally managed to reach her doll at the very instant that it washed up on the beach.

At that moment, the old woman awoke; the knowledge that she did not know how to swim and had never had a doll as a child only spurred her determination, a determination that she had lost for what seemed like ages. At dawn, she was up, prepared for battle. It was imperative she find little Sarah first, then recover the family property with which she had never dealt in all the years she had been in a comatose state.

Three days later, she landed at Orly Airport in Paris. She checked into a modest hotel on rue du Temple, resolved to hire a private detective, and was prepared to wait for months, even years in order to follow all the traces and procedures. France was still buzzing with the scandal of the Finaly children, that had been in the news and had concluded a year earlier with the repatriation of the two boys to Israel. Like Sarah, Robert and Gérard Finaly were born to Jewish parents, but of Austrian origin, who were deported in February of 1944. Nuns had entrusted them to Antoinette Brun, who had converted them. The postwar public had been gripped by the controversy between the biological family and the elderly lady, who had not hesitated to kidnap the children and hide them away, in places as distant as Spain. The resolution of the affair encouraged the aunt, although she did not have any illusions about the difficulty of the enterprise. And her first act was to go to the former apartment of Thamar and Abraham on rue Gustave-Mahler.

She certainly did not expect to find the building in the same state she had left it at the time of their hurried departure in 1942 and the resulting dispersal of the family. The first person who met her eyes when, pale with apprehension, she passed through the front door, was the concierge, Madame Georgette, who was watching over the entrances from her room, as always. The fifteen intervening years had hardly aged her. They recognized each other right away.

Eric Tosca took twenty years to find Sophie after their broken engagement in 1959. Madame Abravanel found Sarah immediately, more than a decade after the disaster. Thanks to Madame Georgette, she was able to more or less reconstruct what had happened on the evening of September 30, 1942, when the false papers made by Monsieur Joseph arrived at the rue Gustave-Mahler apartment. The papers established the identity of Thérèse Sola, born in Salon-de-Provence in April 1914, daughter of Manuel and Solange Caron—the Judeo-Spanish name of Sarah's grandmother was Sol—also of the same city, and those of her children, Daniel, Joël and Renée Sola. Upon the papers' delivery, they realized that little Sarah, whose name they had wanted to change to Sophie so as to sound more French, appeared nowhere, neither on the identification cards nor on the passports.

Changes of heart were not wanting on that tragic evening. Thamar at first decided that this omission was not serious and that an eighteen-month-old baby did not yet need a bureaucratic existence. She managed to reach Monsieur Joseph's go-between after the curfew, with the help of the building concierge. The counterfeiter was not in Paris. The go-between warned her vehemently against the risk of trying to cross into the Free Zone with an unregistered, undeclared person, even a baby. And there was no way to put off the departure which was scheduled for six o'clock the next morning, since their train left the Gare de Lyons at 7:18.

The aunt imagines the long, sleepless night her niece must have spent. Through the intercession of Madame Georgette, Thamar receives the proposal of Thérèse Lambert who lives in the large apartment above them, on the sixth floor: "If you decide to leave the baby, put her in a basket on the backstairs landing. I promise you that we will watch over her as though she were our own child. Think about it, Madame Solal, and do not make a selfish decision. This is a one-of-a-kind opportunity for your little girl."

Thamar probably spent the night next to the cradle, worriedly watching the baby sleep. Sarah was a very happy child; she would have smiled contentedly as she slept, and her little hand that looked sculpted of silk-smooth wax would have trembled with the drift of her dreams. Her mother probably wondered anxiously about the future of this little one who, in all likelihood, would never become a woman, at least not before her eyes. When the first light of that autumn day began to filter through the pale blue curtains of the bedroom, Thamar would have been brutally wrested from the drowsiness that had overcome her vigilance for a few moments. In the meantime, Sarah would have wakened and watched her mother gravely with her golden eyes. Her mother would have taken her in her arms, cradled her, and the child would have fallen back to sleep.

Thamar would have gone to find the changing basket in the coat closet near the entrance to the apartment, a basket she would have made ready with the pillow and pink sheets embroidered with two intertwined s's, her daughter's initials. She would have tucked her into the basket with infinite care, and she would have gone to wake and prepare her other children. At 5:57, she would have knocked, according to the agreed upon signal, on the service entrance door of the sixth floor, and would have placed the basket on the landing. At 5:58, after having heard the creak of the opening door and the rustle of the basket slipping through the doorway, she would have returned to her fifth floor home.

At 5:59, Sarah and Moses Calderon, who only had to cross the street since they lived at number thirteen on rue Gustave-Mahler, rang the bell to the front entrance of the fifth floor apartment. And even as the six members of the family went downstairs for the last time toward the road that would lead them first to Angoulême where they crossed into the Free Zone, and then to Lyons and to Italian-occupied Nice, where they crossed the border and would continue on, still further away, toward via della Botteghe Oscure, Sarah Solal was being transformed into Sophie Lambert and would awaken in the arms of a new mother.

The Disaster

This whole scenario, in which the details might be varied but whose tenor was in keeping with the likely facts, appeared clearly to Aunt Rachel after her first interview with Madame Georgette. She learned, without having to go through the long pursuit she had anticipated, that Sarah, who had indeed become Sophie, was still living in the rue Gustave-Mahler building with the Lamberts, that she was in good health and led the life of a normal child, in ignorance—the Lamberts having forbidden any revelation on the subject—of her origins and of the fate that had cast her some fifteen years ago into the home of a family completely unrelated to her.

Rachel learned also that three days after their departure, seals had been placed on the Solals' office apartment. Inspectors from the Renseignements Généraux had come by for a day to prepare the furniture and other things for the move. Madame Georgette had just had enough time to surreptitiously save one of the albums of stamps that Monsieur Solal collected with such care, and she had kept it all these years, expecting that one day she would give it to his daughter on some pretext or other. Since Madame Abravanel was back, it was to her that this one object, saved from the enemy, by all rights belonged.

She held out to her the album of rare stamps, of which many were postmarked from countries that had been erased from the map: stamps from Bavaria and Bosnia-Herzegovina, Prussian stamps, Serbian, Croatian, Slovenian, Caucasian, Silesian, Wurtemburgian, stamps from Bohemia and Bessarabia, from Kurland and Lithuania. Abraham had started the collection in Burgas, when still a child. At the same time she described to Rachel the speed and efficiency with which the apartment had been emptied the day after the first raid by the police.

"Even the children's toys," she added, "the twins' checkers and Miss Rebecca's broken doll. They took everything, my dear. And we, who watched it happen, could do nothing! It was such a disgrace!"

The totality of the personal possessions and furnishings had been sent to the former Dufayel, a furniture store on Boulevard Barbès that had gone under and was then serving as a warehouse for Jewish property. It was there that everything was put into crates and shipped off to Germany. A little later, the apartment had been requisitioned and occupied by an Italian from the embassy who had been named to manage the Solal property. A German succeeded him. With the Liberation came a French civil servant without a place to live and then victims of the bombings of the Channel and of Calvados who came to work in Paris. After that, the apartment had been given to a former prisoner of war who had just gotten married, succeeded in 1952 by the Fontaine family. Was Madame Rachel going to try to get back the apartment that belonged to her nephew and that should by all rights go to her grand-niece?

Michèle Sarde

"As for the Lamberts," Madame Georgette had lowered her voice and cast an eye around her to be sure there were no listening ears, "think before you go there, Madame Rachel. Be on your guard. They act like generals and look down on less fortunate folk. I tell you, Madame Rachel, those people, they adopted your Sarah, it's true, and it is a good deed they did there, but they are not overflowing with kindness. For starters, all she is interested in is religion. She raised this little girl to please the priests, and for no other reason. She keeps her on a tight rein. When I think she won't even let her play with my Veronica!"

Rachel expected to encounter some difficulties. This situation was very similar to the case of the Finaly children that had taken years to resolve and had divided public opinion. But Robert and Gérard had only been entrusted to Mademoiselle Brun, the director of the municipal daycare in Grenoble, who had them baptized and had been named their provisional guardian, whereas the Lamberts had followed an adoption process that gave them all legal rights to little Sarah.

The first letters addressed to the Lamberts by the aunt got no response and the first moves she made proved fruitless. Nonetheless, after she tried the services of several lawyers, she was referred to Monsieur Delarue who sorted out the matter brilliantly. Upon close examination of the facts, it was found that the adoption procedure had not been exempt from errors or from blundering. Without looking further, it was taken for granted that the whole family had disappeared. Through the Red Cross, it would have been easy to trace the Abravanels who could identify them. The official documentation of the deaths of Thamar and Abraham was a certificate which stated that survivors of Auschwitz had testified to having seen both Solal spouses die before their eyes. The lawyer was able to establish that these testimonies, at the very least, had been extracted, if not bought, via emotional blackmail provoked by the desire to give an orphaned girl a family.

But there was worse. Because the adoption certificate was taking so long, another witness had been convinced to declare, under oath, to having seen Rachel and Raphaël Abravanel get off a train in Treblinka with others who had immediately gone to the gas chambers and within two hours had been exterminated. This false testimony threw the whole adoption process into question. The damning document that the lawyer had discovered became the means by which Rachel gained admittance to the Lamberts' apartment. This time, she decided to strike without warning. With the complicity of the concierge, she came knocking on the Lamberts' door on a Thursday afternoon when she knew both mother and daughter would be at home.

Thérèse Lambert, who at first offered her only the coldest reception, thawed considerably upon seeing the document that Rachel had been able to copy. Nonetheless, her position was unshakeable. At a time of danger, the Jews had fled, abandoning their children to anyone who was good enough to take them in. The Lamberts had taken on the care of this little girl with all of the attendant risks and the costs during that difficult time. They had become attached to this child to the point of wanting her to officially become their own. Most important of all, they had her baptized and brought into the fold of the Church. This sacrament had an absolute value. From now on, Sophie had a spiritual family that was the Catholic family, and a family of flesh and blood that was the Lambert family. It was all too easy for Madame Abravanel to come back like this, after so many years, and attempt to repossess an adolescent who had received all the love and upbringing her adoptive parents had to offer, and who had put down roots in a homeland. With all due respect, what did this woman, a foreigner landing in the lap of a united family, have to offer a sixteen-year-old girl who had truly become both Christian and French? Before discussing this, Rachel asked to see Sarah. As a means to her goal, she used the threat of attacking the adoption process for its use of falsified documents and manipulated testimonies.

It was then that Sophie appeared and disappeared. But that instant of upheaval was enough for her great-aunt to understand that the solution to the problem was not easy. One day, a baby had been left wailing on the doorstep. That baby had become an almost mature human being, raised in total ignorance of the circumstances that had, in a few steps, led her onto unknown ground. Rachel quickly grasped that the first task was not to get Sarah back through a string of trials and verdicts, but to make the road back easier for her, by influencing her and winning her over.

Therefore, from the first day, Rachel negotiated a compromise with the adoptive mother. The child would be told about her origins and her relationship to Rachel Abravanel, who would be able to see her regularly according to a schedule that she argued over fiercely and finally settled on. In exchange, the great-aunt gave up trying to assert her rights and attack the adoption procedure.

And so it was concluded. But this enterprise—the unveiling of a past that one learns is dead before knowing that it had ever existed at all—recovering Sarah Solal at the threshold of life—was by nature enough to trouble a spirit less fragile than that of Sophie Lambert's. Without her knowing it, the chrysalis was hiding another butterfly. Despoiled of her identity by this pseudo-metamorphosis, the destabilized teenager would inevitably meet the child from the opposite camp.

Thus the Solal girl and the Hermesse boy are in position for the masquerade.

Michèle Sarde

Ahead of them, the wrong road, borrowed names, an unsound engagement that disguised a vast game of hide-and-seek with the truth—a truth in which nobody will recognize his or her own people.

Sophie's Notes

In the capital of Nazi Europe, nobody noticed the disappearance of an extravagant ring setting representing the crucifixion of Orpheus.

It was in the middle of the war in what is now the State Museum of East Berlin. The amulet in hematite dated from the third century of our era. The scholars had named it the Gnostic Jewel, because it proved the connection established in early Christianity among Orpheus, Dionysus and Christ: above the head of the sufferer, the crescent moon was crowned with seven stars in an arc. Around the cross, a mysterious inscription was engraved: Orpheus Bacchitos.

During his youth in Samothrace, the poet had been initiated into the mysteries of the one who promised the afterlife. In Memphis, Egypt, he had explored the passageways to the hereafter, the paths of Salvation.

Orpheus, Dionysus, Jesus: all three experienced mystic passion, the descent into Hell, the search for the soul of the world and the solitary resurrection on the third day. Eurydice accompanied all three of them. Eurydice, another name for the Virgin. . . .

— **Translated by Miléna Santoro**

Annie Cohen
(1944–)

Annie Cohen was born in Sidi-bel-Abbès, Algeria, to parents of Sephardic origin. Although she has published over twenty works, it is only in her more recent literary texts that we find references to her cultural origins and her childhood. *Bésame mucho* [Kiss Me a Lot], for instance, is dedicated to the memory of her mother whose Ladino-Hispanic roots influenced Cohen's Algerian childhood.

Cohen's family had been in Algeria for several generations, but when Algeria became independent in 1962, the family left for France. She settled definitively in Paris in the mid-1960s, where she subsequently earned a doctorate in geography, participated in the French women's liberation movement, and worked as a journalist and literary critic for *F Magazine*. In 1979, she published her first literary text, *La Dentelle du cygne* [The Swan's Lace]. While pursuing a career as a writer, she also became known as an artist. Her gouache paintings and Chinese ink drawings have been exhibited in galleries and museums in Paris and Marseilles. Within the context of Cohen's oeuvre as a writer and artist, these scrolls symbolize her personal, intimate struggle with an aspect of the Judaic tradition that forbids representation. As she explained to the writer Chantal Chawaf, her "scrolls" represent the "convulsive side" of her writing, her attempt to capture the roots of the "word" in the face of an adversarial history characterized by persecution, racism, and anti-Semitism. While affirming her physical, cultural, and historical identity as a Jew, insisting that it is her grounding, she admits that she is nevertheless *sans terre* [without roots], in exile, not only physically but also spiritually. She sees herself as outside Jewish thought, law, and tradition which, according to her, limit her self-expression as a woman and as an artist. She admits, however, that to live and to create on the margins of this tradition is an uncomfortable position for her. In order to overcome it, she attempts to re-create the missing links, one by one, and to painstakingly (re)construct her own path. As she says, what counts is the path, not the goal: "For me, writing is graphic, I would even say geographic." In this sense, her "scrolls of writing" reflect the original, physical aspect of her personal, intimate literary itinerary. Though their graphic shape clearly alludes to the Torah, they represent for Cohen her own "sound of written language emerging from behind the words." In short, it is an "anti-Torah" that transcends Judaic law and tradition.

Her internal and external exile are succinctly summarized by a *marabout*

Annie Cohen

[a magician, witch doctor, or soothsayer], who also happens to be the narrator's friend in *Le Marabout de Blida*: "warped *pied noir* [French colonial, born in Algeria] . . . . French on the outside, a crooked Algerian, with an overlay of Jewishness, an African from nowhere, momentarily Parisian, an Algerian from Paris, a Jew from North Africa, a Frenchwoman from Algeria!"[1] That an important figure from the Muslim tradition should be the narrator's friend is symbolic of Cohen's solidarity with all peoples who have suffered, as she has, misfortune at the hands of history. This perspective is manifested in many of her works.

The theme of the legendary wandering Jew is implicit in several of her literary works where he is a positive and a constructive figure. The nocturnal wanderings across Paris of Helena Rojanski in *L'Edifice invisible* (1988) come to mind. With the help of a spool of white thread, the protagonist joyously follows the hidden traces of an underground river, the Bièvre, linking the neighborhoods and squares of Paris. In doing so, she not only links her beloved city to its own past, but she also firmly anchors her own identity in this land of her exile. In subsequent texts, this hidden and forgotten river becomes an all-important preoccupation. In *La Rivière des Gobelins* from which the following excerpts are taken, this preoccupation leads to an act of self-identification:

> Bièvre that I have become
> That I am
> Unknown to me
> Unreadable

Five hundred years ago, the Thirteenth Arrondissement of Paris, where Annie Cohen has chosen to live, was a suburb of Paris along the banks of the Bièvre, a tributary of the Seine. It was the site of the Gobelins manufacturing works and of a cluster of slaughterhouses, tanneries, and tapestry workshops, all of which over time had contributed to the pollution of the river. As a result, the Bièvre was channeled underground in 1910 and covered over with concrete and new construction. Street names and the alignment of the streets, however, still trace the path of this "lost" river.

Cohen's interest in geography, her self-proclaimed "geographic writing," her search for missing links, origins, and roots—combined with her attempts to trace her own path—all seem to point in one direction, namely the search for and creation of her own answers to both physical and spiritual exile.

— **Marianne Bosshard**
Translated by Eva Martin Sartori

Selected Works

La Dentelle du cygne. Paris: Des Femmes, 1979.
Les Sabliers du bord de mer. Paris: Des Femmes, 1981.
Le Peignoir à plumes. Paris: Des Femmes, 1984.
Les Etangs de la reine blanche. Paris: Des Femmes, 1984.
L'Edifice invisible. Paris: Des Femmes, 1988.
Les Mots ont le temps de venir. Paris: Table Rase/Ecrits des Forges, 1989.
Pierre de nuit, rouleaux d'écritures. Paris: Les Petits Classiques du Grand Pirate, 1991.
Histoire d'un portrait. Arles: Actes Sud, 1992.
L'Homme au costume blanc. Arles: Actes Sud, 1994.
Le Marabout de Blida. Arles: Actes Sud, 1996.
Bésame mucho. Paris: Gallimard, 1998.
La Rivière des Gobelins. Tours: Farrago, 1999.
La Douce-mère. Paris: Gallimard, 2001.

Secondary Works

Marianne Bosshard. "Annie Cohen: à la recherche de l'eau, des origines, de la mémoire et du sens caché." In Yolande Helm, ed. *L'Eau: Source d'une écriture dans les littératures féminines francophones.* New York: Peter Lang, 1995, pp. 165–179.

Chantal Chawaf. "Le Geste du verbe: les rouleaux d'écriture de l'écrivain Annie Cohen." In *Le Corps et le Verbe: la langue en sens inverse.* Presses de la Renaissance, 1992.

Edgar Reichmann. "Une Plage incertaine." *L'Arche,* July 1981.

La Rivière des Gobelins

I wish the gardener of the public garden would hire me
I wish I could become his apprentice
wear big shoes all muddied with earth
learn to pull out the bad stock
gather the dead leaves
weed
give a name to rebellious plants
preserve
intact
the (huge)
buds
of the lilacs
stop them from opening
or indefinitely
revive
the first leaf of the climbing (orange)
rosebush
that he planted near the fence

I wish I wouldn't have to miss
any awakening he has prepared
but like every year
I'll understand nothing

once more
I'll spend spring in my little park
and I'll ask questions of the gardener
watch him
surprise him

From: *La Rivière des Gobelins* (Tours: Farrago, 1999), pp. 19–24, 39–49.

La Rivière des Gobelins

walk back and forth on the path
of a new wing not yet made human
not yet in leaf

the new wing
that's how they call it
was some vague empty lot
except for cats and atlantic cedars
behind the ugly fence

women
mostly women
filled the plastic dishes
with milk
and slipped
through the holes
any way they could
tin cans
of kitty chow

you have to know this
the little park on rue Croulebarbe has gotten bigger
it has been expanded
spread out
opened up on the northeast side
to come up to the windows of the factory
just as once before the bièvre
today dead and buried
everybody knows that

the garden has
six entry ways and

Annie Cohen

thirty-two-thousand eight-hundred sixty-eight square meters
32,868 square meters
from rue corvisart to rue croulebarbe
by way of rue cordelières
émile deslandres
berbier-du-mets   that is to say

32,868 square meters

which doesn't mean anything to me
I do my counting with six-liter watering cans
for the lilacs the hibiscus and others
and by fifty square meters of house
balcony included

32868 ÷ 50 = 657.38
I'll round it off to 657

the garden is as big as 657 times my dwelling
that means no more to me
nor less

but the bièvre came into paris
by the back gate of the poplars
forming
where the park is located
an island bordered by poplars

disappeared   the poplars
too old   sick   end of their tether
were replaced by birches
whose life expectancy is longer

La Rivière des Gobelins

should that make us happy
it must

birches follow the flow of a river
invisible to our eyes

invisible building

under the earth of the garden
and for the eternity of stories
that is to say

in the concentration camps
they didn't need glasses
to read
to write
mountains of them were collected there
and the earth from over there
has lost its memory
of glasses and eyes
that's the way earth is
it forgets
doesn't know any more
couldn't care less
about the stories of men
and rivers

tell me why children like to turn
around the vertical bars
turn after turn

the wind of march has dried out the earth
that the gardener crumbles before my eyes

Annie Cohen

earth of paris
survivor of concrete
earth of city dwellers without earth
stateless exiled   refugees
earth of a park
meager   meager   with little substance
earth of the bièvre
dead and buried today
I've already said that
I'll repeat it
I'll never repeat it enough
earth of a river
buried
algeria   algeria
earth of misfortune
without importance
earth of a balcony
that freezes

my gardener's hair is all ruffled

I look at his skin
I find it airy
rather fine
healthy
I count the number of hours he spends outside
in the open air
outside
on the earth
seven hours in winter
ten hours in summer

La Rivière des Gobelins

I like his face
for it catches the wind
a lot of wind today
he tells me
a lot of wind

I forget that the wind is blowing over paris
under a starless sky
cloudy   always cloudy
white sky
even at night
and while the song of birds
reaches only the ears of a few

difficult
today
to follow
its course

impossible

useless

sooner or later
you bump into
streets
intersections
buildings

Annie Cohen

stores
that didn't exist

sooner or later you lose it

under the tar

broken thread condemned done for
interrupted narrative
disconnected
with no logic
with no connection

with fits and starts
river of fits and starts
drowned in its stench
under the asphalt
the cobblestones

sooner or later
under the savings bank
and the pedestrian walkways
you lose it
you lose yourself
you can't find your way

it
today buried
under the weight
of urban
necessities

unfindable

La Rivière des Gobelins

erased from the dictionaries

sacrificed

withdrawn into the city night
underground
into the convent
into its ivory tower

and unable to get back to its bed
its meanders

with no geologic future
with no future
and despite the thousands of years
of flowing differently

once the course of the seine
passed by saint-lazare
rue de la boétie
and the bièvre of the times
occupied the present bed of the seine
it's a crazy story
but it's true

it's like you who comes from afar
who comes from away
who totters under the weight
of histories
and of geographies

who flows flows

Annie Cohen

in an adopted land

and who rushes under the earth
towards the sea
without knowing for what or for whom

that is why when they ask me
how old I am
I answer five centuries
plus a bit
children look at me   stunned
what
they make me repeat
yes   five centuries   plus a bit
I'll tell you
here in algeria
we came from the west
from cordoba
with or without baggage
no lo sé
from cadiz
or granada
maybe we came from granada
andalusian bags
dark circles already blue under our eyes
and when I stroll
today
through the streets of seville
I recognize my mother
look it's mom
and I kiss my grandfather's hand
it's you

La Rivière des Gobelins

you waited for me
you haven't grown old

nos vamos   hasta luego

even when she's done straightening out
cleaning up
polishing
the andalusian woman wears an apron
like mom
she serves me coffee with milk in a glass
in san josé
on the rocky point
across from oran
where I'm to meet my mother
beyond her days and her nights

you'll find me sitting at the café
every morning
emigranté-like
I write it the way it's pronounced
my five-century-old luggage
in my hand
men are playing dominoes
shouting
on a tiled terrace
opening onto the street
azulejos everywhere
as in tlemcen
banging the dominoes on the table
with enough force to wake the dead
as in seville

Annie Cohen

public benches in ceramic
as in granada
music kiosks
as in bel-abbès
smells of the mediterranean sea
that would make you blind
I can't make out the shores of oran

they told me
here   you'll be the closest to algeria

did we leave from here
by the gulf of san josé
what do I know
where we left from
where we boarded
did we board
where from

we did land in algerian land
we were coming from the west
from the northwest

it's at san josé that the distance
between spain and algeria
is the shortest

you'll see
five centuries in algeria
that's not so old
there are some who are even older
and here I am traipsing around with my skirts

La Rivière des Gobelins

and all my teeth
yes my boy

our mother's andalusian earlobe
was particularly long

when they ask me how old I am
I answer five centuries
plus a bit

and I know
how the here
can become the over there

in france we were from over there
but we're still here
for an unknown over there
don't talk to me about over there
talk to me about here
from the depths of your over there
but really
five centuries
make up a lot of heres that you leave
and become over theres
you're making me tired with all your skirts
you're eating my heart out with your heres that keep moving
can't you just hold on
once and for all
to a definitive here   a really down-home here
can't you
I can't
I'm still expecting to move from here to go over there

Annie Cohen

which over there
the over there of yesterday or the over there of tomorrow
you're eating my spleen out with all your
with all your comings and goings to lands
and trying to study history
I tell you
I have a preference for geography
by far
by very far
five centuries
plus a bit
across lands
here or over there

the exit's over here
stories tire me out
you're here even if you come from over there
and over there
you no longer have a here
you can come and go
turn and turn around
you came from over there
from the land of andalusia
from the land of algeria
how can I say it
don't you see I need time

if you come back
in five centuries
I'll tell you
the rest of these stories
and geographies

La Rivière des Gobelins

at san josé
on a clear day
I've been told
you can see algeria

I'm looking   I'm looking
beyond the sea
at the end of the sea

we left andalusia
we left algeria
we didn't leave anything at all
we were a shitful plus fifteen
moving about with our little clay pot

on a clear day
I've been told
you can see the shores of oran

this is the first time I've peered towards the southeast
and that I've blinded myself to the past
and that I'm waiting to see

of san josé I see nothing
andalusia   my sister
our skirts won't stop twirling about
inside out outside in every which way
our torsos proud the way you know the way you see

in all their cafés
you find on the tables
little paper napkins

Annie Cohen

everywhere I go
I slip one into my wallet
name address telephone
especialidad en desayunos
churros con chocolate
nijar mojacar granada
almeria
guadix
on each one of them
you can read
gracias por su visita

from san josé
gracias por su visita

five centuries   plus a bit
that's not much for a river
that's nothing

— Translated by Suzanne Tarica and Ralph Tarica

Translators' Note

Some things are inevitably lost in a poetic translation. The word *terre* here, for example, has been translated as earth or land, depending on the context. The words *rivière* (as in the Bièvre River) and *terre* in French are represented by the feminine pronoun "elle," replaced here by the more prosaic English "it."

Paula Jacques
(1949–)

Born in Cairo in 1949, Paula Jacques was uprooted from her native land in 1958. Of the 90,000 Jews living in Cairo in the 1950s, some 20,000 fled after the creation of the state of Israel in 1948 and the subsequent Arab-Israeli war. Mass expulsions and departures followed the 1956 Suez War. More departures occurred during the islamification of Egypt in the 1960s, which was accompanied by the nationalization of businesses, and again after the 1967 war with Israel. By the 1980s, there remained only 400 to 500 elderly Jews in Alexandria and Cairo.

The death of Jacques's father in Cairo near the end of 1955 coincided with the departure of the Jews and the end of Jewish life in Egypt. Three years later, at the age of nine, she experienced a radical dislocation, not in France, but on an Israeli kibbutz, where she was sent by her widowed mother, who, with her equally widowed sisters, in the classical situation of stateless persons, attempted to find work and lodgings in Paris.

Losing family, cultural identification, language, and the habits of urban life, Jacques felt more isolation on an Israeli kibbutz than she would have in France. In Cairo, she had experienced French culture and had spoken the French language, at home, in school, and with friends of the middle class, whatever their religion. The Egyptian middle and upper classes generally scorned Arabic, which the king himself spoke poorly. The cultivated and the wealthy did study English, the language in which business was conducted, but preferred to read and converse in French, rather than in the detested idiom of the British occupiers. Many sent their children to French schools. Paula Jacques spoke Arabic with her grandmothers who, illiterate like many of their generation, were connected to the ancient culture, as well as the culture of the poor. At twelve, Paula Jacques joined her mother in Paris, where she has lived since.

This Jewish Egyptian Francophone writer has published six novels. A small masterpiece, *Lumière de l'oeil* [Light of My Eye], her first book, was acclaimed by the critics. She received the Femina Prize for *Déborah et les anges dissipés*, and *Les Femmes avec leur amour* won the prestigious German Liberatur Prize for the best novel of the year by a woman.

Paula Jacques's fiction centers on Egyptian Jews, inhabitants of Egypt for millenia, and on the trauma of their uprooting and dispersal. *Lumière de l'oeil* conflates issues of minority status, multilingualism, assimilation, and relocation with problems of individual identity articulated in terms of gender and intensified by the historical events of the 1950s. Those Jewish women who selected French schools for their daughters were motivated in part by an unconscious desire to free them from a patriarchy which confined them to the home, forbidding them access to the public sphere as well as to the religious sphere. The female question intertwines with the Jewish question. In *Lumière de l'oeil*, the narrator's depictions of her Jewish family's life in Cairo, show how being female affects the dialectics of belonging and exclusion—from the personal domain to the wider cultural context—and how it intersects with the issue of language.

Through dialogue and the use of multiple languages, the narrator structures and constructs the narrative as well as her own identity. The text of the following selection is divided into two parts. The first is set in 1952 when Mona Castro is five years old, the second in 1956–1957, when she is on the brink of puberty at the age of ten. Each of these time periods corresponds to critical ruptures for the Jewish Egyptian population collectively and for the child as a female within that community. In this third person text, the narrator never appears. That first person is implied, however, in eight speeches by Mona's mother Rébecca, explicitly addressed to "you," the adult Mona, in Paris in 1977, twenty years after their expulsion from Egypt. Monologues in form only, these speeches function almost like dialogue because they consist of answers to unstated questions about their past put to Rébecca by the narrator. The mother speaks to a daughter present in her Parisian apartment "now."

Rébecca's "speeches" are composed essentially of stories about the family. Indeed, the telling of tales constitutes a key strategy of the novel, as the following selections demonstrate. Storytelling becomes the means to interpret and live history as it happens. As readers, we witness momentous historical events as recounted by those usually silenced: a small yet heterogeneous group of inside outsiders (a Jewish family partly well-to-do and partly poor) and a few of the politically powerless Muslims with whom they interact daily. Together these stories form the composite picture of the Castro family's setting in Egypt and frame the insertion of a little Jewish girl into history. When Mona finally gains her voice as a narrating writer, she intertwines these threads in a language as "braided" as her cultural formation.

Lumière de l'oeil is not written in the standard French of metropolitan France, but in a French inflected syntactically and semantically by the "isms" combining to form her culture: Arabisms mainly, but also Hispanicisms and Hebrewisms. The very title manifests the "creolized" nature of this French, to transpose Aimé Césaire's concept of inflecting standard French with local expressions. A translation from Arabic, the term of endearment "lumière de l'oeil" [light of my eye], also exists in Spanish, reflecting the Sephardic heritage that colors the French spoken by many Egyptian Jews.

The linguistic particularities characteristic of the French in this text include exclamations, colloquialisms, syntactical peculiarities, nominalizations of adjectives, archaisms, and the recourse to verbal flourishes rich in images and to exaggeration rather than to the understatement typical of metropolitan French humor. All of this complicates the customary difficulties involved in translation. Faced with the impossibility of rendering Egyptian-Arabic-Jewish inflections of the French into American English, I have chosen to suggest them, through measured use of what does, at least partially, correspond in spirit: Ashkenazi inflections. In the process, I hope to convey at least some measure of the warmth and humor of the colorful, delightful idiom Paula Jacques brings alive so masterfully.

— Susan D. Cohen

Selected Works

Lumière de l'oeil. Paris: Mercure de France, 1980.
Un Baiser froid comme la lune. Paris: Mercure de France, 1983.
L'Héritage de tante Carlotta. Paris: Mercure de France, 1987.
Déborah et les anges dissipés. Paris: Mercure de France, 1991.
La Descente au Paradis. Paris: Mercure de France, 1995.
Les Femmes avec leur amour. Paris: Mercure de France, 1997.
Gilda Stambouli souffre et se plaint. Paris: Gallimard, 2003.

Translations Into English

"Aunt Carlotta's Legacy." Trans. Michael T. Ward in "Discourses of Jewish Identity in Twentieth-Century France." *Yale French Studies* 85 (1994): 41–50.

Secondary Works

Susan D. Cohen. "Cultural Mixing, Exile, and Femininity in Paula Jacques' *Lumière de l'oeil.*" *The French Review* 67, 5 (April 1994): 840–53.

Light of My Eye

Mona returned from vacation burning with fever and vomiting. Her mother thought she was faking, but the fever persisted. Dr. Lagnado declared it was mumps. Rébecca [Mona's mother] ("your disease is the terror of the virile sex!") immediately sent her to her grandmother's to recover.

So that is how Mona came to spend a month in delicious intimacy with Farida Sardaal. That illness, which made her look like a little frozen seal, left her with the best memories of her childhood.

From the lips of Farida Sardaal, oh beautifully generous one, there issued no nastiness and no scandalmongering, but still you were never bored. For the entire duration of her daughter's illness, Rébecca did not come to see her ("contagious contagion you have!"). Mona wept, complained her mother didn't love her and so much the better, because she couldn't stand her either—she's so mean. Then her grandmother would draw the child into her arms and cradle her with enchanting words: "All drops of water flutter toward the sea. Don't cry, little stream. You, too, are of the family of waters."

Twice a week, Mona would help Farida take a bath. The old lady was afraid of slipping on the tiled floor so the child had to hold her hand. Mona slid the soapy sponge over her superb body, undone like a ravaged countryside; she gently scratched the straight, lean back, caressed with water the thighs sinuate with blue, meandering veins. Filled with horror and hope, she attentively observed the sex, brown, long, hanging between the legs, spread open from giving so much life. She saw its mystery, its beauty, the recesses enfolding a mauve nut, a desert rose. Would she have the same one some day? "Some day," her grandmother would answer. During that stay, Mona acquired the conviction that Farida, so wonderful to look at, would never cease to exist.

After the bath, Mona would knead cakes out of dates, sprinkle slices of oiled bread with cumin and coriander, made for her, "the little one." The two "friends" would eat abundantly and sweeten each other, too, with wonderful words.

"Do you know the story of the child who planted a tree? No? So listen. It was a little boy your age, perhaps a bit older. A poor lamb whose mother died. While he was still a baby in his cradle, an ogress kidnapped his mother and held her captive in a prison. The little boy couldn't stand it any more. No way. He must see his beloved mother. So he searches for the prison for a long time, and when he finds it, he plants a tree. A little tree that grows under the windows of the immured one. He says to the tree: 'Grow fast, so I can sit on your high branch and see my mother at last, inside.' He cares for that tree as for his own

From: *Lumière de l'oeil* (Paris: Mecure de France, 1980), pp. 87–97, 38–50.

eyes. He waters it, kisses it, yanks out the crowding weeds. The tree listens and grows. Finally, one day, the child climbs to the top, his heart soaring with hope. He leans on the window sill and calls. He calls to his lovely mother. But, now hear what I tell you, he sees nothing but an aged woman with a scrunched face, wintry hair, hands spotted by age. Oy! So he weeps in despair and anger."

"Why? Is it the ogress? Did she eat his mother?"

"No, my shining starlight, it's his mother. His very own mother. She has changed. While the tree was growing, while the child was growing, the mother went through her seasons too. That's life. One goes forward, the other backward, and sometimes they never meet. The child doesn't recognize the one who had cradled him with love. So he climbs back down and kills the tree forever."

"What an idiot!"

They laugh together at the little boy's blindness and at time's traps. That subtle demon, sometimes with the speed of an arrow, at others dragging like a cloud, bites the weak, breaks the impatient, rewards those who persevere, and gives to each soul the visage that it deserves.

"And that's why you are as fresh as a rose," Farida's friend Abbo Sapriel would say to her.

Since the death of Raphael Sardaal, his rival and friend, twenty years ago, Abbo Sapriel had been visiting his widow. He would arrive towards evening, bearer of flowers and small gifts, the better to play the sighing suitor. That's what Farida called him. Nice words but inaccurate, according to Mona. Because while he certainly sighed, even a lot, drinking his cinnamon tea without taking his eyes off Farida, he made no suit. And never creased his pants. That suitor made his suit standing. Period. Perched on his little twisted legs, shining in the ancientness of what was once a tuxedo, the vestiges of which included the remains of a lace shirt-front and white spats, the suitor danced dances around the grandmother, mini-dances rather, since everything about him was so tiny. A dwarf he was, to tell the truth, except for his emotions, so immense by comparison. Did he refuse to sit down so as not to diminish his already puny size? Or because of his sciatica, that prize won from fifty years at an ironing board? For families of means, Abbo Sapriel had been the best ironer around. Which he continued to prove, pressing the cherished dresses of his cherished beloved. Who said that, by not sitting down, Abbo meant to show vertically his respect for his chosen one, a flag of love one salutes standing—or lying down, which also counts. Mona would spy on them through the keyhole when they were in the latter position, both Abbo and Farida sighing with pleasure. Both of them stretched out on the bed. Both of them excited and red. Both of them showering each other with tender touches.

Conversation with the dwarf was limited. Thus, when Farida would tell him about the cares of Mme. So-and-So or the bad health of another, Abbo would answer, "Those who give consolation do not catch migraines."

If she complained about the decrepit stove, he would retort, "They sowed the word 'tomorrow' and it did not grow."

And when, annoyed by this laconicism, she would catch him in his own trap, saying, "With you, the bald find nothing but a comb," Abbo would screw up his slanty eyes, the result of a distant ancestress's indiscretion with a passing Mongol, laugh his white-toothed laugh, for he scorned tobacco and wine, among other masculine dissipations, and conclude subtly, "The sigh of a young girl is heard farther than the roar of a lion."

Thus did Mona's illness dissipate deliciously between the two sighing cohorts.

One afternoon, Abbo Sapriel did not come. Farida was rightfully alarmed, for it was his first absence in twenty years. Nor did the next day bring the suitor. Two days later, just when Farida Sardaal was dressing to go find out what was up, she received a little suitcase containing the dwarf's effects and a letter. In it, a neighbor informed her of the accidental death of Abbo Sapriel. Finding himself by chance in the path of a mob about to stone a stealer of oranges, poor Abbo, trampled because of his tiny size, which is no excuse, had had the untoward idea of exclaiming, "You can count the oranges on a tree, but not the trees in an orange!" Taking the little man for an accomplice of the thief, the crowd turned its fury against him and threw him down on the pointy curb of a sidewalk, where he sighed one last time before finding definitive peace.

Mona felt sad and, above all, feared for her grandmother. But Farida said simply: "It's all right. He was old already, with all those good years he lived."

She borrowed a wooden mannequin from her daughter Marcelle, dressed it in the dead man's suit, and placed it near the window. It had no legs, but truly his own were so short one could do without them. The mannequin perpetuated a suitor-like presence. Especially at twilight, when the sun would cast a halo of gentleness over it.

Farida wept little for Abbo Sapriel and spoke no more of him, while all the time taking care to dust off the suit, puff out the empty sleeves, and straighten the hat.

The way Farida was made, her words of sympathy went only to the living. And an enormous task it was at the time, because Marcelle filled the house with her tears. A dressmaker, she suffered the hell of celibacy, pining away for a married man. A producer of musical films, forever in search of gyrating bellies, and who, consequently, put in only furtive appearances at his mistress's place. This mostly fruitless waiting made her cantankerous and a tad mad. Whenever Mona made too much noise, Marcelle would stick her in the hand with a pin, wave her scissors around, and sprinkle tears all over the clothing she was cutting for her rich clientele: dresses, smocks, even Paris-style coats, all of which she cursed as though they were the guilty ones.

"Die, filth, you're gouging out my eyes! No way. I cut you, tailor you, sew you, and to whom do the beautiful outfits go? Paper aristocrats and grocery store lady parvenues. Down-and-out yesterday, today Miss Orderer-of-Dresses. Meanwhile I'm dying! Scissors should stick in your throat, miserable Gabriel. These pins should pierce your stomach!"

Sometimes, struck with sudden elation, she would smile at the absent one and intone an Om Kalsoum song. She would disrobe in front of the mirror and put on her customers' dresses—which, of course, looked better on her. She would call her niece over and ask her to feel how firm her breasts were, or to smell her hair, so luxuriant and sensuous. Then Mona would have to tell her over and over—and it was true—that she was the most beautiful woman in the world. And her aunt would arch her opulent back and execute a few Moorish undulations Mona would imitate, wriggling around the room. To bring the fun to a peak, Marcelle would vary her make-up: Nefertiti eyes or Rita Hayworth mouth, and make up the child next. But she was just playing with Mona—her adorable, perverse little doll. Then for no reason, plunging into an abyss of anger or sorrow, she'd send Mona off to wash her face. In the Boustan el-Said apartment, and and on Mona's arms, there would float the odor of Chabraouichi Number Five, her aunt's perfume.

To this day, Marcelle still reeks of Chabraouichi Number Five. In the same house. Clinging to her home. Her sewing machine, her mirror. And to the old speechless lover. Of the entire family, she's the only one who remains, incrusted in their native land. Obstinate and crazy. She refuses the exodus. What other sun, what other springtime, what other city with some unreadable name could ever shelter her? Oh, that seamstress adroit of hand, sure of her good taste, certified fashion maven, but no decipherer of any parasite alphabet. So she waits, a sleepwalker in her own house. She still test-feels her breasts, the traitors. Inside her head, white beneath the black hair dye, there lives a young woman. Light, lovely, modeler of dresses. Who dolls up for dates with her city. On the balcony. From high up, she rendezvous with her city, observes it, loves it. But doesn't venture into it any more. The streets frighten her. The packed sidewalks expel her. The gracefulness of young girls offends her. The hordes of people crowd her out. Her city no longer belongs to her. She recognizes neither buildings nor men. Still, that's where she wants to remain. Immured in obstinacy. Happy. She has all the time in the world for raving among her memories. A guardian of certitudes. When you die, Marcelle, my childhood will be nothing but a cemetery.

But why argue with the outcome? Let's get back to those sweet hours and to the day when, nearly cured, Mona saw a government worker arrive at her grandmother's place. To record the damage wrought by the arsonists.

Beneath his threadbare suit, he was a polite young man. Removing his tarboosh, he called down the misdeeds of his compatriots on his own head. Took the wretches to task for ignoring the sacredness of private property. In the name of the Republic, he swore to wash away the offense and reimburse the scorched ruins.

Farida Sardaal insisted on nourishing him with the sustenance of hospitality before taking him out to the burnt balcony. Gently she pushed in front of him the fruit syrups, the creamed cheese, the dates, and the coffee, inquiring excitedly after his ancestors and descendants, health and prosperity. Amiably he reciprocated her civilities and strove mightily to eat. Three other professional visits had already stuffed him enough for a lifetime.

When he wiped his forehead, Farida ran to get two Digestbile pills, which he swallowed down in their fizzy water. Espying a missing button on the civil servant's jacket, the grandmother smelled a tragedy of divorce or loneliness. She made him remove the garment, sewed on a new button, and commiserated discreetly but knowingly, over the tortures of love. They proceeded to the balcony and to the composition of the written report. The young man admired the view, went into raptures over the clean air and, marveling, caressed the sickly leaves of the potted shrub. Then he took out a form and inquired about his hostess's nationality.

"What can you mean?" she said in Arabic, "Isn't it obvious? I'm a European from Egypt."

"My congratulations. But your nationality, what is it exactly? French, English, Greek, or Italian?"

"Whatever you wish, sweetie. But in my heart I am Egyptian."

"My compliments. But tell me, my dearest madam, you have a passport?"

"A useless bother! I pass through no ports, and I porter no passes. Boat, plane, train, no way. So no passport either."

"I am your servant. I tremble to dwell on it, such bad manners it would be. But the administration is so picky, Madam, it makes its employees indiscreet ferreters of identity. On my life, show me any official paper and we'll never mention the matter again, very dear madam."

"So let's speak no more about it and no standing on ceremony among friends. Call me Farida. I could almost be your mother."

The civil servant threw a bewildered glance at this woman who could easily have engendered his father and grandfather and asked her age.

"Guess!" answered the coquette. "Never, in the presence of a handsome man, does a woman's age cross her lips."

"At any rate you don't look it. But, on my life, I have to fill in a date in this little box on my form."

"Go ahead, go ahead, so I can see how old you think I am."

He smiled and wrote seventy-two at random. He went on to the other questions.

"Your honored father was called Maurice Benzakein, wasn't he?"

"Yes, and of the purest of origins."

"When did he die, God keep his soul?"

"Do I remember? A hundred and fifty years ago, perhaps."

"Too long ago for the unhappy orphan at any rate. And the cause of death, with eternal regrets?"

"Oy! How curiosity burns. He died of, of . . . of mumps."

"Mumps? Perfect, I'm writing. And your respected mother?"

"Very nice. A great cook. The cake you ate is one of her secrets."

"Fabulous. Even the memory of it is a feast. But, please, the cause of the terrible loss?"

"We will all die one day, won't we? The poor thing was carried off by the plague."

"The hand of God. Which one?"

"Which hand? How should I know?"

"No, dear honored Farida, which plague? Which illness, God protect us?"

"Let's see, let me remember. Chicken pox. There. And now, enough, sweetie, no more questions for my weary head."

"I obey on my knees and kiss your hands."

Highly satisfied with one another, they parted, newly minted childhood friends. The young man promised to keep in touch in the form of a substantial money order.

When he had gone, Mona asked her grandmother the reason for her lies. Farida giggled, her hand over her painted mouth,"No way! He wanted causes and effects, and learned names of diseases. The only ones I know are Sélim's[*] chicken pox last year and your mumps, little flower."

"And your age, Grandma? Your papers? It's true that you don't have any?"

"Truth lies in its own well. I lost everything when I moved once. Age—it comes, it goes, it changes all the time, and so does nationality . What's the use of papers made of dust? Do I not know who I am? Farida Sardaal, born Benzakein, in Cairo, one very fine day."

"And such a happy one for me!" replied the little girl.

---

[*] Mona's older brother

Paula Jacques

§ § §

The family counsel was called. To dispel the general affliction, Rébecca brought out her best dinner plates for the tragic noonday meal. A huge feast of spiced salads, lemon chicken, stuffed grape leaves, meatballs with cumin, rice pudding.

The five Castros, in fancy dress pyjamas, awaited their guests. Aron Castro, a secondhand dealer for the time being, arrived first. His offerings consisted of a one-armed doll and a few pieces of candy. Fortunée Levy, Jacques' older sister, entered, followed by her daughter Bolissa. Dabbing at her reddened eyes, Fortunée groaned so that the astonished Aron queried, "What is it, my dear sister? Are you rehearsing for the last act of Carmen?"

"Evil-hearted man! You don't see the country in flames for our ruin? I have no water left in my body from crying."

"So drink a glass."

They went to table without waiting for Ernest. The governess [Sayeda] settled herself between Mona and Sélim, and sat the little one on her knees. Breaking bread, Jacques launched into the ritual "next year in Jerusalem."

"What Jerusalem?" laughed Fortunée, "what next year? May God kill me, but don't talk calamity even if the situation is shaky as to the future."

Entering, Ernest Castro placed a striped watermelon on the table.

"*Hello you all.*[*] I bring you a watermelon of pure sweeetness, from the king's farm. I was invited to the palace. . . . "

"Of the King?" cut in Aron. "Wow! He must have forgotten to remove the label from Takis's grocery. What royal distraction!"

Sayeda slapped Sélim, who had let out a guffaw like a lout with no upbringing. At every possible occasion, Ernest bragged about his distinguished connections, dropping shaky Anglicisms whenever he could. He *drinked* with Prince Fouad, *lunchered* at her majesty Chivekiar's, *flirted* with Sir Lawrence's *Daddy*. Was he not one of them, he with blue blood that connected him to the Prince of Menashe, benefactor of the Jewish community? Exasperated with this snobbery, Aron declared it was all nothing but lies and hot air. Even Ernest's dentist degree, which he had somehow obtained in Beirut, was probably only a worthless rag certifying his quackery. Indeed, Uncle Ernest had a reputation for supreme brutality in dental pain and his relatives avoided that office of his, decorated as it was with carnivorous trophies. Although Aron maintained that his brother was the best butcher in Cairo, our dental doctor had somehow

---

[*] Appears in English in the original

managed to capture the British officer clientele for himself exclusively. And he was terribly proud of that. Ernest was conscientious. He transplanted in the living gums of his clients the gold he extracted from them in payment. From his pocket to their mouth. His own teeth, to be sure, were as yellow as those of a horse headed for the carcass heap.

Ernest was a man who cared about elegance. He rarely removed his Texan hat and kid gloves, so as "not to inflict on the ladies, during my masterly movements, sweat spots like the prophet's hand prints."

Mona detested the insistent kisses of that uncle, so generous with hugs and so stingy with everything else. Whenever he took her out for tea at Lappas'— we're going to treat *the little dear*—she had to be content with whatever he left of the cake he ordered for himself. On the way out of the pastry shop, he always became afflicted with strange tics. Every three meters, he would shout greetings to invisible passers-by. Tip his hat. Wink. Slice the air with a cordial wave. Salute the streetcar. Bow to the coach. Congratulate the sidewalk. Convey his compliments to the dust. Speak to the statue using the familiar "you." Reprimand the whirling hawks. Shake hands with the mosquitoes. Give advice to the blind beggar. Encourage the overworked donkey, the sweating policeman, the hoarse street hawker. Distribute benedictions to the people with great quantities of tongue clucking. Ernest would deliver monotonous disquisitions to his niece, casting himself as the central figure caught between offended husbands and conquered beauties. Tall, strong, rather grimy, nearsighted and with a sweating face, he would assure her that no woman could resist his charms. Which was why he had always avoided marriage. How could he, for the benefit of one single woman, reduce all the others to despair? At around forty, an arid baldness caused him some uneasiness. Hairpieces, however, assuaged that particular anxiety. In the morning, his hair was a laquered brown, at noon curly blond, and at night wavy chestnut. "He's a veritable Frégoli* in the grips of avarice," sneered Aron. "The butcher has bought himself a batch of wigs and he'll wear out all of them before he dies."

But this was no time for pleasantries. Jacques Castro demanded everyone's attention, and silent attention at that. He said, "Elohim observed the misery of his people in Egypt. He heard them cry out beneath the blows of their slave drivers. He knew their sufferings. Yahweh said: 'I shall go down to deliver my people from the hands of the Egyptians and direct them toward a good land.'"

"There's no place as chic as Paris," approved Aunt Fortunée.

---

*Leopoldo Fregoli (1867–1936), an Italian actor and playwright, famous for performing one-man shows in which he would play as many as sixty roles; his ability to metamorphose himself became legendary.

"Certainly," said Rébecca, "but the river of money flows in New York."

"No!" shouted the dentist, "Brazil is the place for guaranteed prosperity. I go down the Amazon with a pickup truck full of aspirin, and presto! I'm the Dr. Schweitzer of the Indians who are dying like flies of the flu."

"Silence!" Jacques continued. "I'm requesting concentration of the mind, here. The cake has been eaten and the gong of misfortune is striking for us. In my opinion, this is the beginning of great anti-Semitic torments and we have to be united. The situation is serious."

"No, my man, the situation is hopeless, but not serious," said Uncle Aron. Snatching a plate to use as a head covering, he rocked back and forth chanting, *"Auprès de ma bombe, qu'il fait bon mourir."**

"A bomb in your right eye you should get!" cried Fortunée. "Will you please allow your older brother to speak words of wisdom?" She helped herself to another meatball. "Tell me, Becky, you made them with your own hands? They're a dream. What, a dream? An apparition from heaven!"

The stout, gray-eyed lady found consolation from her recent widowhood in a bulimia exacerbated by sadness. She ate quickly, copiously, and musically. Each one of her mouthfuls was accompanied by the tinkling of her valuables, for Fortunée used to go out out adorned with all her jewels, chains, necklaces, rings, even her wedding tiara. Be there riots or peace, she feared thieves more than damnation. "Fortunate Fortunée am I, and my fortune's fortune goes where I go," she would say, constantly feeling the treasures buried in the undulating cache of her cleavage.

Aron pricked her on the breast with a fork.

"When a woman has no more money between her legs, she puts it around her neck. Fortunée, your jewels cry out too loudly, and the revolutionaries are going to take them all. Entrust them to me and, on my life, you'll soon have ten times what you have now."

"May God cut, burn, strangle, drown, and suffocate anyone who dares touch me! Horns on me. May I die if I give the tiniest ring to a thief like you, you accomplice of Al Capone."

"What Al Capone? That spaghetti head? I'm head and shoulders above that circus gangster. He can't come near me."

Aron seemed gratified that his notorious talents as a crook had been brought up. He disclosed his latest misdeeds: He had sold a client back his own pen, which he had forgotten in the store; he had perfected a love potion he hawked successfully to despairing lovers, disguised as a fakir, and, lastly, he'd

---

*"Close to my bomb, oh how nice it is to die." This is a recasting of a traditional French song, "Auprès de ma blonde, qu'il fait bon dormir."

gotten a detested neighbor to decamp, worn out by the banana peels with which our dear second-hand dealer's monkey Mickey continually bombarded him. The family blossomed into laughter. Ernest yelled that such dishonest nonsense was a waste of time. They had to return to the subject of the day's riot and come to a decision.

"*Do you know*, my friends, that ten thousand families, certain Jewish ones among them, and some of the best ones, are wandering about this very day, homeless? Driven out of their burnt houses."

"Really? The poor things," sympathized Rébecca. "At least we can be sure that the dead have found rest from this miserable life. May the days they should have lived be added on to yours, my darlings."

"Thank you," said Ernest. "On the way here, I saw several destroyed synagogues. Cicurel* was still burning and about twenty poor scorched corpses were lying on the sidewalk in front of the Turf Club, with not even a blanket over them. *English friends, I believe*. I have it from the best sources. The poor wretches tried to escape and the crazed rabble pushed them back into the flames, hurling insults at them. Until they sighed their last sigh. *God in heaven. Struggle for life, last but not least*. Have it from the best sources. I recognized dear old Sir Reginald Craig, shrunken smaller than a piece of coal."

"Craig, the British Customs Adviser?" asked Jacques.

"'Himself. *Smart fellow*, I knew him well and it would have given me pleasure, one last time, to. . . . "

"Shake his paw, your highness!" shrieked Aron. "You could have kept a finger for a souvenir."

Ernest rose to his feet, knocking over a chair.

"Enough already! Today's a black day for your mother! Demon, parasitic thief, heartless, uneducated, *poor fool!* May your tongue swell and strangle your breathing!"

Aron tore off his brother's wig and was chased around the table. The little secondhand dealer dodged blows, mimed a boxing match, and Sélim threw himself between the combatants' legs. Rébecca sat on the table so the plates shouldn't fall off. Fortunée pinched a meatball from David's plate. Resigned, Jacques lit a cigarette, an Atlas Coutarelli. Mona decided that adults were unpredictable. The very ones, who that morning were wringing their hands imploring divine protection, were now gorging themselves and fighting in radiant good humor.

Bolissa, mute up to that point, called out in a strident voice: "You blind fools. Clowns. Puppets and henchmen of imperialism. The revolution is

---
*Department store

throwing off its chains and you go on in blindness. How much more of this egotism? How much more oppression?"

The young woman tossed her head of long red hair. Her face, naked as her hands—she despised coquettish subterfuge—sparkled with fury. Heavy haunched, delicate of ankle, long of nose and round of cheek, she became beautiful in anger. To put a stop to the free-for-all, she struck the table with her fist and intoned, "Brothers, follow our banner stained with the blood of innocents."

Catching her bracelet on the neck of the wine bottle, she spilled its contents. Chewing imperturbably, Fortunée sopped up the liquid seeping into the table cloth with a piece of bread. She reassured the gathering: A good marriage would ease her daughter out of this stage of idealism and fury.

"Calm down, light of my eye," she told her, "this too will pass. It's for your own good."

"What good? When I had typhus so I was burning up with fever, you also said that would pass. But you cried like it was your own funeral when you lost your wallet. Here, here's money, take, help yourself!"

Bolissa threw her bracelet on the soaked table, moaning, "I know you, oh my wretched family. You're on the side of money."

"And who are you to spit at money?" exclaimed her mother. "Rothschild's daughter or your father's? Oy, how I sacrificed for her! And this is the thanks a mother gets for so much devotion. Oh, Elie, Elie, why have you forsaken me?"

That was the name of her deceased husband, whom Fortunée invoked in moments of extremity. Her chest heaving with sobs crystalline because of the jingling purse in her cleavage, she seized a dessert knife and held it out to Bolissa, begging her to finish her off. She even bared the top of one breast to facilitate the mortal blow. But Bolissa sneered and turned her head away. At her wits' end, Fortunée covered her face with a napkin, so she wouldn't have to live any more.

Jacques Castro extricated her from behind it so tenderly that Mona shuddered.

"Easy, dearest sister. And you, Bolissa, explain calmly. Like a human. Tell us who set fire to Cairo and ruined the Jews. Muslim fanatics or your communist friends?"

"Papa, what are Communists?"

Rébecca sat Sélim on her knees and answers gushed forth. A bunch of jealous people. People diseased with the cramps of politics. Starving idealists.

"If I should ever get my hands on one of them, damn them, I swear, he won't have a tooth left in his mouth to chomp onto a red commie knife. *Obvious*. Down boy and hands off. All of them, each one more of a groveller than the next."

Light of My Eye

Fortunée clapped her hands in excitement.

"Bravo, Ernest. Let's rid the earth of criminals. How sorry I am Hitler is dead. How greatly I would have made him pay in pain for his crimes against us. I'd impale him on a bellows that would come out of his mouth and I'd give him nothing but menstrual blood to drink with a little jam for taste."

"And me," cried Rébecca, "I'd pour castor oil down the funnel in his mouth until his stomach burst."

"No, no," said Aron. "I'd put him alive in a circus cage and tour the world. To thrill the public even more, I'd tie him up with three big rusty chains and whip him with a horse knout. Then, for ten piasters, the spectator would throw salt and vinegar on his wounds. Justice would be achieved and so would my fortune."

Ernest, striking his forehead with an air of commiseration: "Poor madman. You're dreaming. And what if Hitler escaped? Then what do you do? Huh? No way. Everything would start all over again. Soap from our bodies and gold from our teeth."

"Aren't you ashamed to be so childishly ill with your reactionariness?" demanded Bolissa.

"I know!" screamed Mona. "I've seen jet airplane engines. Yikes, what noise, what speed. . . ."

Rebecca walked around the table and forced a meatball into her mouth.

"Mona you're talking nonsense and you haven't touched your food. You either finish what's on your plate or you'll finish in bed. When one doesn't understand anything, one listens in silence."

"Why don't you say anything when Sélim talks?"

"Sélim's got some sense. Sélim eats everything, even vegetables. Sélim is big. Sélim is a little man."

"I will be too, very soon," pouted the little girl.

Fortunée got up from the table and embraced her niece.

"She is turning out perfectly. God keep her, Becky. A hundred years, let's hope. Now, my apologies, but I am going to do like the Romans."

The aunt went off to vomit, in order to make room in her packed stomach for the coming dishes. You old gorger, you, dead at the age of seventy-two, in Paris, rue des Francs-Bourgeois. Dear Fortunée, felled by an intestinal blockage. Your stomach, source and receptacle of your pleasures, wreaked its revenge for all those upheavals you caused it. Adieu, Fortunée. You expired, scintillating as ever in all your jewels, bemoaning with your final regrets the diet that darkened your last years. Rest in peace and eat again, if you can. In the Jewish paradise, gluttony is not a mortal sin.

For the moment, however, the future dead aunt tripped lightly back from the bathroom. With her stomach unloaded, she seated herself again and lent a benevolent ear to her daughter's analysis.

"In my opinion, the situation is classic. Provocateurs, Muslim fanatics, and the enemies of the propertied, and the English incited the people to torch the city so that afterwards they could accuse the King and his corrupt army of laxity. I couldn't swear to it dialectically, for it's too early for that, but I do declare it to be so."

Jacques shook his head at length and offered Bolissa a cigarette. Since ladies are not supposed to smoke, that was his way of expressing esteem for his young niece, so cultured, intelligent, a reciter by heart of "La Légende des Siècles."* Bored by her job in some ministry, Bolissa read all the classics in the original in her office. Then she would summarize them at the Circle of French Friends, where everyone would admire her Marxist, yet nevertheless personal, interpretations. In her miniscule revolutionary group, they treated her opinions as authoritative. Young intellectuals, Jewish and French, who met twice a week in a secret place, known of course both to their families and to the police. The group maintained cordial relations with the spy sent to keep them under surveillance. He would wait patiently in the street until the meetings ended and then escort them to the Kasr-el-Nil Bridge. Once there, the clandestine members would parade off, fists raised, chanting the "Internationale"— the immediate effect of which was to amuse the neighborhood loafers and make their own throats dry. Then the young people would swill down Egyptian vodka or sugar cane juice and stuff themselves with beans, that food of the people.

"I request a break from mouth stuffing," said Jacques. "Bolissa can't concentrate with all this mastication."

"Everyone look," she said. "This precious table is Egypt. The most beautiful garden in the world."

She quickly improvised a labyrinth, positioning bread, pepper, and salt around the pitcher of water. Then she pointed to the salad scraps, "A garden so fertile that everything grows profusely. What a marvel, this garden caressed by the hand of man. The bread is the working people, gardeners of the Nile. In every group, they are the most numerous, the most productive, the most admirable. I won't belabor the point. But just think what a meal would be like without bread."

Fortunée shuddered, and took another slice of watermelon. "So, let's look at what we have here. The largest group is falling apart. [She scattered the bread.] It's sick. It is hungry. It is burnt by the sun and worn down by vermin. Now let's observe the others. The salt is spreading out, avid and happy. That's

---

*Victor Hugo's epic poem

the English, the colonist, the imperialist manipulator of puppet strings. Next to him, his best accomplice, the pepper. In other words, the feudal privileged, the propertied, government ministers, and members of parliament. The salt and pepper are inseparable on the table of the world. Let us now consider the fourth partner. The water pitcher. The king. Pot-bellied and transparently swollen like his mind. But don't trust it. This pitcher, so full, is nothing but the appearance of legitimacy. If I break it, what remains of the king and all his pomp and ceremony?"

She brandished the pitcher over the heads of the guests and Rébecca stood up: "On your life, Bolissa, don't break it. It's Venetian crystal. Another time maybe."

"Okay, but only if you agree that in order to return the garden to the gardeners, we have to drive out the three bandit partners."

Ernest grabbed the tablecloth and knocked down the whole edifice.

"Get rid of the English? Dances and grimaces in this country of monkeys! This is a black day for Fortunée. Her daughter is mad. Tell me, my dear, what will we live on if our friends leave? With whom will we work? The native tarboosh wearers, sidewalk pissers? *Thanks. Not for me. Last but not least. Bye-bye Egypt.*"

Without losing her self control, Bolissa entreated her uncle to give up cold calculation and join the masses.

"Today or never. It's union with the people or exile with the pecuniary abusers."

"Please!" cried Rébecca. "No dirty words in front of the children!"

"What dirty words? Is this a madhouse or my family? Pecuniary abuser, my dear aunt, means usurer, speculator.

"Never you mind. It's filth."

"Becky, listen to Bolissa. She knows."

"Oh Joucky, you don't love me any more. I'm leaving this table, such humiliation."

Jacques and his sons threw themselves at the offended one's feet.

"I give up," said Bolissa. "You're hopeless. And accomplices of the tyrant. We'll get rid of all of you."

Mona saw her father's face turn purple. He spoke, pronouncing each syllable distinctly: "If you want to make us swim across the desert, I refuse to listen to you any longer. It's a miserable life, going from country to country. Where the exile lives, he can't open his mouth. He drinks nothing but the bitterness of words, for everywhere he is a foreigner. Tell me, my child, what is my crime? What thefts, what speculations, what infamies have I committed in this land where I was born? You want me to burn down my own house and wander around the world?"

"Bravo, Joucky," said Fortunée. "You're totally and completely right. I won't even count to three. Tomorrow I pack my suitcase and I leave these intestine eaters, these sons of dogs. With no hard feelings. First, I'm not the envious kind. Second, Paris is very pretty. Where else can you find the Eiffel Tower? The seven seas I've travelled, I've never seen anything better."

"You, Fortunée? You've been to Paris?" asked Aron.

"Certainly, sir. I went all over on my honeymoon with dear Elie."

"Daughter of a liar! All you saw was Marseilles and even there you didn't get closer than the dock."

"Blindness should be in your eye! What do you know from how I skipped along rivers, streams, and the Champs Elysées? Becky, let's leave for sweet France. Are you coming with me?"

"They should bury me, if I don't fly off too," approved Rébecca.

"Well, I'm staying with Sayeda," said Mona.

"But none of you is going to leave," smiled the governess. "The accursed ones are the English. No way. We'll throw them out to the last drop of blood. One day a mosquito alights on the branches of a date palm. It wants to rest. Fine. It rests. Then it eats all the dates, down to the very last one. When there are none left, green or brown, it says to the tree: 'Okay look sharp, I'm going to fly away.' The date palm answers, 'Go ahead and leave. I never heard you come and if you weren't so close to my ear now, I wouldn't even have heard you speak.'"

"Oh, wondrous!" exclaimed Bolissa. "There lies all the wisdom of a people. Thank you, sister, for your good words. Listen, the peasants and the workers are calling us."

"Yeah, yeah," yawned Aron. "They're calling 'to bed, go to bed.'"

It was midnight. The guests readied themselves to depart.

"A thousand thousand thanks, Becky. I wish you eternal dinners."

"Same to you, Fortunée. My house is yours. Tell me, are you getting the gang together Sunday or are you going to skip it?"

"Sunday without fail. Even should the end of the world come, could you live without cards?"

At the conclusion of this important meeting, the only decision made was to give up the vacation at Tantah. You had to be a fool or a poor wretch to leave your house and roam the streets in such times of iniquity.

— **Translated by Susan D. Cohen**

Brigitte Peskine
(1951–)

Brigitte Peskine was born in Neuilly-sur-Seine to an Ashkenazi mother from Alsace, a "French Israelite for more than three generations," and a Sephardic father whose Judeo-Spanish family came from the Ottoman Empire. Peskine is the last name of her husband whose father emigrated from Vilna, Lithuania. In *Les Eaux douces d'Europe* [The Sweet Waters of Europe], Peskine wishes to bring her father's family to life. Her paternal grandparents had told her nothing of the Turkish Sephardic community, so strong was the desire of these "French-at-heart" Turkish Jews, to forget the four hundred years spent in Ottoman lands. Most of Peskine's Sephardic relations converted or married non-Jews. On the other hand, there have been no conversions in the Ashkenazi part of the family and only one exogamous marriage—to a North African Jew.

A statistician at the INSEE (France's National Institute of Economic and Statistical Information) from 1972 to 1988, Peskine has published seven novels, two essays, and some fifteen works for young people. After having spent several years in Strasbourg and in Caracas, Venezuela she now divides her time between Paris and her house in the province of Berry, writing novels and television scripts.

In *Les Eaux douces d'Europe,* she recreates the atmosphere of the Sephardic community of Istanbul during the early years of the twentieth century. The narrator and protagonist of the novel, Rebecca Gatégno, is born in the city that, in 1898, is still called Constantinople, where she suffers from the triple prejudice of being "female, oriental, and Jewish." The Ottoman Sephardim had lived for four centuries with the memory of that Golden Age for Jews in Spain before the expulsion in 1492, and still spoke its language, Judeo-Spanish or Ladino. Though looked down upon by the native-born French, these minorities—who had received a Francophone education, were not very religious, and were extremely adaptable—sought to assimilate more zealously than the Ashkenazi Jews and those who were called the Zionists. By contrast, the *Alliancists,* as they were called, wanted to be modern and lived *a la franca*. But they were trapped by the Holocaust nevertheless. In the novel Rebecca Gatégno, like her community, journeys toward freedom, in spite of the obstacles.

The youngest in a family of seven—in which girls represent a liability for their parents who must provide them with dowries and husbands—Rebecca, unloved by her mother, tries to escape her ancestral fate through education. Her family's opposition, and later World War I, keep her in Constantinople for an additional two years, but she finally succeeds in realizing her dream of studying at the École Normale Israélite Orientale in Paris to become a teacher and passing the French baccalaureate exams. But at the moment when Rebecca finally seems able to attain independence by studying abroad, her sister Adela suddenly dies in Istanbul, leaving three young children. Sephardic tradition demands that the dead woman's sister marry the widowed husband and bring up the children. Rebecca cannot escape this custom and returns home.

The rest of the novel describes the tribulations of the Sephardic minority which must choose between assimilation and exile when the Turkish Republic is established in 1923. It also follows the adventures of the protagonist and her protracted resistance to a married situation that stifles her, though she assumes the obligation of raising her sister's children. The couple resolves the dilemma by choosing exile to France, where Rebecca contributes to the family's finances by writing serials for newspapers and the radio. After a long period of distress and depression, having divorced her husband and taken refuge with her brother in Venezuela, Rebecca Gatgéno marries the man she loves, a socialist lawyer from the same background—on the day that Hitler becomes Chancellor of the Third Reich. The remainder of Rebecca's story is told in *Buena Familia* (2000).

The Judeo-Spanish minority in the Ottoman Empire is evoked precisely, accurately, and without indulgence. Besides Albert Cohen, few novelists have been interested in describing this community. Yet the French language and Enlightenment had, since the end of the nineteenth century, exerted a profound influence on the Judeo-Spanish community dispersed in places such as Constantinople, Salonika, Smyrna, Rhodes, and Corfu. Its members had been educated by the schools of the Alliance Israélite Universelle and were ready to be integrated into French society, even before the great exodus to France.

Brigitte Peskine deserves credit for her lack of reverence for her ancestors' customs evident in the works of male writers. She demystifies and unflinchingly describes these customs through the eyes, not of an adored son, but of a rejected daughter. From this point of view, Rebecca's mother, Tamar Covo, is exemplary in her dry conventionality and the manner in which she conveys the oppressive experience that has caused her to hate herself and her daughters. Rebecca, on the other hand, succeeds in freeing herself from these traditional prejudices without entirely cutting herself off from her roots, and brings up her children to become free agents. The narrative "I" underscores the feeling of "modernity" that a character born in 1898 inspires.

This novel's charm lies in the re-creation of the life of the *cortijo*, the garden courtyard where the women stay, the evocation of interiors, of clothes, and above all of the delights of the kitchen in which the ancient Spanish culinary traditions mingle with the refinements of the Ottoman cuisine—*borekas, pastelicos,* or rose preserves served on silver trays. Knowledge of Ladino proverbs allows the author to wickedly underscore the patriarchal or macho connotations. For example: *Tiene ijas, tiene ansyas* [he who has daughters has worries]; *tres ijas i una madre, mala vida para su padre* [three daughters and a mother, a bad life for a father]. In the background, the historical context brings to life the great dramas of this vibrant era: the fight of the Young Turks, its disillusionments, as well as the Armenian tragedy—the first genocide of the century. Rebecca also experiences the guilt of having rebelled against the customs of the Judeo-Spanish community about to be exterminated (the subject of the next novel). In this work more than in others, the author cannot defend herself against the sin of having dared to write about future or past victims. It is this tension between the resisting myths and the difficulty in escaping them that gives a historical tragic dimension to Brigitte Peskine's two novels.

The following selection illustrates the opposition that a fourteen-year-old Judeo-Ottoman girl at the beginning of the twentieth century encounters from her family when she desires to study—in France especially.

— Michèle Sarde
Translated by Eva Martin Sartori

Selected Works

Une Robe pour Julia. Paris: Seghers, 1992.
Les Eaux douces d'Europe. Paris: Seuil, 1996.
L'Enfant oublié. Paris: Laffont, 1996.
Sarah, l'enfant perdue. Paris: Hachette jeunesse, 1997.
Buena Familia. Paris: Nil Editions, 2000.
Mon Grand petit frère. Paris: Bayard, 2001.

The Sweet Waters of Europe

In the spring of 1912 my brother had not yet shown any sign of life. The Balkans Wars followed the Tripoli Wars. We knew that cold, hunger, and typhus decimated the armies. My father had a telephone installed at the shop. He impoverished himself by doling out baksheesh in hopes of obtaining information on my brother's whereabouts, but the disorganization of the country and the military's propaganda campaign made all news suspect.

I was about to turn fourteen. Soon Madame Béhar, the director of the Alliance, would recommend that Señor Padre send me to Paris to pursue the program at the École Normale, and I had not yet informed my family of my plans. The moment had come to confront the paternal authority.

I took advantage of an afternoon when my mother was shopping at the Bon Marché to settle myself in the kitchen. I filled the *cezve** with water, coffee, and sugar, then stirred the fire to life. At the first simmering of the water, I poured the beverage into the cup, taking care to spoon out the froth. On the silver platter, I placed the *charope,*** the glass of water, the spoon, and the cup covered with foam. I brought everything into the dining room where my father, chased out of the other rooms by the Passover cleaning, read the newspaper.

He sighed. *"Kaves alegres!"****

"Oh yes," I thought, "let the coffee bring cheerfulness!"

I waited to formulate my question while father sipped the coffee, dipped his spoon into the preserves, and drank the cool water.

Had I forgotten that in our home women were not made to be heard? Without doubt, my father loved me and would cry for me if I died. But alive, I was only supposed to keep quiet. As I explained my request, for which my gender and our respective roles had not prepared him, he looked at first bored, then insulted, then resentful.

How dare I bother him like that? Wasn't it enough that he had found me a husband? That he had given me a dowry that would bring honor to the family? Even though, because he could pass on to me neither rights nor responsibilities, I would be of no help to him in his old age?

---

*A small pot for making Turkish coffee

**A thick sugary syrup flavored with extract of lemon, orange, and roses. It is served on Passover and other special occasions.

***May you have joyous occasions on which to drink coffee.

From: *Eaux douces d'Europe* (Paris: Seuil, 1996), pp. 111–118.

The departure of Vitali tormented him, business went less profitably, and logically I should have used my feeble strength to alleviate his great suffering. I should have filled the platter with the rarest sweets: for example, quince paste, watered lozenges that ran through the fingers but deliciously coat the stomach, and a little glass of *raki** accompanied by *bunuelos*** soaked in honey. I could have also washed his feet, as done in ancient times. Instead, I added to his worries!

"Paris? Why Paris?"

"I just told you. To earn my diploma and become a teacher!"

"You want to work for money? You, the daughter of Señor Gatégno?"

"Rachel Abravanel said that . . ."

"I don't care what she says! This is a woman without respect, who speaks like her husband!"

"But . . ."

"Silence! Tell Señora Béhar to come to see me next Saturday after *desayuno**** and see to it that she is well received. This coffee had no taste. You have much to learn, my daughter."

My hands still trembled when I rang at the Abravanels' home under the pretext of returning their books. Their living room was littered with boxes. Standing on a stepladder, Nissim was going through his library. I thought that they were getting ready for their vacation on the Princes' Islands.

"No, Rebecca," Rachel said to me in a sad voice. "This time, it's over. We are leaving Constantinople. Don't cry, *querida*, we will write you. . . . And you will come join us in Paris. Consider this: you have only a few months to wait. Soon, you will take the French and mathematics examinations. Then Madame Béhar . . ."

"Excuse me, it's the director in person!" cut in Nissim smiling. "The one who treats the ambassadors as equals! It is the *bachi-bouzouik***** of the Alliance who comes to announce your admission to the ENIO!***** But . . . what is going on, my little one? You're crying?"

"My father refuses to let me go!"

I recounted my interview with the Señor Padre. Nissim, embarrassed,

---

*Anise-flavored Turkish brandy
**Fried potato fritters
***Breakfast
****Soldier in the Ottoman army
*****Teachers' seminary for Jewish girls

promised to intercede in my favor. Rachel stuffed me with Passover cake and kissed me tenderly.

"Élie is waiting for you, you know…"

"Élie?" I cried. "He has forgotten me! And you will forget me too! When you leave here, you will no longer look back!" I slammed the door as I left.

Every day we learned of a new departure. And never did a son or brother return, even for an ordinary visit. The parents boasted, in the *cortijo,* or at the synagogue, about the success of their progeny. The emigrants wrote, they sometimes sent money to repay the cost of their studies, or for being set up in business: we thanked them with "Turkish Delights" and rose-flavored preserves that probably rotted in their packages covered with wax seals, postage stamps, and rubber stamps. Everything happened as if, once settled in Europe, the Ottoman Jews wanted to forget the *juderia** of Haskeuy, the dust of Andrinopoulos, or the vineyards of Smyrna, as if the past four centuries in the Empire had only been an accident of history, a detail of no importance.

I had trouble understanding. We were all so imbued with the notion of family. . . . Jewish mothers were so possessive and fathers were so jealous of their authority. Several thousand kilometers transformed the most loving and respectful son into a perfect stranger. He was not cursed, in fact to the contrary. And I, who was neither respectful nor loving, I remained a prisoner in this decaying city.

Madame Béhar visited us, as planned, the following Saturday. Mama offered her *bimuelos de patata* and canapés on unleavened bread.

"Coffee or anisette?" she asked.

Indeed, how was one to know if women who work for money did not drink and smoke like men?

"Coffee with sugar, thank you," answered Madame Béhar without responding to the insult.

My father laid claim to a brown egg to accompany his beignet.

"Lengthy mastication guarantees good digestion," he stated, his mouth full, while we waited in silence for him to finish eating.

"Certainly," approved the school director.

And she congratulated Mama on her cooking. I fidgeted nervously. Long minutes elapsed. Then my father cleared his throat. "I am grateful for the interest that you have shown in my daughter. I am a simple man and poorly educated, but I have always urged my sons to pursue an education. Alas, you know of the bad luck that has stricken us."

---

*Jewish quarter

Mama groaned.

"My wife here has a weak constitution. It will soon be necessary to help her with her eldest daughter's first childbirth. No, I cannot entrust Rebecca to you right now, I regret it, given the circumstances."

I fell on my knees. "Think again! I beg you!"

"Your daughter is our best student, Señor Gatégno," said Madame Béhar, "and she wishes with all her heart to serve the Alliance. Think of the future of your grandchildren. . . . They will need teachers like Rebecca. . . . "

My father rose. The interview was over.

"Another beignet?" asked my mother.

Ernesta brought the platter, a jubilant smile on her lips. I shoved her on purpose as she left the room, but my sister had a steady hand and nothing fell.

In my room, I remained seated on my bed, shocked, incapable of envisaging the consequences of this refusal. I felt nothing. Only a profound rebellion, too ancient, too buried to explode in the form of anger.

I don't think that my father took the time to reflect on the proposition that had been made to him. Nor do I think that he had spoken with Mama. He refused because he was absorbed in other things and it was easiest to keep me home, not to change any of our practices. He refused because he had earned money these last years, but had begun to earn less and, in accepting that his youngest daughter become a teacher, he risked appearing poorer than he was. He refused because this conversation—a woman speaking to him as an equal—made him ill at ease. He refused because, in *buenas familias,* women did not work.

What reason would there have been to agree? To make me happy? Happiness was not in our vocabulary. My father was neither happy with nor proud of my scholarly accomplishments. A learned daughter is difficult to marry off. That she had inherited intellectual capacities was looked upon as a kind of genetic error. It was as if she had taken it from her brothers. Yes, truly, why would he have agreed?

Simone opened the door.

"Mama is taking us to the Fresh Waters," she murmured.

"Leave me alone!"

In response, she sat down beside me and put her arm around my shoulders. Finally the tears escaped, drowning me in their salty warmth. "We will go to Paris together," replied Simone. "Next year. Like Mama says, *paciencia es pan y censia.* Madame Béhar will save a place for you. We will go together, do you hear?"

In the tram that took us toward the Ortakoy pier, I took my sister Nita's hand and brought it brusquely to my lips. She had understood that I had to get out of the house, at least for the afternoon. The Fresh Waters of Asia.... Undoubtedly she remembered last year with Nahum sick, the walk postponed from day to day.... Nita was good. Intent on consoling me, she agreed to transgress the Sabbath law of weekly repose. How had she preserved her generosity in a house where distrust and envy reigned?

I had more experience than she with the wharf and the ferrymen. But I let her shift for herself. I hurt all over. We climbed into a caïque. The Bosphorus, an unflagging blue, wrinkled by little waves, seemed to want to pull me into its depths. What a difference from the gray, stagnant water of the Golden Horn! Dozens of boats, from the most humble to the most luxurious, sailed toward the Black Sea. The spring was radiant; the birds dove adroitly between the boats, the calls of the seagulls covered the insults of the oarsmen.

I watched the pontoons file by, the escuelas and the sumptuous wooden palaces constructed on the banks of the water. To my left, in a caïque with four oarsmen dressed in gold and velvet, floated veiled silhouettes. What was I doing here? Did I have a place in this languid, nostalgic Orient?

A tributary of the Bosphorus, that cut its course through a clearing, constituted the Fresh Waters of Asia. It was a place for refined promenades. The Turkish women reclined on their barges that were so entangled at this point that they transformed the river into a suspended moving bridge. Levantine families picnicked under the Judas trees. Some elegant women strolled by, parasols in hand, and men in straw hats swung their walking sticks.

I looked at Nita, somberly dressed, her hair pulled back in a heavy ungraceful headband, and Leon, lost in the sailor suit that he had inherited from his uncles. They looked so Jewish! And how I hated that one could recognize us at first glance, categorize us, assume that we were all the same....

Nita took out an embroidered cloth that she stretched out on the grass. It was one of the rare pieces of her trousseau that had escaped the fire in her house. She sat down with a thousand precautions. Her high buttoned shoes were threadbare and out of fashion. I was ashamed of my sister and my nephew. And ashamed to be ashamed. What a bad idea it had been to come here! Didn't Nita know that the Sephardim did not frequent the Fresh Waters of Asia, that they preferred to relax among themselves on the hills of the European shore?

Sorrow made me unjust to my own people. My sister knew that I was suffocating in the *juderia*. She naively thought that I would feel better in the midst of Turks and Christians. Poor dear Nita!

A child with her soles stained with dirt walked on the white sheet: a little French girl accompanied by her governess, who offered no word of apology. I looked at the imprint. The scene of that washday came back to my memory. *Mano pezgada.**

"I will go to Notre-Dame-de-Sion," I declared.

Simone gazed wide-eyed.

"With the nuns?"

"Grandpa would never want it," declared Leon in Ladino.

He had a sententious tone, too old for his age, that exasperated me.

"I want to pursue my studies. The Sion secondary school is the only institution where I could prepare for the French baccalaureate.

"But it is exclusively for Catholics!" said Simone.

"They don't care, as long as you pay," I retorted.

Nita looked at me with horror.

"You are not afraid of the nuns?" she asked.

Oh, and how! I was terrified in advance. But if Greek, Turkish, and Armenian girls studied at Sion, why couldn't I? I was as capable as the others of putting marks on paper.

My decision was made. I had buried my disappointment under a new defiance because, of all the kinds of suffering, powerlessness is the worst.

— **Translated by Nancy Shale**

---

*Clumsy oaf

Chochana Boukhobza
(1960–)

Born in Tunisia, Chochana Boukhobza is a journalist by profession. She has also published a number of novels that have been well received by an appreciative and loyal public as well as by critics.

How do you come to terms with your feelings as a woman when you are rebelling against your family's traditions, while at the same time remaining attached to them? How do you define yourself as a Jew when you are haunted by the horrific images of the Holocaust? When exiled from your native country, do you grow up with memories of a land forever lost? These are some of the questions that give power and coherence to Boukhobza's novels.

Un Été à Jérusalem, from which an excerpt follows, is a short narrative work written in the first person and sustained by the powerfully moving imagination of someone seeking to express an incurable spiritual pain. It exhibits the deeply felt knowledge of a particular kind of parent/child conflict that can sometimes exist in the Tunisian Jewish community—the result of the last three generations having been exposed to two, and often three, different cultures and realities: Judeo-Arabic, French, and Israeli. This knowledge extends further to an ambivalence toward Israel felt deeply by any Jew who, despite an acute sensitivity to the fate of that country, is no less aware of the moral contradictions aroused by its policies, and may, at one time or another, reject them. Chochana Boukhobza speaks from personal experience. Though her book has an authentic tone, it is not an autobiography; it is fiction.

The narrator is a young woman of Tunisian Jewish origin who, for a few weeks one summer, returns to her parents' home in Jerusalem after being away from her family and country for three years. Her inner crisis is brought on by dual feelings of belonging and separation toward both. It is only in the very last lines of the story that we learn the young woman's name is Sarah. And it is just at that point, when one of her relatives calls her by this name, that she affirms that, henceforth, she will no longer go by the name Sarah but Mavrika. Mavrika is the last word in the novel.

In a sense, *Un Été à Jérusalem* is the story of a search for identity that leads the narrator from rejection of her real name to adoption of a name that she gives herself. "Sarah" represents her identity as a divided self in conflict with her own people, primarily with her father, for whom she has real hatred. Her father is locked into the rigidity of moral taboos and sees only shame in his daughter's will to lead her own life. This hatred, however, sometimes gives us the impression of being the mirror image of unexpressed tender feelings. She is also in conflict with her mother, because she cannot stand seeing her mother submit to the exigencies of married life at the expense of stifling her own self. In addition, there is conflict with the older generation which we encounter when, following the grandmother's death, the family gathers together during *shiva,* the traditional period of mourning. Sarah sees in all of them—in their obsessive diligence in following the rituals—the last traces of a Tunisian Judaism where faith and superstition are confused in a version that seems to her totally archaic. Finally, her conflict extends to the State of Israel, culminating in her severe and unambiguous condemnation of Israeli defense policies—in this case, relating to the 1983 war in Lebanon—and in a kind of pro-Palestinianism, so to speak, expressed not so much in terms of a real political analysis of the situation, but as a deep sympathy for the Arab population of Jerusalem.

Sarah is the name of the woman who tries to shake off her chains, but who nonetheless remains shackled. Mavrika is the name she chooses to represent her liberated self, with all its complex implications. The Mavrika with whom Sarah identifies does not exist in reality, but paradoxically Mavrika has always existed. Mavrika is "a form of pleasure banned in Jerusalem," says Sarah. She is the slut, the prostitute of yesterday, today, and tomorrow. She is the woman damned by the rabbis, cantors, priests and imams. But Mavrika is also, according to Sarah in reference to beliefs in mystical Judaism: "This woman for whom Kabalists and Talmudists have been searching for twenty centuries. In Hebrew she is called the Shekhina, the divine Presence." There is therefore something like divinity in Mavrika. And the Shekhina, the Presence, is the compassionate listening post. Embedded in the assumed stance of revolt by Sarah, there is thus a deliberate ethical claim.

— **Joseph Brami**
Translated by Ralph Tarica

Selected Works

Un Eté à Jérusalem. Paris: Balland, 1986.
Le Cri. Paris: Balland, 1987.
Les Herbes Amères. Paris: Balland, 1989.
Bel Canto. Paris: Seuil, 1991.
Pour l'amour du père. Paris: Stock, 1996.
Sous les étoiles. Paris: 2002.

A Summer in Jerusalem

A verdigris sky hangs over Lod. Rundown gray cement buildings are scattered haphazardly over the airfield, separated from one another by sand or sparse grass. As they meander about with their rifles slung over their shoulders in the pale dawn, the soldiers, too, appear to be dressed in gray. Amid my four suitcases, I smile vaguely, still hesitant, as I watch displays of affection that made this corner of the earth famous a few years ago. For me, Lod has become an ordinary place. It has ceased being the airport of final refuge.

The taxi drivers, fat and sloppily dressed, leaning over the hoods of their cars, look at me ironically. They recognize me as a tourist, perched on heels that are too high, with no one outside the windows of the large hall waiting to pick me up. They call out their prices and points of destination with thick voices: "Haifa, Tel-Aviv, Jerusalem."

They can't know that, in front of these doors opening silently, two ghosts wander about: a seventeen-year-old girl arriving, burdened under her backpack, her ponytail held in place by a rubber band, a touching figure with all her ideas about Zionism; a twenty-year-old departing, her mouth hard, carrying a cardboard suitcase tied with string, her convictions gone astray.

I lift my suitcases onto a cart. Bernard had watched me with amusement as I loaded up on bars of soap, jars of cream, electrical appliances, little gifts that I had bought at ridiculous prices by rummaging through the sales at Tati or the Galeries Lafayette, but highly valued by my family in Jerusalem who were impatiently waiting for them.

"Daughter? Where are you calling from? Daughter, are you here?" Her voice breaks. It seems that my whole life is held in my mother's cry, new and yet already old, an enormous cry that my memory can reproduce with its accent and tone even before I hear it.

But her voice has already disappeared, snatched off by the distance, drowned out by the static of a telephone demanding another coin. I hang up sharply.

The strip of new highway built between Tel-Aviv and Jerusalem stretches out over plains and hills. Civilian vehicles are rare; we pass military trucks, half-tracks, assault tanks. The driver slowly raises his rear view mirror to meet my eyes. He starts a sentence in broken English, but I interrupt him immediately in Hebrew. Astonished, he turns around, risking a swerve. He smiles.

"An Israeli? Well now, I would have sworn you were French. Excuse me!"

"There's nothing to excuse."

His black eyes, bloodshot, topped by bushy eyebrows, are not laughing. An uneasy flame flickers at the back of the iris.

"Did you have a nice vacation?"

"I wasn't on vacation," I say, reluctantly. "I'm on vacation now."

The man speeds up angrily. His hand slides out the window and his fingers stir the air.

"You weren't happy here? Maybe the war scares you?"

"Maybe."

"You're all the same," he blurts out bitterly. "You abandon us while we.... What's so great about Europe, anyway? After they put all the Jews in a ghetto, then...."

His palms pressing hard on the steering wheel, the man drives on in silence. The light is still diffuse on the fields, sprayed by crooknecked sprinklers with a carefully controlled economy of water.

Staring straight ahead at the road, the man mutters grumpily, "Well, as far as I'm concerned, when it comes to war, when our lives are at stake, I'm all for it! I don't have any problems with that!"

I smile as I light up a cigarette.

What catches my eye as I get out of the taxi, in front of the cut-stone façade of the apartment house where my parents live, is the presence of the Arab gardener, his eyes aimed upward, his face straining as he splashes a scrawny shrub with a wildly aimed water hose. Hasn't anything changed since I left? The trees are still scrawny. And the Arab, with his orange and green knit cap over his frizzy hair, is still ruefully watering them.

My mother, hearing the rumbling of the motor below, rushes down the stairway. Her shape has filled out. Only her legs are still long and thin. She doesn't care how she looks, rigged out in a flower-print house smock decorated with large mother-of-pearl buttons from the collar down to the waist. The mules on her feet flap against her skin at every step. I see only the look in her eyes, opaque, shifting, animated by a flicker of madness. I see only the tired and haggard look in her eyes, trying to look joyous, but filled with infinite despair.

She rushes towards me out of breath, her arms widespread. But she won't say anything to me; she won't even talk about the defeats she has suffered. And suddenly, feeling ill at ease, I turn around, grab my suitcases from the taxi trunk and throw them on the ground with a bounce.

The driver, standing stiffly, stares at me accusingly. He seems to feel sorry for my mother.

I don't kiss her. It is she who takes me by the waist, with a hoarse moan, she who turns my face towards her to hug me, she who pays the driver and

From: *Un Eté á Jérusalem* (Paris: Balland, 1986), pp. 131–137, 150–152, 183–185.

insists on taking my suitcases into the house as she repeats, "You look worn out, my little girl. Your skin is as yellow as saffron!"

It is barely nine o'clock on this first morning in August, and the sun in the sky has begun to whiten the wash hanging on the apartment terraces and in the courtyards. My mother moves about the jumble of suitcases scattered around, delighted, but disturbed by my silence. The first thing she does is draw the blinds and suddenly there is a lot of shade, with ladders of light on the wall where the slits and little holes of the blinds go up and down.

"Sit down! Do you want coffee? Some cake?"

Above the sideboard there are cheap paper prints, yellowed and worn, protected under glass, representing scenes of Moses crossing the Red Sea. There are pictures of rabbis, too, with their respectable beards and spiritual eyes. Towering over the television is a black and white portrait of *saba*, grandfather with a *kaboush* on his head, draped in his *gandourah*. Hanging from plain nails in the wall are oil lamps made of bronze and cheap silver, vestiges of a lost Tunisia.

My mother returns from the kitchen with a Turkish coffee and a bowl of freshly rinsed fruit. She kisses me again, steps back, bends over the suitcases, shakes the clasps, and gives up trying to open them. Flopped down on the sofa, my feet resting on the low, green onyx table, I don't react. She almost tells me, "Be careful with the furniture," but stops in time, resigned. She comes over to sit by my side, her two hands clasped under her knees.

"You're wearing the scarf now? It's ugly. You look old."

She blushes. The light in her eyes has gone out and it's as though I had created an eclipse over the entire room. Suddenly, it feels cold.

She was hoping for an outpouring of warm feelings, but has once more found my biting voice, my sarcasm.

"I decided to do it a few months ago," she says apologetically. She explains hurriedly, speaks about the neighborhood rabbi, about a vow, a commandment from the Bible that she was late in honoring.

I express my doubts. "From the Bible, Ma? You really surprise me!"

But what surprises me especially is this irritation burning my eyes. What do I care, after all, about this new zeal of my mother? Why should I ridicule it? I was not unaware of this centuries-old tradition of hiding the newlywed's slightest wisp of hair underneath a flannel, nylon, or cotton headcover or a wig. But I had always known my mother with hair like a queen's, thick and black.

This one is a white cotton scarf hastily tied at the back of her neck, with the two ends hanging limply over her shoulders like two crumpled tails. It has slipped to one side, hiding one temple while exposing the other.

"You have it on wrong. It makes your face look lopsided."

She sighs, declaring that a forty-five-year old woman is not supposed to be worried about her beauty. Beauty, a word, startling in its modesty, has crept into the conversation.

"Was it your husband who asked you to do it?"

She retorts with dignity: "First of all, my husband is your father. How you hate him, girl! You're wrong about him. He didn't ask me to do anything. I made the decision by myself."

I laugh with a sneer. "Sure! By the way, is he still jealous?"

My hand pulls off the scarf. Her hair that used to be so thick has been ruined by scissors. Thin, sad-looking wisps jut out messily.

"Mom? I'm sorry!"

She smiles. Slowly, she places the cotton square back on her head, and this time, with a bit of coquettishness, ties it around her forehead.

"Don't cry dear, it's nothing!"

That's the way my mother is, she even apologizes for my insolence. I light up a cigarette, sip my coffee, look at the portrait of *saba*, my grandfather—who looks on the scene with an enigmatic smile—for an answer to my anxiety. But he is from another century, another exile, and offers me no protection.

"Tell me about you, Ma!"

"About me? I missed you. Your absence is like a hole in my life!"

"Come on, Ma, tell me. Your letters are so rare and you only talk about me. How did you live through the war?" She leaves me and gets down on her knees to examine the contents of the suitcases. She takes her time in answering, a stubborn expression on her face. Then, in a hoarse voice, she tells me about the electric outages, the young men—Emma's son, Clara's son—who disappeared, the courage needed at the cemetery gates when the two women dug their nails into their cheeks and pulled out their hair. And then, after their frenzy, the sense of numbness as the two tombs were sealed.

I stretch out on the sofa, my eyes fixed on the little crack in the ceiling. It has become even wider and the separated edges now look like two lips sneering.

In Jerusalem, a few years ago, I met a prostitute. She went by the name Mavrika, "sparkling." She had simply spelled the consonants of her former Arabic surname, which meant blessed, into Hebrew, changed the vowels, and came up with a new title for her condition as a woman. It was at that time that she had begun to burn up her life. At first, she had only lit little torches, just a few blue sparks, to study her own reactions. Then she cropped her hair and widened her mouth into an artificial smile. There were times when she would sleep for four days and four nights, her face buried in the pillow, her body curled up with her hands cupped shell-like over her sex.

A Summer In Jerusalem

During the following days, she would wander about the city like an insomniac, brushing against the doors of houses, scratching the stone walls with her sharp nails. Men would approach her: "Mavrika!" She gave in to their desire, followed them mutely, penetrated the interiors of houses behind them into the cool shade of the rooms. First, they would take her on the stone floor. Then they would stretch her out on a bed, wrapping themselves around her hips, forcing themselves into her with gasps of pleasure, spreading her legs to enjoy her more deeply. She would get up to take her leave, but they toppled her down again and split her sex wide open with brutal thrusts. On the bed sheets, they would leave wet traces, white, or black when she was impure. They laughed as they commented on the firmness of her breasts, the heavy curve of her belly, or the fineness of her ankles decorated with golden chains. Some of them covered her with jewelry, others draped cloths of black or red silk and scarves about her waist. She remained limp, giving herself over to their skillful hands that shaped other images of her. A public girl, she sometimes accepted the ropes that tied her body to the bedstead.

But no cry ever left her lips. I caught sight of one of her lovers. His name was Michael. His skin was withered, seamed with scars. His forearms were tattooed with poisonous flowers. He begged her, in his heavy, indecent voice, to shave off the hair of her pubis, preferring, he said, hairless women. Then he confided that he hated old women with drooping, flabby bellies and the gray mop below. "I'll kill you if you lose your beauty," he would threaten. The whore's eyes would smile and she would get away.

"Mavrika!" She represented a form of pleasure that was banned in Jerusalem. She was becoming like a wild bramble and I dreamed of seeing her invade the barrels of sub-machine guns and cling to the smoking muzzles of tanks. "Mavrika!" She would stand in the street, perched on her high heels, one leg folded up like a heron on an imaginary lake. Impassive, Mavrika flouted the sunsets. She was the prey of soldiers, drunken businessmen, and foreign diplomats. Her cropped head fascinated them. With a little imagination, they could imagine they were possessing one of those women from the religious quarters who wear wigs.

I look for her in the Street of the Prophets, the Via Dolorosa, Omar Ibn El Katteb Street, and at the gates of the old city. I look for her in dark nooks, dead end alleys, beggars' dens, sun-drenched squares. I interrogate the shoeshine boys who set out their metal cans and laugh as they work, the *begalé* merchants who watch the flow of passers-by from behind their parked carts.

I go to the Greek Abu Christo's, a place visited by nargileh smokers, stretched out on horsehair mattresses, daydreaming beneath a gigantic photograph of Yasser Arafat. Other women are there, with their facile laughter and their pearl-studded loincloths. But no one has her depth, that light in the eye. Mavrika. I want her to teach me the art of dissembling. I look like her now, rebuffed by my father who, since the death of my grandmother, watches me with eyes contracted with anger. He does not forgive me for running out of the house decked out like this. He hasn't understood that my fetish colors are meant to trick death. But he has to respond to those unhappy old men who have taken him to task for the way he brought me up. "She's not dressed like a Jewish woman, one of our own women," they reproached. Others went further still: "She is giving way to sin. Break her before she consumes you."

So my father, to justify himself, complained over and over again about my rebellion and the torments I was causing him. In one of the rooms where he dragged me in the hope of making me listen to reason, he slapped me, this man who for years had foregone lifting his hand against me. But he could not look me in the eye.

Mavrika! The stories she once told reverbrate in my head, while I stumble through the streets, along walls that evoke the unjust eyes of my father.

A grinder sharpens his knives, bent over by his effort. With every scrape of the stone a shower of sparks shoots off the blades. I want to find the thread of this despair that dulls life. I flee toward the edge of the city where, behind the Abu Tor quarter, scrawny sheep graze on thorny bushes, their flat udders scratched by the brambles. Arab children, floating in their djellabas, raise their heads up from their games, and their hands make obscene gestures to discourage me from approaching. I lose myself in Jerusalem, as I drift through the meanders of my memory.

In the main street of Mea Shearim there exist certain people who may seem eccentric with their black, glossy coats, their round hats covered with a plastic bag on rainy days. They seem to be hopping, their backs tightened, revealing a fear so profound that all the stretching in the world could not straighten them up. They glide through the sunlight like shadows coming out of nowhere and going who knows where, fierce, distrustful, angrily protecting the texts of the law squeezed under their arms.

One often hears them talking to the occasional birds in the street which, perched on the low walls, seem to listen to them lovingly. One can also see them stop suddenly, as though moved by a memory, and shudder. On their lips is a prayer. With a finger to their mouths, they force themselves into silence to avoid revealing a secret. Then they take off again, bent over, a hand behind their back, and with the tips of their shoes busy themselves with kicking aside the ice-cream wrappers littering the street, or the marbles that children have left lying around or fruit-juice bottles. Still later they come to a sudden standstill and laugh quietly in a quavering voice, while pulling at their beards.

They mutter hatefully as they stare at the white posters with black borders that are pasted crooked on the walls, proclaiming religious decrees.

"Cover yourself, shameless woman."

For them, too, I am an intruder.

Jerusalem doesn't lead to anything. The stones say nothing. The sky remains splendidly silent. Men fluster about in the acrid dust, eat like gluttons, forget to laugh, go to great lengths to blaspheme against death, but their words come out mangled. And death passes by, royally, and death mows down young men. They are borne into the earth in the revolt of mothers who sink into ecstatic madness and put scarves on their heads or renounce God, but the result is basically the same. I have seen some who throw themselves frantically under car wheels, saved by a sudden braking, getting back up distractedly only to begin anew somewhere else, provoking fate and cursing the day they were born. Some of them start to climb one step on a stairway, and there, grotesque and touching, flap their arms for a long time, ready to fly off.

Fathers in mourning simply let their hair turn white and their shoulders sag, become old from having to say the kaddish at the graves of their sons.

Mavrika had loved only one man. When he began to show the first signs of insanity, she kept her misfortune from her neighbors. If she had to go out, she would tie him to a chair, gagging his mouth to smother his cries. But one day, the hospital attendants came to drag Isaac off to the asylum of Talbia. She gave herself to men while her mind thought about the madman, convinced that he would get well one day and return to her with his old smile and his fingers that knew how to make love. Once, when she was dancing at Abu Christo's to stimulate a state of bliss in the *nargileh* smokers, she told me that passion was an insurmountable ordeal. She thought that by offering pleasure she could come closer to the interned man. Talbia. She pronounced the name of the asylum with her eyelids half-closed, as if nails were penetrating her body. She claimed that sperm purified her. Mavrika resembled that unfathomable woman for whom kabbalists and talmudic scholars have been searching for twenty centuries. Draped in black, her face hidden, she enters the most protected forts, trembles in front of the Scrolls, forgets herself in the presence of the disciples who moan their prayers, gives herself to the bearded soldiers doing their watch rounds. In Hebrew, her name is the Shekhina, the Presence.

Mavrika is the padlock of Jerusalem. She gashes the city with her sharp laugh, the laugh of a woman crazed by love for a madman who probably no longer remembers her. When she would visit him, he would look at her with pupils dilated with fury. But she would just excuse him. She would say, "He has lived through terrible moments. He could not stand spilled blood, friends who disappeared . . . violence. He simply forgot that he had abandoned me, left me behind, destroyed."

The doctors allow her to hope. But Mavrika danced more and more heavily at Abu Christo's. Was she perhaps, like me, dragging the insults—like cannonballs around her ankles—of the old men who accused her of too much looseness? It was at that time that she disappeared from the city, leaving us her madman as a security pledge.

Mavrika. In her coal-black eyes, one could see her insomnia. She was from that Jerusalem disowned by rabbis and cantors, priests and imams, from that nocturnal city that comes alive when the iron shutters of the shops in the narrow streets come down like blind gray eyelids. Then she would join other Mavrikas in dark cafés where naked light bulbs, hanging down from electric wires, barely bit into the shadows. Here one could smell alcohol, opium, women. Discreet waiters officiated, filling the nargilehs as needed with water or *kif.* Sometimes one of the men lying down would swear "Allah!" or "Adonai" and the whores would bow their heads as though in a temple. But this was still a holy Jerusalem vibrating, while in the desert soldiers were being taught how to advance silently from one hilltop to another without moving a single stone, how to handle the breech of their rifle, how to shoot at a target in the dark, how to live without thirst, without hunger, disembodied, without a sound. On the other side of the border, other soldiers dressed in other uniforms were training to kill the men who, in the desert, were learning how to kill them.

I went down into the Old City to resist the desire to telephone Henri. In the gardens of the mosque, I felt close to him. Women wearing the *chador* strolled about in the narrow streets with furtive footsteps. In front of the fountain, barefoot men were carrying out the ritual ablutions. I love this place—the peace of the stone benches lined along the verdant shrubs, and this tiny minaret, like a rare trinket of white sugar that the faithful walk around with devotion.

Sometimes, Mavrika would come to dream here. She let her hand float through the water of the fountain, looking at the sky. Isaac was already at Talbia. She said she would have liked not to think about anything, to become this bench, this shrubbery, an element that was an integral part of the landscape, that one could not remove without leaving the impression of something missing.

She noted, with a bitter voice, "With Isaac gone, I felt I was in a daze. For whole days, I couldn't get any further than my rug. If they hadn't come to fetch him, I could have brought him back to himself . . . and saved myself."

She was carrying the word of the devil into these gardens. Mavrika's face was always changing. Sometimes it became just eyes, at other times an enormous mouth. She was the witness, or else the prophet. Sometimes both. Wherever she walked, she would stir up riotous feelings—for men, in their sex, for women, in their hearts. For she was a whore of abundance. And yet her hands were like a sieve—she did not know how to possess. In these very alleyways, she had confided to me, one day, "I feel like seeing the sea. They say it is immense and blue. But, you know, I'm afraid of getting there and finding it all dried up."

— Translated by Ralph Tarica and Suzanne Tarica

ADDITIONAL JEWISH WOMEN WRITING IN FRENCH

Soazig Aaron. Novelist. *Le Nou de Klara.* Paris: Maurice Nadeau, 2002.

Eliette Abécassis. (1969–). Novelist and essayist. *Qumran.* Paris: Ramsay, 1996. *L'or et la cendre.* Paris: Ramsay, 1997. *Petite métaphysique du meurtre.* Paris: Ramsay, 1998. *La répudiée.* Paris: Albin Michel, 2000. *Mon Père.* Paris: Albin Michel, 2002.

Odette Abadi. (née Rosenstock) (1914–1999) Author of a memoir. *Terre de Détresse: Birkenau, Bergen-Belsen.* Paris: Editions l'Harmattan, 1995.

Marlène Amar. (1949–) Movie critic and novelist. *La femme sans tête.* Paris: Gallimard, 1993. *Des gens infréquentables.* Paris: Gallimard, 1996.

Myriam Anissimov. (1943–) Novelist and biographer. *Comment va Rachel?* Denoël, 1973. *Dans la Plus stricte intimité.* Paris: Editions de l'Olivier, 1992. *Primo Levi, Tragedy of an Optimist.* Translated by Steve Cox. Woodstock, NY: Overlook Press, 1999.

Myriam Antaki. Novelist. *Les caravanes du soleil.* Paris: Gallimard, 1991. *La Bienaimée.* Paris: Orban, 1985. *Les versets du pardon.* Arles: Actes Sud, 1999.

Dominique Arban. (1909–1991) Journalist and novelist. *La cité d'injustice.* Paris: Julliard, 1945. *Le passé défini.* Paris: Morgan, 1964. *Je me retournerai souvent. Souvenirs.* Paris: Flammarion, 1990.

Estréa Zaharia Asséo. Author of a memoir. *Les Souvenirs d'une rescapée.* Paris: La pensée Universelle, 1974.

Fanny Angel. (Mme Collet) (19th century) Novelist and translator. *La pupille, roman de moeurs.* 2 vols. Paris: H. Souverain, 1845. *Trois nouvelles de Disraëli.* Paris: Mongie, 1821. *Un premier pas.* Paris: H. Souverain, 1842.

Nathalie Azoulai. Novelist and screenwriter. *Les cordées de Paris: une histoire d'ramoneur.* Paris: Editors Ouvrières: Turbulence, 1989. *C'est une histoire de Femme qui a un frère.* Paris: Seuil, 2004.

Myriam Ben. (Marylise Ben-Haïm)(1928–2001) Poet and short story writer. *Ainsi naquit un homme.* Algiers: La Maison des livres, 1982. *Reed.* Paris: Editions l'Harmattan. 1993. *Quand les cartes sont truquées: mémoires.* Paris: Editions l'Harmattan, 1999. *Le soleil assassiné.* Paris: Editions l'Harmattan, 2002.

Simone Benda. (known as Simone) (1877–1985) Actress, playwright, and novelist. *Jours de colère.* Paris: Plon, 1935. *Emily Brontë, pièce en trois actes et neuf tableaux.* Paris: Editions Nagel, 1945. *Sous de nouveaux soleils.* Paris: Gallimard, 1957.

Appendix

Blanche Bendahan. (1903–1975) Poet and novelist. *Mazeltob*. Paris: Ed. du Tambourin, 1930. *Poèmes du Mzab*. Setif: Ed. Continents, 1955. *Messieurs, vous êtes impuissants*. Paris: Debresse, 1961. *Sous les soleils qui ne brillent plus*. Blainville-sur-Mer: L'Amitié par le livre, 1970.

Berthe Benichou-Aboulker. (1866–1942) Poet and playwright . *La Kahéna, reine berbère*. Algiers: P. G. Soubiron, 1933. *Pays de flamme*. Algiers: P. G. Soubiron, 1935. *Louise de Lavallière, Pièce en trois actes et cinq tableaux*. Algiers: P. G. Soubiron, 1935.

Simone Benmussa. (1932–2001) Stage director and playwright. *La vie singulière d'Albert Nobbs*. Paris: Ed. des femmes, 1977. *Le Prince répète le prince*. Paris: Seuil, 1984. (with Viviane Forrester) *La Traversée du temps perdu*. Paris: Seuil, 1978.

Sarah Bernhardt. (Pseud. of Henriette Rosine Bernard) (1844–1923) Actress and playwright. *Ma double vie,* 2 vols. Paris: Fasquelle, 1923, Des Femmes, 1980. *L'Art du théâtre, la voix, le geste, la prononciation*. Paris: Eds Nilsson, 1923. *Adrienne Lecouvreur, drame en six actes*. Paris: Charpentier et Fasquelle, 1980.

Claude Cahun. (Pseud. of Lucy Schwob)(1894–1954) Photographer, essayist, and novelist. *Aveux non avenus*. Paris: Editions du Carrefour, 1930. *Les paris sont ouverts*. Paris: J. Corti, 1934. *Ecrits*. Paris: Jean-Michel Place, 2002.

Pauline Caro. (1835–1901) Novelist and short story writer. *Le péché de Madeleine*. Paris: M. Lévy frères, 1865. *Pas à pas*. Paris: M. Lévy frères, 1898. *Aimer c'est vaincre*. Paris: Hachette, 1900.

Muriel Cerf. (1950–) Novelist. *Amérindiennes*. Paris: Stock, 1979. *Maria Tiefenthaler*. Paris: Albin Michel, 1982. *Deux oiseaux de Galilée*. Paris: Albin Michel, 1988.

Denise Chalem. (1952–) Actress and playwright. *A cinquante ans elle découvrait la mer*. Paris: Actes Sud-Papiers, 1985 *(The Sea Between Us*. Translated by Danielle Brunon, Adine Sagalyn and Catherine Temerson. New York: Ubu Repertory Theater Publications,1986). *Selon toute ressemblance*. Paris: Actes Sud-Papiers, 1986. *Couki et Louki sont sur un bateau*. Paris: Actes Sud-Papiers, 1987.

Elisa Chimenti. (1883–1969) Storyteller, novelist, and translator. *Chants de femmes arabes*. Paris: Plon, 1942. *Légendes marocaines*. Paris: Editions du Scorpion, 1959. *Le sortilège et autres contes séphardites*. Tangiers: Editions Marocaines et Internationales, 1964.

Catherine Clément. (1939–) Philosopher, essayist, novelist and diplomat. *Les fils de Freud sont fatigués*. Paris: Grasset, 1978. *Vie et légendes de Jacques Lacan*. Paris: Grasset, 1981. With Hélène Cixous, *La jeune née*. Paris: UGE, 1975. *La Senora*. Paris: Calmann-Lévy, 1992. *Cherche-midi*. Paris: Stock, 2000.

Sylvie Courtine-Denamy. (?–) Philosopher. *Hannah Arendt*. Paris: Belfond, 1994. *Three Women in Dark Times: Edith Stein, Hannah Arendt, Simone Weil*. Translated by G. M. Goshgarian. Ithaca, NY: Cornell University Press, 2000. *La maison de Jacob*. Paris: Phébus, 2001.

Appendix

Paule Darmon. Novelist. *Baisse les yeux, Sarah.* Paris: Grasset, 1980. *L'Homme adultère.* Paris: Presses de la Renaissance, 1985.

Degracia (Pseud. of Gracia Cassou née Cohen) (1911–1985) Novelist. *Retour sur un monde perdu.* Paris: Paris. Les Presses du Temps Présent, 1971. As Gracia Cassou, *Un sacré métier.* Paris: Les Presses du Temps Présent, 1974.

Lise Deharme. (1898–1979) Biographer and novelist. *La Marquise d'Enfer.* Paris: Grasset, 1976. *L'amant blessé.* Paris:Grasset, 1966. *Les années perdues 1939-1949.* Paris: Plon, 1961.

Eve Dessare. (1926–1990) Writer of children's books. *Bintang et l'oiseau malin.* Paris: Eds. G.P., 1971. *Mon enfance avant le déluge.* Paris: Fayard, 1976. *Cet amour-là.* Gembloux, Belgium: Duculot, 1983.

Rachel Ertel. Scholar and translator. *Le shtetl.* Paris: Payot, 1982. *Dans la langue de personne; Poésie yiddish de l'anéantissement.* Paris: Seuil, 1983. *Une maisonnette au bord de la Vistule et autres nouvelles du monde yiddish.* Paris: Albin Michel, 1988.

Patricia Finaly. Novelist *Le gai ghetto.* Paris: Gallimard, 1970. *Tropique du Valium.* Paris: Julliard, 1978.

Annie Fitoussi. (1950–) Novelist. *La mémoire folle de Mouchi Rabbinou.* Paris: Mazarine, 1985. *Le bureau des longitudes.* Paris: Fayard, 2001.

Ania Francos. (1938–1988) Journalist and novelist. *La fête cubaine.* Paris: Julliard, 1962. *Sauve-toi, Lola.* Paris: Barrault, 1983.

Nadèjda Garrel. (1939–) Actress, author of books for young people, and novelist. *La peau du ciel.* Paris: Gallimard, 1994. *Ils reviennent.* Paris: Mercure de France, 2001.

Claire Goll. (1891–1977) Poet and novelist. *Education barbare.* New York: Editions de la Maison française, 1941. *Les larmes pétrifiées.* Paris: Seghers, 1951. *Le ciel Volé.* Paris: Fayard, 1958. With Yvan Goll, *Duo d'Amour, 1920–1950.* Paris: Seghers, 1959.

Nina Gourfinkel. (1898–1984) Literary critic and translator. *Aux prises avec mon temps.* 2 vols., 1953. *Gorki.* Paris: Seuil, 1977. *Lénine.* Paris: Seuil ,1959.

Katia Granoff. (1895–1989) Poet, travel writer, and art critic. *Reflets d'Israël.* Paris: Seghers, 1951. *Anthologie de la poésie russe.* Paris: Gallimard, 1961. *Naguère.* Paris: UGE, 1977.

Gisèle Halimi. (1927–) Lawyer and essayist. *La cause des femmes.* Paris: Grasset, 1973. *Le lait de l'oranger.*, 1988. *Une embellie perdue.* Paris: Gallimard, 1994.

Appendix

Jacqueline Harpman. (1929–) Psychoanalyst and novelist. *Orlanda*. Translated by Ros Schwartz. New York: Seven Stories Press, 1999. *Moi qui n'ai pas connu les hommes*. Paris: Stock, 1995. *L'Orage rompu*. Paris: Grasset, 1998.

Myriam Harry. (1875–1958) Novelist and travel writer. *La Conquête de Jérusalem*. Paris: Flammarion, 1903. *La Petite Fille de Jérusalem*. Paris: Fayard, 1913. *La Jérusalem retrouvée*. Paris: Flammarion, 1930.

Claudine Hermann. (1926–) Novelist and critic. *L'étoile de David*. Paris: Gallimard, 1959. Edited *Ma Double Vie: Mémoires de Sarah Bernhardt*. Paris: Edition des Femmes, 1980.

Lily Jean-Javal. (1882–1958), Novelist, poet, travel writer, and author of books for children. *Le Brasier*, 1922. *Noémi*. Paris: Plon, 1925. *Sous le charme du Portugal. visages et paysages*. Paris: n.p. 1931.

Luba Jurgenson. (1958–) Novelist, short story writer, teacher, and translator. *Avoir Sommeil*. Paris: Gallimard, 1981. *L'autre*. Paris: Albin Michel, 1984. *Une autre Vie*. Paris: Lieu Commun, 1986.

Nelly Kaplan. (known as Belen) (1936–) Novelist and film director. *La reine des Sabbats*. Paris: E. Losfeld-Le Terrain Vague, 1960. *Le réservoir des sens*. Paris: La Jeune Parque, 1966. *Mémoires d'une liseuse de draps*. Paris: J-J. Pauvert, 1973.

Sylvie Korkaz. (1939–) Novelist. *Ma jolie Palestine*. Paris: Denoël, 1972.

Evelyne Krief. (1932–) Writer of a memoir and sculptor. *Une Enfance interdite ou la petite marrane*. Paris: Editions l'Harmattan, 1997.

Aleksandra Kroh. (1939–) Novelist and translator. *Les Guerres sont loin*. Paris: L. Levi: Scribe, 1993 (*Lucien's Story* trans. Austryn Wainhouse., Evanston, IL: The Marlboro Press/Northwestern, 1996). *L'Aventure du bilinguisme*. Paris: Editions l'Harmattan, 2000.

Raïssa Maritain. (1883–1960) Essayist and poet. *Lettre de nuit. La vie donnée*. Paris: Desclée de Brouwer, 1939. *Les Grandes Amitiés*. Paris: Desclée de Brouwer,1949. *Journal de Raïssa*. Paris: Desclée de Brouwer, 1962.

Nora Mitrani. (1921–1961) Novelist. *Rose au coeur violet*. Paris: Losfeld-Terrain Vague, 1988.

Nine Moati. Novelist. *Mon enfant, ma mère*. Paris: Stock, 1974. *Les belles de Tunis*. Paris: Seuil, 1983. *La passagère sans étoile*. Paris: Seuil, 1989.

Noémi Mossé. (1860–1953) Novelist and poet. *La clé du caveau, roman d'aventures*. Marseilles: Hachette, 1921. *Poésies. Essai de moeurs comtadines israélites*. Cavaillon: Musée Juif Comtadin, 1984.

Gabrielle Moyse. (Madame Armand Lipman) (1870–1964) Playwright, poet, and biblical scholar. *Les Sanédrin, 2 actes en prose*. Poligny: Imprimerie A. Jacquin, 1910.

Appendix

La morale dans les prophètes. Nancy: Imprimerie L. Stoquert, 1950. *Le Talmud de Babylone*. Angoulême: Imprimerie Ouvrière, 1926.

Clarisse Nicoïdski. (1938–1996) Novelist, poet, and art critic. *Le désespoir tout blanc*. Paris: Seuil, 1968. *Amadeo Modigliani: autobiographie imaginaire*. Paris: Plon, 1989. *Couvre-feux*. Paris: Ramsay, 1981. *Une histoire des femmes peintres des origines à nos jours*. Paris: Lattès, 1994.

Amélie Pollonnais. (née Cohen) (1835–1898) Educator. *Rêveries maternelles*. Paris: Plon, 1864. *Philosophie enfantine*. Paris: Librairie Internationale, 1869. *A Travers les Mansardes et les écoles*. Paris: Perrin, 1886.

Rachel. (Elisa Rachel Felix) (1821–1858) Actress. *La vie sentimentale de Rachel d'après des lettres inédites*. Paris : Calmann-Lévy, 1910.

Katia Rubinstein. (1944–) Novelist. *Mémoire illettrée d'une fillette d'Afrique du Nord à l'époque coloniale*. Paris: Stock, 1978.

Nathalie Sarraute. (1902–1999) Novelist, essayist, and playwright. *Tropismes*. Paris: Denoël, 1939. *Portrait d'un inconnu*. Paris: Robert Marin, 1948. *Le Planétarium*. Paris: Gallimard, 1959. *Oeuvres complètes*. Paris: Gallimard, 1996. *Childhood*. Translated by Barbara Wright. New York: George Braziller, 1984.

Marianne Schreiber. Novelist. *La passion de Myriam Bloch*. Paris: Fasquelle, 1947.

Beatrice Shalit. Novelist. *Lisa, Lisa*. Paris: Barrault, 1990. *L'Air du Brésil*. Paris: Flammarion, 1993. *Familles et autres supplices*. Paris: Julliard, 2000.

Simone Signoret. (1921–1985) Actress and novelist. *Nostalgia Isn't What It Used To Be*. New York: Harper & Row, 1978. *Le Lendemain elle était souriante*. Paris: Seuil, 1979. *Adieu Volodya*. Paris: Fayard, 1985.

Reine Silbert. (1942–) Novelist. *L'inexpérience*. Paris: Laffont, 1967. *Il faut toujours quitter la Pologne*. Paris: Olivier Orban, 1980. *De Mémoire*. Paris: Denoël, 1995.

Téreska Torrès. (1921–) Novelist. *Le Sable et l'écume*. Paris: Gallimard, 1946. *Les Années anglaises: Journal intime de guerre, 1939–1945*. Paris: Seuil, 1981. *Le Choix: mémoires à trois voix*. Paris: Desclée de Brouwer, 2002.

Elsa Triolet. (née Kagan) (1896–1970) Novelist. *Le cheval blanc*. Paris: Denoël, 1943. *(The White Charger,* London: Virago, 1947). *Le premier accroc coûte deux cents francs*. Paris: Denoël , 1945. *(A Fine of Two Hundred Francs*. New York: Rinehart, 1946). *Le rossignol se tait à l'aube*. Paris: Gallimard, 1970.

Cécile Wajsbrot. (1954–) Novelist and biographer. *Marianne Klinger*. Paris: Calmann-Lévy, 1976. *Une vie à soi*. Paris: Mercure de France, 1982. *Violet Trefusis: biographie*. Paris: Mercure de France., 1989.

Appendix

Louise Weiss. (1893–1983) Politician and journalist. *Mémoires d'une Européenne,* 6 vols. Paris: Albin Michel, 1968-1982.

Sabine Zlatin. (1907–1996) Novelist. Author of a memoir with François Mitterand and others, *Mémoires de la "Dame d'Izieu."* Paris: Gallimard, 1992. *L'Expiation, roman sentimental.* Paris: Ed. Diderot, 1945.

CONTRIBUTORS

Sonia Assa grew up in Morocco, studied in Paris, and settled in New York City. She teaches French and Spanish literature at the State University of New York, College at Old Westbury. She has published and lectured on women writers and film makers, particularly Leïla Sebbar, Assia Djebar, Monique Wittig, and Agnès Varda.

Stella Behar is Associate Professor of French at the University of Texas-Pan American, Edinburg, TX. Her research and publications have focused on twentieth-century avant-garde and post-Holocaust French literature. She is the author of *Georges Perec: Ecrire pour ne pas dire* (1995) and of articles on Perec, l'Oulipo, Surrealism, and Nelly Kaplan.

Michèle Bitton holds a Ph.D. in sociology. Her research focuses on Jewish women. Her publications include *Etre Juif en France aujourd'hui* (Hachette, 1997), *Poétesses et lettrées juives. Une mémoire éclipsée* (Publisud, 1999), and *Présences féminines juives en France: Cent itinéraires* which received a prize from the Hadassah Research Institute on Jewish Women (2M Editions, 2002).

Marianne Bosshard is Professor of French and Francophone Literatures at the U. S. Naval Academy in Annapolis, Maryland. Her publications include a monograph on the contemporary French author Chantal Chawaf (Editions Rodopi, 1999).

Joseph Brami is Professor of French at the University of Maryland, College Park. He is the author of *Les Troubles de l'invention. Essai sur le doute poétique de Joë Bousquet* (Summa, 1987), and with Michèle Sarde edited and prefaced the first volume of Marguerite Yourcenar's correspondence, *Lettre à ses amis et quelques autres* (Gallimard, 1995). He is currently working on a series of volumes of Yourcenar's letters and on an essay on the question of Jewish identity in Proust's work and correspondence.

Lauretta Clough holds a Ph.D. in French from the University of Maryland, with a specialization in translation theory. Her translations include Pierre Bourdieu's *The State Nobility: Elite Schools in the Field of Power* (Stanford UP, 1997). She has taught French language, culture and literature at UMD since 1990, most recently developing the French Writing Center,

Susan D. Cohen taught for many years at Barnard College, Sarah Lawrence College, and New York University. She has published a book *Women and Discourse in the Fiction of Marguerite Duras* (University of Massachusetts Press, 1993), and numerous articles on twentieth-century French and Francophone authors.

Madeleine Cottenet-Hage is Professor Emerita of French at the University of Maryland, College Park. She has written on twentieth-century Francophone women writers, in particular surrealist writer Gisèle Prassinos. She is also the editor, with Christiane Makward, of *Dictionnaire littéraire des femmes de langue française: De Marie de France à Marie Ndaye* (Karthala, 1996). In 1995 she edited *Penser la Créolité* with Maryse Condé (Karthala).

Elissa Gelfand is Professor of French and Chair of the French Department at Mount Holyoke College, where she also teaches in the Women's Studies Program. She is the author of *Imagination in Confinement: Women's Writings from French Prisons* (Cornell UP, 1983) and co-author of *French Feminist Criticism: Women, Language and Literature* (Garland, 1985). She has lectured on Jewish women writers in interwar France and is currently exploring representations of women and aging in works by French women.

Patricia Le Page holds a Ph.D. in French Language and Literature from the University of Maryland. She teaches at the Catholic University.

Pauline Reychman has a degree in comparative literature from the University of Paris III and an M.A. in French from the University of Maryland, College Park. She has taught French at the School of Advanced International Studies at Johns Hopkins University and is now teaching American University students in Paris.

Miléna Santoro is Associate Professor in the French Department at Georgetown University. She has written articles on authors such as Hélène Cixous, Jeanne Hyvrad, and Esther Rochon and has translated poetry. She recently produced and introduced a video on Quebec feminist writers entitled *La Théorie un dimanche: Sweet Suite (ACQS* and *Le Conifère têtu, 2002).* Her first book, *Mothers of Invention: Feminist Authors and Experimental Fiction in France and Quebec,* was published in 2002 by McGill-Queen's University Press. Santoro is currently serving as the Secretary for the American Council for Quebec Studies and is the Book Review Editor for *Women in French Studies.*

Michèle Sarde is Professor Emerita at Georgetown University. An essayist, critic, and novelist, she has published extensively. In particular, she is the author of a biography of Colette (Stock, 1978; English translation by Richard Miller. Morrow, 1980), *Regards sur les Françaises* (Stock, 1983), *Vous, Marguerite Yourcenar: La passion et ses masques* (1985), and the recent *Jacques le Français, Pour Mémoire du Goulag* (Cherche Midi, 2002). Her novel, *Histoire d'Eurydice pendant la remontèe* (Seuil, 1991) was considered for the Prix Goncourt.

Eva Martin Sartori is Professor Emerita of Libraries at the University of Nebraska-Lincoln. With Dorothy W. Zimmerman she edited *French Women Writers* (Greenwood Press, 1991; University of Nebraska Press, 1994) and was editor-in-chief of *The Feminist Encyclopedia of French Literature* (Greenwood Press, 1999). She has also published articles and edited books on Western European librarianship.

Contributors

Judith Morganroth Schneider is Associate Professor of French and Spanish at the University of Maryland, Baltimore County. She is the author of *Max Jacob: Clown at the Altar* (University of North Carolina Press, 1978) and of essays on French Jewish writers, including Liliane Atlan, Alain Finkielkraut, and Albert Memmi. She has also written articles on several Latin American Jewish authors and edited a special issue of *Folio* (September 1987) entitled *Latin American Jewish Writers*.

Nancy Shalen received an M.A. with a specialty in literary translation from the University of Texas, Dallas. In addition to Brigitte Peskine's *Les Eaux douces d'Europe* she has translated Amélie Nothomb's play *Les Combustibles*.

Ralph Tarica taught at Brandeis University before coming to the University of Maryland, where he served as Professor of French and Department Chair for a number of years. His research has centered on the work of André Malraux, Antoine St.-Exupéry and other French writers of the 1930s and 1940s. Since his recent retirement and Emeritus status, he has collaborated on numerous translation projects with his wife, **Suzanne Tarica,** who has also taught French at the university level and has extensive experience in English-French translation.